Missouri Folklore Society Journal

Special Issue

Emerging Folklorists

Volumes 40-41
2018-2019

Missouri Folklore Society Journal

(Volumes 40-41, 2018-2019)

Special Issue

Emerging Folklorists

edited by

Adam Brooke Davis

General Editors
Dr. Jim Vandergriff (Ret.)
Dr. Donna Jurich
University of Arizona

Missouri Folklore Society
P. O. Box 1757
Columbia, MO 65205
2021

This issue of the *Missouri Folklore Society Journal* was published by Naciketas Press, 715 E. McPherson, Kirksville, Missouri, 63501

ISSN: 0731-2946; ISBN: 978-1-952232-59-6

The *Missouri Folklore Society Journal* is indexed in:
The *Hathi Trust Digital Library*: Vols. 4-24, 26; 1982-2002, 2004. This library essentially acts as an online keyword indexing tool; only allows users to search by keyword and only within one year of the journal at a time. The result is a list of page numbers where the search words appear. No abstracts or full-text incl. (Available free at http://catalog.hathitrust.org/Search/Advanced).

The *MLA International Bibliography*: Vols. 1-26, 1979-2004. Searchable by keyword, author, and journal title. The result is a list of article citations; it does not include abstracts or full-text.

RILM Abstracts of Music Literature: Vols. 13-14, 20; 1991-92, 1998. Searchable by keyword, author, and journal title. Indexes only selected articles about music that appear in these volumes only. Most of the entries have an abstract. There is no full-text.

A list of major articles in every issue of the journal also appears on the Society's web page. Go to *http://missourifolkloresociety.truman.edu/MFS-Jcnts.html*.

Notice to library subscribers and catalogers:
Notice to library subscribers and catalogers: Though the cover date on this volume is 2018-19, the volume was actually published in 2021. The Society's board is working to produce enough issues to catch up with the journal's publishing schedule as quickly as possible.

Contents

Preface to Emerging Folklore, Emerging Folklorists
Adam Brooke Davis

The present volume showcases outstanding work in folklore from 2010-19, roughly the first decade of the folklore minor program at Truman State University. These projects came primarily from folklore courses and capstones, with others from our signature interdisciplinary seminar. As long-time MFS secretary Don Lance demonstrated, and as further witnessed by projects overseen by Dr. Greg Richter, folklore and linguistics have considerable overlap.

These papers represent a range of topics and approaches, from the rigorously quant to humanistic studies that ask to be validated by the reader's recognition of sound insight and empathetic understanding. We have oral history, family history, archival study and fieldwork. Because the papers were produced in various disciplines, the different citation styles are respected.

We had in mind something like the discipline of history provides, with their estimable journal, *The Apprentice Historian*. Some of these inquiries are in spots naïve, in the same sense art historians use the term, work that shows the marks of the newcomer, or that may not have the range of historical reference of more senior practitioners – but also rides on a freshness and freedom from preconception (even from the cant and cultural politics) – of professionals. These are people still learning how to imagine their audience – they do not always know what needs to be explained and not. But in folklore they have found one of the places where an undergraduate can make genuine contributions to knowledge.

Not many of these writers thought then of going into academics generally or folklore in particular, and in fact, few have, thus far. That's fine – academics is not a growth field, and we're all a little uncomfortable with the fact that serious art of all kinds seems too often to be the purview of very small elites (in fact, mostly academic). Folklore, more than any other cultural enterprise, should be studied by people who plan to do something else with their lives than study.

I have had the pleasure, and the honor, of working with each of these young scholars, mostly in person, some via this miraculous interwebs thing. The future is in good hands.

As always, the society is in debt to the indefatigable Betsy and Neal Delmonico, our editors and conscience.

Adam Brooke Davis,
Kirksville, December 2020

Tales at Tapawingo: A Place of Joy
Maple Adkins-Threats

This essay was written by a pre-med student in 2015, in response to shared experience and memories that bonded several generations of women in her family. Despite the personal inspiration, it works from an ideal of objective distance.

While Boy Scouts camps are known to have their own culture, rich with history, traditions, and badges, Girl Scouts camps can feature the same cultural richness. Girls have been attending Camp Tapawingo in Metamora, Illinois since it opened in 1958 (Kendall). Over the past almost 60 years, hundreds of girls have attended the camp, both learning and contributing to the culture and lore of the camp. As different generations have attended the camp, specific stories, songs, and traditions have come and gone. Today many traditions can be observed and analyzed to show their functions and importance to the camp.

In order to gather information about Tapawingo, women who attended the camp when they were young and women who were counselors were interviewed. Many of the eleven interviewees served in both roles. Women ages eighteen to sixty-nine who attended the camp between 1965 and 2014 were interviewed. Interviews were conducted via email, phone, and in person. A questionnaire was sent out, asking the women demographic questions and questions focusing mainly on Tapawingo history and legends behind the traditions, landmarks, and sites. The interviews also focused on how the women learned the songs and legends and the activities they did around the campfire. The women were encouraged to include what they could without the help of outside sources. Phone interviews were also conducted with those who requested them. The phone interviews, like the in-person interviews, allowed for more in-depth questions and gave the informants a chance to elaborate on their answers.

The name of the camp signifies the attitude reflected by many of the women as they recounted their experiences at the camp. Strangely, only two women were able to elaborate on what the word "Tapawingo" means and to give possible insight as to why it was chosen. These women explained that the name meant "Place of Joy," and one informant reported that it was a name chosen by the first girls at the camp. The informants knew that the name had some Native American origin, but were uncertain of the specifics. The same origin of the name is shared by an informant in *A World of Their Own Making: Myth, Ritual, and the Quest for Family Values* who reports that as far back as in the 1930s the name meant "House of Joy" in some Native American languages (Gillis, 107). Regardless of the fact that only a few informants were able to remember the meaning of the name, the fact that it has been remembered bears significance. The time difference between when the two informants attended the camp was nearly twenty years and yet both of them were at some point taught the meaning which was conserved. The name is not specific to the camp in Illinois; there exist Camp Tapawingos in Oregon and Maine. The other camps dating back as far as 1919 also conserve the "Place of Joy" meaning of "Tapawingo." The name possibly serves as a reminder of the purpose of the camp, as a place of pleasure and to make memories.

A major part of the culture associated with the camp was the name of the campground sleeping units. Until recent years, there were five sleeping units with tents, one lodge, and a unit house (additionally there was a unit with just the unit house itself). Currently, only three units are being used, but the names and origin stories of old still remain with some women. Katie Stobaugh, an informant who attended the camp as both a camper and a counselor from 1991 to 2008, and whose mother went to camp, reports that she was taught that the names were picked by the first girls and were influenced by their location. Few women remembered all of the units, even fewer were able to recall the origins of the names. Many of the women who remembered the origins of the names belonged to the older group (attending as campers before 2005 and only serving as a counselor or faculty since). However, there was a consensus among those who could remember origins of the names. *Setting Sun* was the best place to watch the sun set, *Shining Star* was the best for star gazing, *Rustling Oaks* was surrounded by oak trees, *Crooked Tree* was named for the crooked tree behind the unit, and *Many Moons* was the farthest unit from the entrance. Concerning the origin of the *Many Moons* name, there is slight variation. Some women reported that the name was given because the unit was "many moons away from anything else" while other women reported that it took many moons to hike to the unit. The first references "many moons" as a distance to be traveled while the other refers to "many moons" as the passage of time. Despite the fact that the use of the phrase "many moons" may change, its use is still conserved as a camp-wide, well-understood descriptor. Strangely, *White Cloud* was the only sleeping unit that was recalled by a majority of the women, but only one person could explain that it was named for the clouds. The most recalled unit was *Crooked Tree*. Ten out of eleven women were able to talk about that unit while eight of those ten reported knowing that the unit was named after the Crooked Tree found behind the unit. The legends surrounding this tree may have been one of the more well-known stories from the camp.

The Crooked Tree located at Camp Tapawingo

Crooked Tree has a tree with a crooked, humped trunk after which it is named. Women who attended the camp from the mid-1960s to this past summer of 2014 were able to recall the stories they were told about the tree. Two main explanations for how the tree came to be crooked have been circulating around the camp. While the explanations differ, both claim to have Native American roots. The older explanation—reported by Marie O'Connor, who attended Tapawingo as a camper and as a counselor from 1965-1975—claims that the tree got its crooked form because it was used as a Native American marker tree to indicate the presence of a water source or trail. Native Americans would bend the trunk of a young sapling and keep it tied down with animal hide so that it would grow to have the humped shape (Houser). Similar trees have been observed in Texas and deemed Indian Marker Trees or "thong trees." It is reported that the Comanche people would bend or alter the tree to point in the direction of a campsite (Gelo and Pate, 45). The explanation was still being circulated in 1990 as other women who attended at the time remember being told the marking tree explanation as well.

However, by at least 1998, and until the present, a second tale, involving a Native American woman, has surfaced as an explanation for the hump. Both campers and counselors report telling various versions of this story. The concept of variation within conservation is apparent; the basic core elements of the narrative, including a Native American female waiting at the tree, remain fixed. The variation lies in minor details. The narrative consistently involves a Native American woman/princess whose lover/husband/warrior has gone off to war. She has chosen/promised to stay resting on the tree until he returns. Unfortunately he dies/gets lost in battle and she is not told. She continued to wait, resting on the tree, and it grew around her, forming the hump. In some versions, the woman dies there and in others, her fate is left undisclosed.

Why these stories continue to be circulated may lie in the fact that people want explanations for phenomena that are witnessed and the strong localization of the legends keep them believable and alive. In Orlik's *Principles for Oral Narrative Research*, it is explained that the narrative type of legends can exist in two forms: origin legends and anecdotes (3). When we examine the two explanations it is evident that they are both origin legends since they both are used to explain the origin of the crooked tree in a fixed location. The legends remain believable because of visual evidence that both of the stories could have taken place (Orlik, 79). The credibility of the legends also contributes to why both are still being circulated around the camp today. A major reason why campers keep the marking tree legend is because the Crooked Tree does actually point in the direction of a nearby creek that runs behind the camp. Additionally, it helps place emphasis on recognizing the Native American presence and history of the land before the camp was there. The fact that the land on which the camp rests would have been inhabited by the Pimiteoui before French settlers in late 1600s adds to the importance of localization in the story (Couri). Consequently, there could have been a Native American princess/woman who lived in the area, validating the Native American love story. Nevertheless, it does not matter to the campers which legend is true; it is merely the fact that both are possible explanations for the crooked tree that is important.

While both origin stories are still circulated, there have been reports of each story being told to different demographics of campers, showing that the stories may serve different purposes. Multiple counselors report that the Native American love story was told to the younger girls, while the older campers were told the explanation of Native American marker tree. One counselor explains that they tell the Native American love story to the younger girls because it has the tall tale, fairy tale element: "There is the truth and then there are fairy tales we tell to entertain kids" (Staley). A purpose for the Native American love story could be that it displays a dedicated woman. The legend fits the mold of the Aarne-Thompson Tall tale type 888: the faithful wife. The legend features a woman who is completely devoted to her husband. When considering this tale type, the story could serve the function to teach the girls about being a devoted lover or wife. Because this woman remained loyal to her husband she was remembered decades later, making her seem like a role model. This function aligns with the fourth function mentioned in Dundes' *The Study of Folklore* (294). The story aims to support and glorify the social expectation that these girls grow up to be wives who are faithful to their husbands.

Regarding the transmission of the crooked tree origin stories, like most of the stories told at the camp, they are transmitted orally. Counselors told campers the stories as they visited the tree or when campers asked about the name of the unit. An interesting trait of both legends is that there exists little variation within each over the past 50 and 25 years. Even within the Native American love story, the variation arises only in specific words. According to Orlik, no verbal narrative or story exists in its original form; by being transferred verbally, it is prone to being altered in some fashion since no person tells a story the same way twice. Nevertheless, there may be forms or versions of the narrative that are remarkably close to the original as witnessed in the love story legend (90). Within this lies the principle of variation within conservation. The core essence or ideal of the narrative may be present, but its presentation may be altered by time, region, or audience. Alterations of the original can serve either to help the story maintain its original purpose without becoming obsolete or serve to indicate a new purpose. At Camp Tapawingo, the two stories may have arisen separately to serve different purposes, or they help maintain the relevance of the unit name and the actual tree. It is not the truthfulness of these stories that is important, but the role they play for the campers.

A tradition of the camp that has popped up repeatedly from 1991 until the present is the stories of fairies. Multiple informants mention the wood fairies as being "present" during campfires. The wood fairies would sprinkle fairy dust on the fire, turning it different colors. The campers were told about fairy houses in the grass and tabletops. Katie Stobaugh, who attended as a camper from 1991 to 2001, recalls that she was taught table manners using the fairies. Table fairies lived on the table and if you put your elbows on the table you would crush them. Wood fairies built their houses in the grass, therefore girls were supposed to stay on trails and off the grass or risk crushing the fairies. Examining the reported stories, the function of the fairies is seen as pedagogical tool (Georges and Jones, 189). The counselors are using the fairies as a way to teach the campers lessons. The table fairies teach the girls table manners like refraining from putting their elbows on the table. The 'presence' of fairy homes trains the girls to avoid walking on the grass. This method is commonly used to subtly teach children rules or manners. Additionally, the youngest informant who attended the camp in 2012 explains that the fairies dislike the use of technology on the camp grounds. This new development functions as a way to endorse the rules culture of the camp even in the technological age. The use of technology at camp is prohibited because camp is supposed to serve as time with nature. In this case, the folklore discourages the girls from breaking the rules at the risk of upsetting the fairies.

Another major tradition of the Camp Tapawingo is the opening and closing campfires. O'Connor remembers the all-girl weekly campfire as early as 1965, and many women report the campfire ceremonies as being a special part of the week, and even sacred. However, the role of the campfire gathering is not specific to Tapawingo or even Girl Scouts. In his publication in the *Journal of American Folklore* entitled "The Magic of the Boy Scout Campfire", Jay Mechling reports the significance of the campfire event for Boy Scouts and his observations are mirrored in what the women interviewees reported about their experience with the opening and closing campfires. The ceremonial campfire functions as a method to gather and creatively share experiences and bond through multiple mediums. By comparing the campfire events of the two scout groups, the conservation present can be observed as well as the variance that occurs.

Mechling explains that the event of a Boy Scouts campfire could be broken into six distinct elements: the opening, songs, skits, yells, story, and closing (with benediction). The opening is often characterized by the gathering of scouts, the lighting of the fire, and the greeting. O'Connor, who retired from Tapawingo in 1975, reports that the opening and closing campfires would be held at the creekbed somewhere behind the camp. The counselors would lead the girls down a trail that ran behind each unit, using torches made with sanitary napkins dipped in kerosene. Many times the counselors would dress in pajamas or as Native Americans with bells around their ankles. The fire pit would already be constructed, the logs ready to be lit. There would be chemicals in the pit to make different color flames. Usually they would sing "Rise Up Old Flame" or "Fire's Burning" to start the occasion. At some point the permanent location of, and the quest to, the all-camper campfire must have changed, because no one after O'Connor reports the event being by the creek. Instead, by 1991 the campfire site called Bullfrog is specified. While each unit has a fire pit, Bullfrog is special. The site contains a central, large fire pit, surrounded by full-sized logs to be used as seats, and a wooden stage. The area is set in front of the Mary Morgan dining hall at the center of the camp. The campfires held at Bullfrog did not function just as a place to cook meals or provide warmth, but as more. Despite the fact that the site of the campfire has changed over the years, as stated by the current camp director Katie Noland, "what happens around that campfire between the girls and their councilors is universal and timeless."

The song-element of the campfire event is very apparent in the Tapawingo tradition. Women report that as campers, they learned the songs only by hearing them sung by other campers or counselors. Counselors often used the call and response method to teach songs and marches. And even though counselors were given standard camp songbooks, informant counselors report mainly learning the songs by hearing them from others. Additionally, international counselors or counselors from other camps would bring new songs. O'Connor recalls one co-worker who specialized in Native American songs that she taught to campers, while other transferred counselors would bring songs with them which they would adapt for Tapawingo. Both Boy Scouts and Girl Scouts report learning through the call and response method; however, the prompt to initiate the learning differed. One former Boy Scout reports being prompted by the phrase, "This is a repeat-after-me song" (Dryden). The phrase, "I sing a line, you sing it back," often prompted the teaching of a new song for Girl Scouts (Nelson, Trimble, and Merz). Songs mentioned by informants were Scout originals, general camp songs, marches, and even mainstream songs. Songs like "G for Generosity," "Barges," and "On My Honor," were songs identified by informants as well as found in a recently compiled *Girl Scouts Song Book* (Lefebvre, Stobaugh, and Peck). Certain songs were also accompanied by motions or gestures, like "The Princess Pat," "Boy and Girl in a Little Canoe," and "I'm a Little Coconut." While many songs were generic, they carried the themes of love, friendship, and adventure. Songs were mostly sung *a capella* with the occasional help of counselors who could play guitar (O'Connor). As observed by Mechling, the song list is not fixed. Depending on which campfire, the songs would differ and not all of the same songs are sung at each event. Women reported having happy, loud, quiet, and tranquil songs that could be used to set a range of moods.

A skit section was also reported by informants. The skits were performed by both counselors and campers. While skits were mentioned by informants, little was said about them. Despite the fact that little was said, a function will be inferred later in the paper as the content of the skits may not have been the element that held the most importance.

Yells–as described by Jay Mechling in his 1980 article on Boy Scout campfires–were a way for the Boy Scouts troops to be competitive with each other. However, yells (or anything similar) were not reported by any of the women in my study. The lack of yells in the Girl Scout campfires may be attributed to a difference between how boys and girls play. In *Feminist Theory and the Study of Folklore*, the different ways boys and girls behave in their own groups are examined. This research–published in 1993–showed that girls focused more on constructing and maintaining relationships. The yells are supposed to be loud and active, yet nothing of the sort was reported by female informants. For females, games were characterized by being passive, symbolic, including turn-taking, and attempting to maintain unity–which seems counterintuitive if the goal is competition (Hollis, 130). Additionally, Boy Scouts traditionally attend camp with their troops. At larger camps, troops would have their individual yells to use as a way to identify themselves and proclaim their pride (Dryden). At Camp Tapawingo, while girls can sign up with their troops, it is more common for girls to go as individuals or with a friend. Consequently, there would be no pre-determined troops to be in competition, and yells would not serve that competitive function for the Girl Scouts at Tapawingo.

As far as stories are concerned, the informants were asked mainly about the stories surrounding the history of the camp, but not necessarily those told at the campfire. The stories told had the characteristics more of legends. The final part of the campfire was the closing and benediction. Similar to Mechling's findings for the boys, the women report singing slower songs for this part of the evening. As the ceremony draws to an end, the mood becomes softer and comes down like the inflection of a voice as one gets closer to the end of a statement.

Mechling's analysis of Boy Scout campfires also focuses on the shifting roles of the campers and counselors as both audience and performers, leaders and followers—as a way to form bonds among all members of the group. For examples, the importance of the skits lies not so much in the content, but in the function skits exercise in allowing the campers to switch roles. As campers, interviewees report that they would be part of the audience as they were watching skits such as the Raisin Bran skit, or Introduction skits, done by the counselors on the stage. These skits were usually done during the opening campfire. The campers were predominantly in the role of the audience. They would watch counselors display skills like juggling, singing solos, or playing instruments. However, at the end of the week, the campers would be expected to take up the role as performers and to give their own skits, reviewing the events and experiences of the week. By this time, the campers were bonded closer with the counselors, each other, and camp. This bond is reflected by the fact that they are no longer audience members looking up at the performing, distant counselors, but that they are both performers and equals. Even the role of campers in songs shares this dichotomy. Campers are audience members for songs like "Rose, Rose, Rose" which was only sung by counselors, but are performers in call and response songs and marches.

While the whole campfire event was able to be broken down into segments, it is evident that the all-camp campfires played a role in how the week went for the girls. Each campfire can be analyzed using a lens similar to the one that Mechling uses. The first campfire serves as the opening for the whole week. The girls are introduced to all of the staff, told the rules, and introduced to the camp as a whole. The songs sung at this ceremony are more upbeat and generally louder. At this campfire, the sillier songs like "I'm a Little Coconut" would be sung.

This is still a bonding time, but it is clear who is the audience and who is the performer. However, the closing campfire is the closing and benediction for the week-long camp session. Informants report this being more of a solemn, meditative night, a night to reflect on the week and say goodbye. At this campfire, slower songs were usually picked by the counselors. Traditional closing songs included "Linger," "Make New Friends," "Rose," and Dean Martin's "My Rifle, My Pony, and Me." Even lullabies were sung. One informant reported singing "Make New Friends" while in a circle holding hands. Everyone would close their eyes, hold hands and a hand squeeze would go around the circle. When you felt your hand squeezed, you stick your foot in the middle and pass it on (Trimble). Similar to what Mechling reports, this time serves as a chance to reflect on the week, to reflect on the time spent with each other, and to acknowledge the end of an experience. While some elements are shared between the Boy Scouts and Girls Scouts, for females the ceremony is overall less aggressive as seen by the lacking yells. Instead, if the campfire is an arena, the arena is more of a "domestic hearth" where the campers and counselors can gather and bond through a range of activities (Mechling, 55).

Currently, Camp Tapawingo is undergoing much physical change. As time has passed, older units have been retired, the Crooked Tree has been cut, and new buildings are being constructed. Nevertheless, the camp stories and traditions surrounding all parts of the camp should be preserved for their value. The specific legends like those of the Crooked Tree, the Many Moons unit, and the fairies all serve a purpose for those who attend the camp. Although it is not as well explored or advocated, Girl Scouts camp folklore can be just as rich and powerful as the folklore found at a Boy Scouts camp. Using Mechling, the difference and similarities in the campfire ceremony between the two groups of Scouts can observed, analyzed, and further appreciated.

Works Cited

Couri, Peter J. "The First European Settlement in Illinois." *Peoria Historical Society.* 1992. Web. 19 March 2015. www.Peoriahistoricalsociety.org.

Dundes, Alan. *The Study of Folklore.* Englewood Cliffs: Prentice-Hall, 1965. Print.

Dryden, Phillip. Personal Interview. 20 March 2015.

Gelo, Daniel J., and Wayne Pate. *Texas Indian Trails.* Lanham: Republic of Texas, 2003. Print.

Georges, Robert A., and Michael Owen Jones. *Folkloristics: an Introduction.* Indiana University Press, 1995. Print.

Gillis, John R. *A World of Their Own Making: Myth, Ritual, and the Quest for Family Values.* New York: Basic, 1996. Print.

"History and Philosophy." Camp Tapawingo.com. American Camp Association. n.d. Web. 19 April 2015. www.camptapawingo.com/Summer-Camp-History-Philosophy.

Hollis, Susan T., Linda Pershing, and M. Jane Young, eds. *Feminist Theory and the Study of Folklore.* Urbana: University of Illinois Press, 1993. Print.

Houser, Steve. "What is an Indian Marker Tree." Dhtc.org. Texas Historic Tree Coalition. n.d. Web. 18 March 2015. www.txhtc.org/trees/indian-marker-tree/indian-marker-trees/.

Kendall, Jeanette. "Women Recall Time at Camp Tapawingo in Metamora." *East Peoria Times Courier.* 26 March 2014. Web. 21 March 2015.

LeFebvre, Julianne. "RE: Tapawingo." 9 March 2015. E-mail.

Mechling, Jay. "The Magic of the Boy Scout Campfire."*Journal of American Folklore*, vol 93, no. 367, 1980, pp. 35-56. JSTOR. Web. 19 Feb. 2015.

Merz, Gwen. "RE: Tapawingo Interview." 13 March 2015. E-mail.

Nelson, Kelly. "RE: Tapawingo Interview." 13 March 2015. E-mail.

Noland, Katie (Katie Bugs). "Camp Continues to Grow and Change." Facebook, 21 March 2015, 8:54 a.m.

O'Connor, Marie. Personal Interview. 21 March 2015.

Olrik, Axel. *Principles for Oral Narrative Research*. Trans. Kirsten Wolf and Jody Jensen. Bloomington: Indiana University Press, 1992. Print.

Peck, Cori and Troop 8420. "Girl Scout Songs." 2013. PDF File.

Staley, Bobbi Jo. "The Story Didn't Evolve." Facebook, 13 March 2015, 3:12 p.m.

Stobaugh, Katie. "RE: Tapawingo Interview." 10 March 2015. E-mail.

Summers, Candace. "RE: Tapawingo Interview." 18 March 2015. E-mail.

Trimble, Macy. Personal Interview. 12 March 2015.

Please Stop Feeding: Folklore and Language Used in *League of Legends* and Other Online Games
Madeline Barrow

This paper, written in 2015, is a classic participant-informer report of the content and creative dynamics of a folk-group's lingo—except that it studies a kind of folk group that could not have existed even a few years earlier: online role-playing games.

League of Legends is one of many online games that have become massively popular in the last few years. Naturally, with the exponential growth of online games and players, a culture has developed around many of these games, most notably the language and commonly seen terms used in the communication between players. The fascinating nature of these terms comes from the fact that they are not terms that came from the game, but were created by the players themselves for various purposes and spread to all other players by mere online chat. One gamer makes up a term for something and types it so that other players around him or her can see it. Other gamers pick up the use of this term, and soon it becomes a standard part of the online game to use the term, though nowhere in the game is this term listed or verified. This is seen with many terms in the game *League of Legends*, and in many other MMOs as well. The similarities in language, and the way a term warps and changes as it is passed on, are what makes this online language an interesting form of folklore.

When considering MMO's, or Massively Multiplayer Online games, it is important to first mention the game *Warcraft. Warcraft* is often credited as the mother of all modern day MMOs, the game that inspired most if not all modern online games and turned many early gamers on to online gaming, especially once the upgraded *World of Warcraft* was released in late 2004. Robinson Mills, who started his gaming journey with *WoW* before moving onto other MMOs, says that "a lot of terms on *League of Legends* originally came from *Warcraft* games." He says that terms like "Smurf" and "OP," terms to be discussed later in the paper, originated in the *Warcraft* games and have spread to attach themselves to other online games, likely transferred as players moved on from *Warcraft* to other games, taking their new terminology with them.

League of Legends is not as old as *Warcraft*, or even as old as *World of Warcraft. LoL* was released in 2009 and is actually classified as a MOBA (Massive Online Battle Arena) rather than an MMORPG, which is the full classification of *World of Warcraft*. While *WoW* is a multiplayer game, it is largely focused on the individual and the individual's progress. There are numerous bosses and events that cannot be defeated by a single player, events that require groups; but with an RPG (role playing game) like *WoW*, if a person is determined enough, they can get very far alone. Performance in an RPG is largely based on personal skill rather than the skill of others around them. *League of Legends*, as a MOBA, is very different. While an RPG is more about the individual's skill, MOBA's are highly competitive team-focused games that depend on the skill of every member of the team. If even one person in a MOBA is unskilled, he or she can keep their whole team from success. This is important to note because it changes the way that the invented terminology is used. When the nature of the game changes, the language and the meaning of the language for the game changes, though the way it is transmitted remains the same. All transmission is player to player. In this way, we can see conservation and variation of the language used throughout different online games.

Before discussing some of the terms, it is important to note that this research relies very heavily on my own personal fieldwork. I have been playing *League of Legends* for almost two years and have been immersed in its language and culture. Though I also cite many online forums that list terms and their meanings, language changes meaning so rapidly in the online gaming world that these forums can quickly become outdated. I have interviewed many people who currently play online games and have also compared their language experiences with mine.

One of the terms that became popular in *Warcraft* and later spread to other games is the word "noob." With many variations, such as newbie, newb, n00b, noobie, nub, and neeb, this term probably originated with the form "newbie," which was thought to be used by some US troops in the Vietnam War as a slang term for a new man in a unit (Elting 209). It is unknown exactly when this word was picked up by the internet, though in the early 1990's it was known to be widely used by computer programmers "with the emergence of l337speak...which led to the birth of its variant "n00b," spelled with two zeros instead of O's" (*Know Your Meme*). The word seems to have been popularized in the gaming community by early MMOs like *Warcraft II*, and has since spread to other games from there. What is really interesting about the term is that in many games, including *League of Legends*, it has evolved so that the spelling of the word will change its meaning. In *League of Legends*, when a person uses the term "newb" or "newbie," it is generally known to refer to a player who is new and/or inexperienced at the game. It is not a mean or a derogatory term, rather, a factual or even a fond one. The word "noob" used to mean the same thing. Now, however, when the spelling changes so that the word looks like "noob," "n00b," or "nub," the meaning changes to one much more derogatory to the player. While "newb" still refers to an inexperienced player, "noob" has come to mean someone who is experienced at the game but is extremely unskilled. Though both spellings used to hold the same meaning, time has changed one to become more derogatory, though it can be used in both a playful and a hurtful manner.

It is then important to note how the word "lol" can completely defuse or change the meaning when applied to a derogatory term like "noob". Calling someone a "noob" directly would be an insult, while saying, "Lol noob" could suddenly be considered playful. This difference is crucial in a game like *League of Legends* where players are extremely dependent on mutual cooperation with each other. Calling other players on the team "noobs" could potentially cause them to turn on the offender, thus losing the game for their whole team. Thus the word "lol" can make a phrase or an outburst less harsh while still allowing frustration to be vented at an unskilled teammate or teammates.

This is where the interesting difference between the two main types of MMOs comes into play. In an RPG like *WoW*, the word "noob" is generally a neutral term. This is because the skill levels of those around you do not matter in an RPG, whereas in a MOBA like *League of Legends*, if a teammate fails it can mean that everyone fails, and the language changes to become harsher and more degrading. Robinson Mills said that the only time he encountered the word "noob" in *World of Warcraft* was when he and his friends were teasing each other. I have seen the word used multiple times in *League of Legends*, both to demean other players and as a playful joke. Context and the word "lol" can change everything about this word's meaning, and all of this is heavily embedded and understood in gaming culture.

Korean gamers actually have a phenomenon similar to the American one we have been discussing, though without using a spelling change to differentiate between meanings. Instead, they have two separate words, "hasu," or literally "low hand," and "chobo," which means "beginner." Though neither of these words actually seems derogatory when taken literally, in the Korean gaming world, "chobo" has come to be the way to insult someone, in the exact same way that the word "noob" is used in English. "Hasu" would then be the polite way to call oneself a "newbie" (*Ask a Korean!*). Though the English and Korean languages are nothing alike, human nature in relation to competitive video gaming remains the same. People will insult each other's gaming skills by implying that they are like "newbie" players, but without actually insulting true new players.

The Japanese MOBA servers also have a word similar to the English "noob" called "chu". "Chu" comes from the Japanese word "chugakusei," which means "junior high kid" (*Vocaforum*). In their MOBAs, this word is used in the same way "noob" is used in *League of Legends*, to degrade unskilled players. It is interesting that Americans insult other players by mutilating the word for a newbie, while Japanese gamers insult other players by changing the word for a middle school kid. In both cases, the word used to put down others comes from someone seen as either inexperienced or immature.

Another term that changed meaning when it moved from the more individual based RPGs to competitive team-based MOBAs is the word "smurf." This is where some very interesting meta-folklore begins to circulate. While many sources seem to agree that this term originated with one of the old *Warcraft* games, some fascinating stories arise about just how this term came to be. The definition of the term "smurf," also called "smurfing," is generally an experienced player making a new account and posing as a newbie player. The experienced player likely has far more skill than new players and can easily destroy them. One of the stories that people tell is that "this definition of smurfing comes from 1996 and the game *Warcraft II* when certain well-known players made up new names, pretend[ed] to play badly, then beat the other players. They picked the names PapaSmurf and Smurfette" (*English Language & Uses*). Another person seemed to agree with this account, stating:

> that this kind of thing was started in *Warcraft II* days by Shlonglor and his buddies, who seem to be demi-gods for some people. They called it smurfing and Shlonglor's stated reason for it was because they couldn't find anyone who wanted to play

them. So they started picking on newbies and having great fun 'smurfing' them, that's the name they gave it. (*English Language & Uses*)

Allegedly, a group of well-known expert players were having trouble because no one wanted to play with them anymore; too many people knew that they were the best at the game. They then created new accounts, and labeled their actions as "Smurfing." Regardless of whether this is true or not, the term now exists almost twenty years later in almost every type of MMO game.

The way this term changes as it spreads is very interesting. *Warcraft II*, if that is indeed the game it originated in, is an RTS game (real-time strategy). It is like a MOBA in that anyone can sit down at level one and instantly be the best player in the world. It is nearly entirely skill based, rather than level-and-skill based like RPGs, which require time and effort before a player can become strong. A "smurf" account in an RTS like *Warcraft II* would have been devastating for the new players just beginning the game and being continuously crushed by experts. However, when this term spread to RPGs like *World of Warcraft* (not to be confused with its older cousin *Warcraft*), the negative connotation behind the term disappeared entirely. Robinson Mills first encountered the term "smurf" while playing *World of Warcraft* and said that "it wasn't like a bad thing. People made smurfs to play with their low-level friends." Smurfing in an RPG was seen as a neutral thing to do. Expert level players could make new accounts at any time yet would have to start at level 1 like everyone else. However, "smurf" again became a negative term when it appeared in MOBAs like *League of Legends*, games which, like *Warcraft*, are skill-based games that would make new players suffer if they had to play against an expert posing as a noob. The word "smurf" has gone through the whole spectrum from negative to positive and back to negative again, and there is no doubt that video game culture has taken a powerful ownership of this interesting word.

Unfortunately, like with the word "noob", there also seems to be a trend across languages when it comes to harsh and unsportsmanlike players declaring a victory. This is seen a lot in MOBAs like *League of Legends*. When a very powerful and easy victory of some sort is achieved, one player might type to the enemy team the word "pwned" or "pwnage." "Pwned" seems to come from a distorted form of "owned", perhaps even "perfect ownage" or "perfectly owned" (*InternetSlang*). It is used most often when a player achieves a "perfect" victory over an opponent. It is a way of saying they dominated and destroyed the other player. It can come as no surprise, then, that—though rarer nowadays because of the attempts of the game banning system and more conscientious-minded players—the even more demeaning word of "raped" will sometimes be substituted for "pwned."

This is no different in Korea. The most similar word in the Korean language to the English "pwned" is "gang-gandanghada." This is a corruption of the phrase "gang-gan gotong" which means literally "rape suffer" (*Ask a Korean!*). This is an awful word to say to somebody, especially to a stranger over the internet. However, in the world of online text, zealous players in both languages will overstep normal verbal boundaries that would prevent them from saying anything like this to a person's face. Something as simple as an online battle arena can cause people to insult both other players on their team and members of the enemy team in order to feel emotionally validated.

This universally aggressive use of the language can create some misconceptions about the gamer folk group. Nathan Schellenburg, Krishna Ganim, Robinson Mills, and Grant Simon are all Truman students who play *League of Legends* and other video games. They are, in my opinion, nice and ordinary people. However, all of them at some point have used semi-aggressive language on the chat box in *League of Legends*. Playing a game involving unknown teammates can change the way that players interact with others. This is hard to spot in RPGs but negatively affects everyone in MOBAs, because MOBAs actively require the player to communicate with others. It also explains why a lot of the language can seem unreasonably aggressive. One can be more aggressive to a stranger over online text than one would during a face-to-face interaction. The language spreads the way it does because of the anonymity factor.

On the brighter side, I have played *League of Legends* for two years, and while I have personally seen "pwned" and "rekt" ("wrecked") used, the community does seem to be more politically correct, in that I have never once seen someone claim that they "raped" the other team. Matt Barth, who has been playing *League of Legends* for about a year, has also never encountered the word "raped" in his experience with the game. "There's more substitutes for that word," he says. "Gaming has evolved past that [word]." We both believe that as banning and honoring systems have been introduced into the game, the community as a whole has gotten more politically correct. However, the highly-competitive nature of the game and the need to rely on others to win has still led to some emotional and aggressive language when communicating with teammates.

This leads into the *League of Legends*'s (and many other MOBAs') term, "feeding." The term "feeding" seems exclusive to MOBAs, leaving World of *Warcraft* and other RPGs safe from such words. The term is clearly to be used in a competitive team-based game. To "feed", in the most basic sense, is to die repeatedly to the enemy team. This places the team with the "feeding" player at a disadvantage, because the more kills the enemy team gets, the stronger they become. In fact, when a player gets a lot of kills, they are considered "fed." To die is to feed, to kill is to become fed. Nowhere is this stated in the game's rules; this is something that players have made up and spread through communication to other players. One of the most common phrases said to a repeatedly dying player is "please stop feeding." The funny aspect of that statement is that though it may sound at least a little bit polite, it is one of the cruelest insults in the game. To say that a player is "feeding" is inherently implying that they are so incompetent it is like they are dying on purpose. The verb "feed" itself is an action verb; it is a word that one must "do." When a person is said to "feed" or is "feeding" another player, this makes it sound not like an accident, but like it was their intent to sabotage the game by purposely dying to the enemy team.

The word "fed" also works in an interesting way. According to all interviewees, a player on the enemy team is very rarely complimented. They are never simply a good player. They won because they got "fed." By saying "the enemy champion *name* is fed," a player is implying two things. Firstly, that his (the player's) team or someone on his team is incompetent and losing the game. Someone on his team had to "feed" in order for the enemy to become "fed." The second implication of this statement is that the enemy is as worthless as the players on his team. They are not good. They did not earn their kills. They were passively "fed" by the people on his team. They are only winning and doing well because people on his team are screwing up, and not because they are more skilled. No one wants to admit that the enemy team is better, so they blame their own teammates. This shows an interesting psychological dynamic of many people who play MOBAs like *League of Legends*. It demonstrates the human's unwillingness to admit personal fault and the need to pass blame onto others, be it their own team or the opposing team.

The term "OP" is another "blame" word like "feeding" and "fed," though it has existed long before MOBAs, likely since the dawn of online gaming itself. It is important to talk about this term because it is extremely well known and widely used in nearly every MMO where it is possible to use such a term, and everyone has learned it, like the term "feeding" from each other. "OP" stands for "Over-Powered" and has always been used to refer to a monster, a boss, an ability, or a player, as being designed by the game to be more powerful than everyone else even though the game is supposed to be balanced. In *League of Legends*, this term is thrown around frequently. In *League of Legends*, this term often describes different "champions" that players choose to play, usually champions that are difficult to play and are hard to play against. For example, in *League*, there is a champion that a player can choose to play called "Master Yi". There are over 100 champions to choose from in *LoL* when playing the game, and anyone can choose to play Master Yi, like any of the champions. *LoL* is constantly being reworked to make sure that all of the champions are balanced with one another, and for the most part, they are. With the right skill, any champion can be played very well. However, in the case of Master Yi and others like him, when he is played against players of lower skill he is very hard to defeat, especially if he is played well. That is when the frustrated players will cry out into the chat box, "Master Yi OP!" This is very common when being defeated by a known "hard to play, harder to play against" champion. It is used like the words "feeding" and "fed" to pass along blame, to absolve the self from responsibility for poor game performance. Everyone knows that they could have chosen Master Yi, or any other so-called "OP" character, but rather than admitting fault in themselves, they blame the foundations of the game, the inherent flaws in the game's balancing system, and even the opposing player for choosing an "easy-win" champion.

To avoid pointing too many fingers at the toxic behaviors that persist in MOBAs, it is important to remember that the term "OP" is in nearly every online game. Just asking around the building I live in, people have heard this term used in *World of Warcraft, Starcraft, Diablo III, Call of Duty,* and even in *Smash Bros.* Since the beginning of video gaming it seems, whether playing with friends or with strangers, no one wants to appear unskilled. They blame the game instead, and crying, "OP!" is the quickest way to say, "I lost, but it wasn't really my fault."

The language passed down from game to game can be aggressive, rude, demeaning, and blame-giving. It can also be beautiful and fun. The marvelous part of online gaming is that it is easy to play with friends, and groups of friends create their own culture when they get together. Though gamers are always part of the large community of the game they are playing, they also can become part of a smaller community—a community of friendship. It may sound a bit cheesy, but what happens with the language that develops between friends is every bit as fascinating as what happens with language in large groups. For example, Krishna Ganim, Truman State University student and avid player of *League of Legends,* came up with the term "Jeff." In *LoL,* there are creatures called "minions" that one can kill for experience and money. They also have the unfortunate habit of getting in the way, and can block a person's "skill shot" (ability that requires aiming and skill, like shooting a gun or an arrow). Many who play *League* have experienced aiming their weapon at the enemy team only to have their well-timed shot unintentionally blocked by a minion. Krishna affectionately calls all minions who block skill shots "Jeff." This was picked up by the group of people playing with Krishna, and the word "Jeff" has actually evolved. One can say "Damn it, Jeff!" or "Man, I got Jeffed!" when blocked by a minion. No one else in *League of Legends* says this. It is a special term invented by one person and used by a small group of people living on the fifth floor of Centennial Hall. People say it without thinking, and some do not even know that the word was invented by Krishna. Language and terminology evolves and spreads more quickly than imaginable.

Amazingly, after several over-the-internet interviews with strangers, one person told me that they too have a term for the annoying minion that gets in the way. He and his friends call those minions "the secret service." This is also not a widespread term, just something used between friends. Gaming allows folklore and culture to develop in small groups as well as large, and it is interesting to see how different people perceive different parts of *League of Legends* and come up with their own terminology to pass on.

MMO's are a world rich and thriving with an ever-changing language and lore behind the language. Though the language can be cruel and degrading, it can also be positive and inspiring. Every word has its own story, and individuals learn the language from each other. No matter how mocking the words, it would still be amazing if in one hundred years gamers are still begging each other to "please stop feeding," whatever that may mean!

Works Cited

"Beginners Phrases and Acronyms in *LoL*." *League of Legends Community RSS*. Riot Games, Inc., 10 May 2010. Web. 22 Feb. 2015. forums.na.leagueoflegends.com/board/showthread.php?t=110065.

Elting, John Robert, Ernest L. Deal, and Dan Cragg. *A Dictionary of Soldier Talk*. New York: Scribner, 1984, p. 209.

"Gosu." *Wikipedia*. Wikimedia Foundation. Web. 14 Apr. 2015. en.wikipedia.org/wiki/Gosu.

"Japanese Internet Slang [Archive]." *Vocaforum*. 30 May 2009. Web. 23 Feb. 2015. www.vocaforum.com/archive/index.php?t-238.html.

K.T. "Ask a Korean!" *Blogspot.* 20 Aug. 2013. Web. 23 Feb. 2015.
    askakorean.blogspot.com/2013/08/here-are-some-korean-slangs.html.

"MMORPG Lingo." *Almar's Guides.* 1 Jan. 2008. Web. 22 Feb. 2015.
    almarsguides.com/eq/gettingstarted/mmorpglingo.cfm.

"Noob." *Know Your Meme News.* 2014. Web. 14 Apr. 2015.
    knowyourmeme.com/memes/noob.

"What Does PWNED Mean?" *InternetSlang.com* Web. 14 Apr. 2015.
    www.internetslang.com/PWNED-meaning-definition.asp.

"Where Does the Term "Smurfing" Come From?" *English Language & Usage.*
    Stack Exchange Inc., 20 June 2012.Web. 14 Apr. 2015.
    english.stackexchange.com/questions/17209/where-does-the-term-
    smurfing-come-from.

Yo Momma So Y That Z: A Linguistic Analysis of Yo-Momma Humor
Chris Buerke

Folklore is at home equally in the social sciences and the humanities. The study of verbal folklore ranges from belletristic and impressionistic to rigorously linguistic. Buerke's 2013 study of a type of humorous verbal performance exemplifies theory-driven analysis, and can serve as a model for other genres.

Abstract

This analysis will focus strongly upon the topic of "yo-momma humor," applying a cognitive linguistic approach to determine both the humorous and non-humorous properties of formulaic insult humor when used in states of conflict. The television program, *Yo Momma* was analyzed for the sake of discussion and a collection of jokes which exemplify the yo-momma form were gathered. Through an examination of these jokes, as well as an investigation of modern humor theories (incongruity theories, conflict theories, and relief theories), this paper will attempt to answer the question, "Why are yo-momma jokes humorous?" The results of this analysis should lead to a greater understanding of linguistic humor, and should determine the effects of divergence on language.

INTRODUCTION

What is funny? If you were to ask a group of people on the street this question, you would likely hear a variety of answers—one liners, dirty jokes, good stories, slapstick movies, goofy babies, and possibly even anti-humor, which prides itself on being the opposite of funny. Chances are that the things that one person finds humorous are unique to them, and that someone else, despite the shared forms of humor, would have difficulty relating completely to the other individual. The question becomes then not "what is funny?" but rather "what is humor?" What is the element that makes anything, on a basic scale, worth laughter?

What is humor?

According to Bergen & Binsted (2003), it is this particular question that causes humor to be held amongst the most intriguing and least understood of our cognitive capabilities. Attardo (1994) attempts to answer the question by examining a historical yet philosophical perspective. First looking at the Greeks, he states that Plato (427-347 BC) believed humor to be a "mixed feeling of the soul" for example, a mixture of pleasure and pain that causes laughter through overwhelming—something Plato condemned absolutely. Aristotle (384-322 BC) disagreed, condemning only the excess of laughter and stating that the humor found within comedy can be seen as a "stimulation" of the soul that puts the listener into a state of good will. It is within the works of Aristotle that humor is given a purpose, and that purpose is to create a relaxing mood despite the argument presented by a speaker.

Attardo (1994) goes on to make claims about the Greek influence on Roman humor theory, mentioning the works of multiple Latin philosophers. Primarily, he quotes the works of Cicero (106-43 BC) who "introduce[d] the distinction between verbal and referential humor," explaining that jokes can be "about what is said" (*dicto*) or about "the thing" (*res*). Cicero's claims implied that humor was not only an element of comedy, but a conscious act performed by a speaker through a variety of different methods. Attardo (1994) lists the following genres of humor assumed by the Roman thinker:

> [Cicero] elaborates his taxonomy by stipulating that referential humor (*in res*) includes anecdotes (*fabella*) and caricature (*imitatio*). Verbal humor includes ambiguity (*ambigua*), paronomasia (*parvam verbi immutationem*), false etymologies (*interpretatio nominis*), proverbs, literal interpretation of figurative expressions (*ad verbum non ad sententiam rem accipere*), allegory, metaphors, and antiphrasis or irony (*ex inversione verborum*).

Years later, Quintilian (35 – 100 AD) introduced a definition of humor that dealt with three subjects: (1) plays at others, (2) plays at ourselves, and (3) a middle category which involved neither ourselves nor others. Within this third kind (the neutral category), Quintilian implied that words or phrases could be interpreted in multiple ways, hinting at the modern linguistic ideas of both polysemy and ambiguity. Claims were also made about using language to state differently what was right and true, similar to the current ideas of Raskin (1985), who categorizes humor as real/unreal, normal/abnormal, and possible/impossible. Attardo (1994) assumes that what Quintilian referred to as right and true were closely related to the ideas of real and normal. It is here that one realizes that the study of humor on a scholarly level existed long before any formal linguistic analysis, as philosophers attempted to understand the humorous quality of their own work. And while this is by no means a full historical account, Attardo (1994) ends by taking note of the Middle Ages, in which linguistic theories of humor were rarely discussed, and the study of communication seemed to fade away.

Fortunately for the current linguist, in considering the various theories of humor that have been offered in the past, as well as the present-day understanding that humor is a conscious communicative effort, the subject has been reborn through cognitive linguistics. And while various forms of notable linguistic humor do exist, and have existed for some time, this paper will focus primarily upon a variation of formulaic insults by the name of "yo-momma humor." The general structure and linguistic qualities of these jokes will be discussed in the following section.

Yo-momma jokes

Yo-momma humor is a form of linguistic humor that references a maternal figure through the use of phrases such as "your mother" or "yo momma" in an attempt to insult the target by way of their family. Frequently used when "playing the Dozens" (Abrahams, 1962), various insults concerning obesity, age, race, intelligence, unattractiveness, poverty, and many other topics are implemented to create the hilarity of a particular "snap," or joke. The Dozens, according to Cole (1974), is a spoken word game, common among African-American communities, where participants insult each other until one concedes. Typically, the game is played in front of an audience of one's peers, who encourage the participants to reply with more offensive insults so as to increase the tension and humor of the play. Also referred to as "sounding," "sigging," "wolfing," or "joning," the Dozens serves as an important part in the linguistic and psychosocial development of African-American youths (Abrahams, 1962). The most prominent linguistic features include (1) the reliance upon formulaic patterns, which will be discussed later in terms of syntax, (2) the use of rhyme within these patterns, and (3) the change of speech rhythms from natural ones to ones that show differences of pitch, stress, and syntax. Some examples of yo-momma humor, collected through personal experience, are shown in (1) below:

(1.) **(a)** Yo momma so fat when her beeper goes off, people think she's
        backing up.
      (b) Yo momma so stupid it took her 2 hours to watch *60 Minutes*.

Within (1), the formula is immediately evident. An entity (*yo momma*)
is described in the first clause as possessing a great deal of some property. The first clause is then followed by a second clause that provides
the punch line (Bergen & Binsted, 2003). In (1a), the mother is described
as possessing a great deal of weight within the first clause. The second
clause references the fact that a beeper sounds similar to the sound that a
large vehicle would make when in reverse. When the two clauses are read
in conjunction with one another, the joke suggests that the mother is so
hefty that she is comparable to the size of a large vehicle, causing other
people to believe that when her beeper is going off, she is backing up like
a truck might. In (1b), the mother is described as possessing a great deal
of stupidity, or a lack of intelligence. The second clause implies that *60
Minutes* is a show that should only take an hour to complete; however, the
subject takes two hours to finish the episode. When the phrases are read
together, the joke suggests that the mother is so unintelligent that she cannot even adhere to the unchanging, temporal restrictions that have been
placed upon a television program. While both (1a) and (1b) are highly
absurd and impossible, the jokes employ the use of imagery to create a
situation that many would find humorous.

A more in-depth discussion will take place in the Data and Discussion
section of this paper in an attempt to discover which specific elements of
humor elicit laughter, and which do not.

METHODOLOGY

For the sake of determining which elements make yo-momma humor
funny, a collection of jokes was gathered from the MTV reality show, *Yo
Momma* (Valderrama, 2006)—an American reality television game show
from 2006, based upon the black urban tradition of insulting one's opponent's mother. This unscripted comedy competition series puts individuals
up against each other in a battle for $1,000 in cash and a chance to ad-
vance to the final tournament. Participants are allowed the opportunity
to investigate the life of their competitor's mother, in order to enhance
the quality of their jokes. They are then brought together and exchange
yo-momma jokes in attempt to thwart each other. Five episodes were observed, and thirty-four yo-momma jokes that displayed the "X is so Y that

Z" construction were then transcribed. All jokes pertaining to characteristics of the opposing player were omitted in an attempt to focus strictly on yo-momma humor, and not all jokes are included in the discussion. For a complete list of jokes used to form conclusions, see the Appendix section.

The purpose of this research project was to analyze and determine the humorous properties of yo-momma jokes. In order to gather this data, the jokes were subjectively rated based on audience reaction. Jokes received either a "successful," "average," or "unsuccessful" rating. Those which received sustained, loud laughter were given a rating of "successful." Those which received booing or very few responses were given a rating of "unsuccessful." Those which received little laughter and were followed quickly by an opposing joke were given a rating of "average." For the sake of discussion, the "successful" and "unsuccessful" jokes were closely examined, as well as various jokes gathered through personal experience.

DATA AND DISCUSSION

This section will deal primarily with the question of "Why are yo-momma jokes humorous?" and will be divided into two parts. The first will attempt to explain yo-momma humor from a linguistic perspective, discussing the general categories of linguistics (syntax, morpho-phonological changes, pragmatics, and semantics), the humorous and non-humorous qualities used within MTV's *Yo Momma*, and the patterns that exist within moments of conflict. The second part will attempt to answer the question from a theoretical perspective, discussing modern incongruity theories, conflict theories, and relief theories.

I. Linguistic Perspective

Syntax

Considered a variant of scalar humor, yo-momma jokes make use of the following syntactic structure, with some alternate forms: **X is so Y that Z**. Within yo-momma humor, the X quality of the construction always pertains to *yo momma*—an African American dialect (AAE) form of the Standard American English *your mother*—or various other referential devices, such as *his mom* or *this dude's momma*, when addressing a crowd; the Y quality involves a negative characteristic such as *poor, lazy, fat, stupid,* etc.; the final Z quality is the varying component of the joke, offering the greatest source of humor. Many of the jokes, due to the strong use of AAE, lack various aspects of the standard English structure through the omission of morphemes such as *is* and *that*. However, the structure is still present, as seen in (1a). *Yo momma* signifies the X quality; *fat* seems to be the Y quality; and *it took her two hours to watch 60 Minutes* represents the Z quality.

As mentioned when discussing the initial structure, some variations of the "X is so Y that Z" formula do exist, as seen in a joke told by a participant of *Yo Momma*:

(2.) Yo momma's like Geico, she's so easy a caveman could do her.

Rather than existing separately as its own sentence, the formula appears after the clause *yo momma's like Geico,* which is included for semantic purposes. The X quality which typically appears as *yo momma,* is represented by the pronoun *she* instead. The primary clause which appears before the actual yo-momma joke references both the Y and Z qualities of the sentence. One must understand the popular slogan of the company in order for the joke to make sense (i.e. "It's so easy, a caveman could do it."). Semantic narrowing is also imposed in (2), using the word *easy* to imply a certain level of non-difficulty in relation to sexual availability. Despite the added semantic information that exists prior to the clauses necessary for yo-momma humor, the "X is so Y that Z" formula is required in order for yo-momma jokes to take place. However, not all utterances that use this structure are considered humorous; many are simply scalar structures (Bergen & Binsted, 2003):

(3.) **(a)** It was so cold where I live, we found dogs huddling for warmth.
       (b) The film's ending was so shocking that it physically hurt you.

One can assume that the syntactic elements found within yo-momma jokes are not central to the humorous utterances, though without these essential components, the joke would not even be allowed to exist.

Morpho-phonology

In addition to the syntactic structure being morphed to fit the constraints of yo-momma humor, morphology and phonology are both affected as well. In most constructions of yo-momma jokes—which rely on the "X is so Y that Z" formula—both *is* and *that* are omitted. The first (*is*) seems to disappear due to the conjunction of *is* and *so*. Over time, the emphasis was most likely put upon *so*, causing elision to occur and the *is* to fade away. The omission of *that* occurred for the sake of combining the two clauses into one joke. Rather than using the complementizer, a speaker instead takes a pause, building suspense and allowing themselves to play upon surprise theory as seen below in (4a).

In terms of phonology, certain vowel phonemes are lengthened and strong emphasis is used in certain places to produce a particular way of speaking within the first clause, *yo momma is so*.... Take for example the successful joke (4a) versus the unsuccessful joke (4b):

(4.) (a) Yō momma **sō fat**//she bought her bras at AutoZone.

(b) Your mother's so nasty that she brought crabs to the beach.

In (4a), the sentence was spoken with the emphasis on the bolded morphemes. It is assumed that the first *yo* is emphasized and lengthened in order to draw attention to the fact that a new joke is beginning. The *so* is lengthened in order to imply that the mother has a great quantity of the Y quality, *fat*, which is then emphasized to signify the scale that will be used for the remainder of the joke. The speaker takes a pause between the first and the second clause, giving the audience time to assume what he might say, and allowing himself to take advantage of incongruity theory (Ross, 1998). The speaker in (4b), however, does not use any specific emphasis within his joke. He begins weakly by not placing phonological stress on *yo*, which marks the start of a new "snap," and then omits stress on *nasty*, which is shown to be the relevant scalar system. Because the audience is not given the time to dwell on what the speaker might say, the joke loses its humorous appeal.

Within (4b), the speaker neglects to follow the expected omission of phonology and morphology, including unnecessary linguistic components for these types of jokes. The speaker also maintains the standard *your mother* rather than *yo momma*, or another variation, causing him to appear as if he does not know how to "play the Dozens" (Abrahams, 1962). Another fact worth mentioning involves the loss of the contracted *is*, as well as the present progressive *–s* and past tense *–ed* morphemes. For example, <*she's walking down the street*> becomes <**she** *walking down the street*>; <*she sits on an automatic toilet*> becomes < *she* **sit** *on an automatic toilet*>; and <*when I looked on her MySpace page*> becomes <*when I* **look** *on her MySpace page*>. For the sake of simplifying sentence structure and improving the flow of speech, these morphemes often tend to disappear from most Z quality constructions.

Participants might also imitate the mother's voice in order to intensify the image being created within the joke. For example:

(5.) (a) Yo momma so poor I asked her what's for dinner, that b**** lit my pocket on fire, "Hot Pocket!"

(b) Yo momma so fat and stupid when the judge says order in the court, she says, "Yeah, let me get a hamburger..."

(c) Yo momma so stupid when she had you and saw the umbilical cord, she say, "Ooh it come with cable?"

These jokes rely heavily upon the phonological use of imitation, rather than any semantic or syntactic structure. Only by enhancing the imagery of the mother do these jokes become humorous, and surprisingly all were perceived as highly successful.

Pragmatics

Bergen & Binsted (2003) claim that a major portion of the pragmatics used with the construction of yo-momma humor depends upon the knowledge of linguistic scales—"a set of words of the same grammatical category which can be ordered by their semantic strength or degree of informativeness" (Horn, 1972; Levinson, 1983). Examples of such ordered words are:

{warm, hot, burning}
{dim, dark, pitch black}
{big, huge, colossal}

Within yo-momma humor, a scale of Y-ness is first identified (for example, *poor*) and the X quality is then placed high on the scale (...*she can't even afford to pay attention*), with the full utterance reading as < *Yo momma so poor she can't even afford to pay attention* >. One might view the scale of *poor* as poor, bankrupt, homeless, etc., extending so far as to being unable pay for something that is always free. The greater the level of intensity that exists, the funnier the utterances appears to be. As the scale increases in intensity, the use of imagery is imposed for the sake of creating context-independent rankings (Bergen & Binsted, 2003). While these context-independent labels allow the jokes to be more creative, it tends to affect the scalar implicature that should exist. No longer can a linguistic scale be visualized; instead, interpretation of the punch line depends upon how funny the audience believes the hypothetical situation to be. Take for instance, the following successful (6a) and unsuccessful (6b) jokes:

(6.) (a) Yo momma so fat, yo dad proposed to her with an onion ring.
        (b) Yo momma so fat she got hit by a school bus and 23 kids died.

In (6a), the speaker makes use of semantic vagueness by expressing the idea of an engagement ring as an onion ring, which is not typically an item used for engagement. Additionally, the speaker takes advantage of fantastic hyperbole by assuming that the mother's fingers are so large that she would need an onion ring in order for the ring to fit. This joke works on multiple layers by suggesting (1) that the mother loves food so much that she would actually prefer an onion ring to a diamond ring and (2) that she is so large that she requires a wrist-sized ring for her fingers. In (6b), imagery is again used, as it is commonly used within yo-momma jokes; however, no pragmatic or semantic tools are being used to enhance the quality of the joke. (6a) appears to be more humorous, not because it is on a higher scalar level than (6b), but because the image it produces is more humorous since it employs more semantic devices.

When analyzing the humor found within *Yo Momma*, certain Y qualities were found to be used more prevalently. All of the included terms were used by participants of the show: *big, nasty, fat, sleazy, stupid, ugly, easy, black, poor*, and *lazy*. The terms were then grouped into certain categories and the following chart was compiled to determine which Y qualities were used most frequently:

Y Categories	Total References	Successful (+)	Average	Unsuccessful (-)
Body size (fat, big, large, etc.)	15	8	2	5
Sexuality (easy, sleazy, nasty, etc.)	5	2	1	1
Intelligence (stupid, dumb, etc.)	6	2	2	2
Race (black, dark, etc.)	2	0	2	0
Miscellaneous (poor, lazy, ugly)	7	1	3	3

The chart shows that "body size" was the most referenced quality. Based on the use of scalar implicature, one can make the assumption that body size allows for the greatest linguistic expansion. A mother can be referred to as big, large, huge, ginormous; the list goes on. In terms of imagery and metaphor, body size has the greatest potential for visualization as size is an easily comparable measurement. The chart also shows "race" to be the least referenced quality. While a large scale system can be implemented to refer to levels of darkness, one might assume that jokes of this category were avoided because they could be seen as offensive rather than humorous. A few other qualities, not found within the show but worth noting, include: *skinny, bald-headed, crazy, old, dark, short, hairy, slutty, greasy, teeth so yellow, glasses so thick, hair so nappy* (Percelay, Dwek, & Ivey, 1994).

Pragmatically, the use of yo-momma humor also intentionally flouts the maxims proposed by Grice—quality, quantity, manner, and relevance (Aarons, 2012). Concerning *quality*, one can assume that the humorous utterances being made are completely untrue. Even if the mother is indeed

overweight, poor, ugly, lazy, or any other insulting term, participants using this form of humor within conflict take advantage of hyperbole, un-
derstatement, and indirect relation to increase the hilarity of their "snap"
(Bergen & Binsted, 2003). Abrahams (1962) claimed that the less true an
utterance was, the more likely it was to be considered humorous. Because
yo-momma jokes are not meant to be harmful, participants focus more
on being creative rather than insulting the mother; in fact, those who do
make serious claims within their jokes might create violent situations.

In terms of *quantity*, this maxim is the least flouted of the four, as a
particular length of yo-momma humor has not formally been established.
When a joke exceeds a particular amount of time while being told, it tends
to lose its humorous appeal, causing participants of the Dozens to believe
that short and fast snaps are best when playing against each other; however, lack of detail also carries less semantic meaning, often causing the
joke to become less relatable. In instances where detail is omitted, contes-
tants of *Yo Momma* often attempted to compensate by making particularly
crude references that they hoped would elicit laughter. In most cases,
these attempts were seen as uncreative and participants were then booed.

Concerning *manner*, pitch, stress, and syntax are often molded to fit the
demands of this type of humor; however, the topic of manner is discussed
in more detail within the morpho-phonology section of this paper. In addition to changes of speech, participants may also use non-verbal language
when telling these jokes. For example, when telling his "final joke" on *Yo
Momma*, a participant uttered the following:

(7.)   This dude's momma so fat she got a rest in peace t-shirt for all her
        favorite foods.

He then proceeded to reveal the shirt underneath his jacket which displayed cartoon images of food, with eyes crossed out and tombstones behind their "bodies," as if he had taken the shirt from the other contestant's
mother. While the joke would likely not be very humorous, the visual
action included within the telling of the joke caused it to succeed among
the listening community. While this aspect of yo-momma humor is non-
linguistic, it seems notable as it often affected the audience reaction when
certain jokes were told.

The final maxim, *relevance*, is flouted slightly, as most of the jokes do
not logically follow others. Within one episode of the show, the following
exchange took place:

(8.) (A:) Yo momma so poor her checks bounce like basketballs.
     (B:) Yo momma so lazy, she just like butter, easy to spread.

(A:) Yo momma so poor she was the leading lady in 50 Cent's video, "Window shopper."

(B:) This dude's momma so lazy, her best friend's a Chinese delivery guy.

While both speakers remained relevant to the Y qualities that they were separately portraying through their humor (A used *poor* consistently while B used *lazy*), neither speaker addressed the jokes of their opponent. However, the jokes were relevant in that they all pertained to the mother.

Semantics

In terms of semantics, a variety of jokes will be discussed for the sake of determining which qualities cause a joke to be humorous, and which cause a joke to fail. Because each joke contains varying semantic information, not all thirty-four jokes will be discussed; instead, this section will focus upon a select few, and the remaining jokes can be found in the Appendix. In the following, (9) will contain successful jokes; (10) will contain unsuccessful jokes.

(9.) **(a)** Yo momma so big, when she walking down the street, her stomach's doing the Bankhead Bounce and her ass is doing the East Side Stomp.

(b) Yo momma so fat I told her I gotta new grill, she started pulling steaks outta her pocket.

(c) Yo momma so fat when I looked on her MySpace page, her top 8 was all her favorite restaurants.

All three jokes rely heavily upon the cultural knowledge that the audience holds. (9a) refers to two cultural phenomena, known primarily to the black community. The Bankhead Bounce was "a dance that originated in a neighborhood on the west side of Atlanta known as Bankhead"; and the East Side Stomp was "a walk used to 'represent' the eastside in which a person slowly picks up one foot, waggles and shakes it as if it is heavy, stomps the ground (with the heavy foot), and repeats with the other foot" (Peckham, 2005). The joke implies that the mother is so large that she can simultaneously perform two very different dances with two different parts of her body; and not only is able to accomplish this feat, but she is also in two different areas while performing them. (9b) assumes that the audience understands that a *grill* can refer to either (1) an instrument used for cooking or (2) a set of gold or silver teeth worn in one's mouth. In order to find the joke humorous, one must understand the use of polysemy and the lexical ambiguity of the word *grill*. The joke implies that the mother cannot differentiate between the two terms and instead assumes what she would like to hear—that the *grill* in reference will be used for cooking food—and because the mother is so overweight, she most likely carries food with her in convenient areas, such as her pockets. (9c) reaches a more general audience, as most people are familiar with MySpace, including those outside of the black community. One must understand that an individual's top eight usually involves their best friends. The joke implies that the mother's best friends are restaurants because she frequents them so often and perhaps enjoys their company over that of actual people.

When semantic intention is misunderstood, lost, or even absent from a joke, it suffers drastically when received by an audience.

(10.) **(a)** Yo momma so stupid she measures height with a thermostat.
     (b) Yo momma so stupid she thought she needed a degree to become a vegetarian.

In (10a), the speaker is attempting to make a stab at the mother's intelligence level; however, it seems to fail. While it is understood that a thermostat tracks and sets temperature, the more appropriate word would have been *thermometer*, which actually measures temperature. Regardless of the speaker's incorrect word usage, the joke does not contain any cultural references and lacks creativity within the imagery, causing the joke to fail. (10b) also lacks any cultural reference, and contains a weak semantic relationship. The speaker believes that the audience should be able to interpret the connection between a profession, such as *veterinarian*, and a lifestyle, such as *vegetarian*; however, considering that most professions do not end with the final–*arian* ending, the relationships does not appear to be very strong, causing the audience to lose sight of the connection that the speaker is attempting to convey. While believing that one needs a degree to become a vegetarian is "stupid," the utterance is hardly funny.

II. Theoretical Perspective

Incongruity Theory

Made famous by both Kant and Shopenhauer, the incongruity theory states that humor is perceived when the incongruity between a concept involved in a certain situation and the real objects thought to be in some relation to the concept are realized. In other words, the theory depends upon the expectations of an audience, and offers an unexpected twist. As

Aristotle put it, "[t]he effect is produced even by jokes depending upon changes of the letters of a word; this too is a surprise. You find this in verse as well as in prose. The word which comes is not what the hearer imagined" (Smuts, 2009). According to incongruity theory, the humorous aspect of jokes depends upon the realization of the resolution. In order for a joke to succeed, it must give the audience a chance to ponder what the resolution might be. Only by surprising the listeners with an unanticipated punch line is humor achieved.

Within yo-momma humor, a rather large portion of the humor comes from the strong delivery of a joke within a heated situation. As discussed in the morpho-phonological section, a pause needs to exist between the first and second clause. This gives the audience an opportunity to ponder what the resolution might be. One might assume that players of the Dozens focus strongly upon particular Y qualities because they allow the listeners to assume the punch line(s) that they have heard in the past. While the audience contemplates the multiple ways that they expect the joke to go, the speaker surprises them with a new alternative, which then elicits laughter. It is through the resolution of incongruity that the audience finds the joke humorous.

In terms of a conflict setting, the incongruity theory allows for an increase in humor as the jokes continue. While one speaker may produce a joke referencing the size of the mother and succeed, the following player is given the opportunity to create an even bigger twist. The jokes possess the potential to build in hilarity until a non-humorous resolution is presented for an incongruity. Outside of a conflict theory, yo-momma humor still depends upon the incongruity theory as each joke contains the opportunity to separate the X and Y from the Z quality.

Relief Theory

The relief theory focuses primarily on humor as a pragmatic tension-relief mechanism. The two most prominent theorists within this idea were Herbert Spencer and Sigmund Freud, as the theory deals with the essential structures and psychological processes that produce humor. Attardo (1994) states that relief theory (or as he describes it, release theory) is particularly interesting to linguists because it accounts for a liberation from the rules of language, and allows the individual to use word-play outside the principle of Cooperation proposed by Grice. In terms of yo-momma humor, Abrahams (1962) would believe that playing the Dozens serves as an important relief technique for children growing up within African-American communities. The tension that would typically be built up in youth is expressed through yo-momma jokes by means of targeting a fictional mother character, and expressing "liberation" by means of playing a game. The humorous aspect of these utterances occurs when in conflict with another individual, allowing both players to incrementally reduce the amount of tension that exists between them—assuming that they are friends already or have a mutual understanding of the game—by continuing to challenge each other's creative abilities. This lack of tension then draws forth laughter from the audience. Humor, according to relief theory, is used mainly to overcome sociocultural inhibitions (Attardo, 1994). In addition, Freud (1901) might argue that participants in this form of humor may comment on the negative qualities of one's mother in order to reveal suppressed desires. By acknowledging this fact within a community and within conflict, relief is achieved and humor is obtained.

Conflict Theory and Superiority Theory

Conflict theory, as described by Bergen & Binsted (2003), "hold[s] that humor evokes two conflicting impulses—the impulse to proceed and the impulse to draw back. These may be more specifically the results of conflicts between feelings of friendliness and hostility or play and seriousness." The other, superiority theory, appears in two forms according to Smuts (2009), the first maintaining that all humor involves a feeling of superiority, and the second that the feelings of superiority appear in many cases of humor. In a way, these two theories disagree with each other. Conflict theory states that humor arises from the mere play that exists between two individuals in an attempt to maintain a level of homeostasis; superiority theory finds humor not in the balance of conflict, but within the idea that one overcomes the other and can view oneself as superior.

Both theories, however, are seen within yo-momma humor. Unfortunately, in some hostile instances, these jokes are used in states of conflict. Humor arises when individuals realize that the pragmatic use of language is being implemented, not to insult, but to play a game. It is when that balance of conflict is uneven that jokes become rather unfunny. For example, if an individual takes the game too seriously while the other attempts to poke fun, the player who is acting with the intent to offend will appear to be non-humorous; whereas, the player who pokes fun will be seen as comical, and will likely have more subject material for future jokes. Superiority theory can arise from an unbalanced conflict, as one individual might be favored over the other. In many of the episodes of *Yo Momma*, the community shown would not laugh at the jokes of a white person, regardless of how humorous they actually were. Instead, humor arose when the audience chose to favor one person over the other, and used their laughter to mock the less-funny white individual.

FUTURE RESEARCH

Suggestions for future research include analyzing a larger sample of jokes and focusing primarily upon a specific linguistic feature. Many notable aspects seemed to arise throughout the research; however, for the sake of this paper, all topics could not be discussed. A more elaborate discussion over phonology and the use of prosody might be interesting. Also, a more conductive study could be produced from someone who grew up within the African-American culture and took part in the Dozens, as they might understand the semantics of yo-momma humor better and be able to better analyze the pragmatic mechanisms used in these jokes.

Future research might also focus on creating a comprehensive theory of humor, as many theories tend to overlap when studying a particular genre of humorous language. In addition, linguistic topics (such as Grice's maxims and other linguistic features) tend to merge in discussions of particular elements of yo-momma humor. If certain aspects were contained and focused upon, a more detailed and comprehensive view of the subject could likely be produced.

The final point of research that one might suggest could consist of observing and recording the Dozens being played. While gathering jokes and responses from a television show was convenient, one runs the risk of editing bias and may misinterpret the audience reaction. Transcribing yo-momma jokes when used in conflict would aid the linguist in better understanding the emotion, prosody, and non-verbal cues used within the game.

CONCLUSION

Many humorous features exist within yo-momma humor, and any exclusion of these features can cause the joke to be perceived as "unsuccessful." The general requirements necessary to create successful yo-momma jokes include factors within varying linguistic categories. Within syntax, the joke must follow the "X is so Y that Z" construction. Variation may occur, but only to add semantic meaning for the sake of humor. In terms of morphology, certain free morphemes such as *is* and *that* must be excluded, as well as verbal suffixes (*–s* and *–ed*) and most contractions. Phonology requires that tellers of yo-momma jokes lengthen most vowels within the primary clause, phonologically emphasize the crucial features of the joke construction (such as the X, *yo momma*, and Y, *so* , qualities), and allow for a crucial pause between the first and second clause so that the audience may have time to form their own resolutions to the incongruity that exists. The process of imitation may also be used to enhance the creative imagery within the Z quality of the joke. Within pragmatics, yo-momma jokes require the individual to flout Grice's maxims with the exception of quantity, use non-verbal actions to accompany jokes, and maintain creativity when referencing the scalar implicature of the Y quality. Finally, semantics dictates that the jokes be relatable to the culture in which they appear, allowing speakers to understand where they come from and make appropriate references to aspects of the African-American lifestyle.

In terms of theory, all three (incongruity, relief, and conflict) work together to create a unified view of humor that elicits laughter in multiple circumstances. Incongruity theory is present in yo-momma jokes as the audience attempts to resolve the given incongruity between the first and second clause. Relief theory states the jokes are made for the sake of relieving unwanted psychological tension, causing linguists to see the Dozens as an important linguistic and psychosocial speech act for African-Americans to experience. Conflict theory assumes that one must find balance amidst conflict, and through this balance, humor is achieved. When the balance is not achieved, superiority theory can be applied as one participant is seen as more humorous than the other.

In terms of what specifically causes yo-momma jokes to be humorous, no definite answer exists; however, many factors are certainly observable, and should continue to be observed within the cognitive linguistic field.

Appendix: Humor Rankings

0 — booing or little laughter
1 — mild laughter
2 — sustained, loud laughter

(Editor's note: a color-coding scheme in the original Appendix was changed to a numerical one for this printing format.)

Episode 301 (College Park vs. Union City)

4:56 –This girl's momma so big she can't call a taxi, she gotta call a tractor trailer. 1

5:19 – Yo momma so nasty, that b**** don't have crabs, she got lobster. 1

5:31 – Yo momma so big, when she walking down the street, her stomach's doing the Bankhead Bounce and her ass is doing the East Side Stomp. 2

8:25 – Yo, this man's momma so fat when she sit on an automatic flush toilet, the toilet don't flush till she leaves the room. 1

8:34 – Yo momma so fat she got an HD TV just to watch the food network. 0

9:00 – Yo momma so fat I told her I gotta new grill, she started pulling steaks outta her pocket.

18:33 – This dude's momma so fat she got a rest in peace tshirt for all her favorite foods. [takes off shirt] 2

19:03 – This dude's momma so sleazy me and Wilmer dropped her off at the Clear Mount Lounge so she could jump on the pole to get my thousand dollars cash money. 2

Episode 302 (Marietta vs. Jonesboro)

1:57 – His momma so fat I f***ed her via satellite. 0

2:08 – Yo momma so nasty she ain't got the clap, she got standing ovations. 0

2:23 – Your mother's so nasty that she brought crabs to the beach. 0

2:30 – Yo momma so stupid she thought Osama Bin Laden was three different terrorists. 1

2:35 – Your mother's so fat she got hit by a school bus and 23 kids died. 0

4:14 – Yo momma so ugly the shrink make her lay face down on the couch. 1

6:26 – Yo momma so fat she bought her bras at AutoZone. 2

6:56 – Yo momma so ugly she look like she got kicked in the face with a cowboy boot. 0

7:15 – Yo momma so fat when I look on her MySpace page, her top 8 was all her favorite restaurants. 2

7:57 – Yo momma so fat, yo dad proposed to her with an onion ring. 2

8:10 – Yo momma so fat I asked her what her favorite food was, the broad said seconds. 0

8:28 – Yo mom so stupid she took a jigsaw puzzle back cuz she said it was broken. 1

14:57 – Yo momma so fat when she calls I gotta put her on three way. 0

15:13 – Yo momma's like Geico, she's so easy a caveman could do her. 2

Episode 303 (Ben Hill vs. Cabbagetown)

7:00 – Yo momma so stupid she measures height with a thermostat. 0

7:30 – Yo mom so black she sweats tar. 1

15:32 – Yo momma so fat I asked her what's her favorite color, she screamed out "Long John Silver!" 2

Episode 304 (Dunwoody vs. Southside)

6:43 – Yo momma so black she get her facials done at Jiffy Lube. 1

6:49 – Yo momma so poor I asked her what's for dinner, that b**** lit my pocket on fire, "Hot Pocket." 2

7:07 – Yo momma so fat and stupid when the judge says order in the court, she says "Yeah, let me get a hamburger..." 2

15:32 – Yo momma so stupid when she had you and saw the umbilical cord, she say "Ooh it come with cable?" 2

Episode 305 (Best of the Week)

4:41 – Yo momma so stupid she thought she needed a degree to become a vegetarian. 0

7:40 – Yo momma so poor her checks bounce like basketballs. 1

7:45 – Yo momma so lazy, she just like butter, easy to spread. 0

8:00 – Yo momma so poor she was the leading lady in 50 Cent's video "Window Shopper." 1

8:21 – This dude's momma so lazy her best friend's a Chinese delivery guy. 0

REFERENCES

Aarons, Debra. (2012). *Jokes and the linguistic mind.* New York, NY: Routledge.

Abrahams, Roger D. (1962). Playing the dozens. *The Journal of American Folklore*, 75(297), 209-220. Retrieved from http://www.jstor.org/stable/537723?seq=1

Attardo, Salvatore. (1994). *Linguistic theories of humor.* Berlin: Mouton de Gruyter.

Bergen, Benjamin & Binsted, Kim. (2003). The cognitive linguistics of scalar humor. *Language, Culture, and Mind*, p.1-14.

Cole, Robert W. (1974). Ribbin', jivin', and playin' the dozens. *The Phi Delta Kappan*, 56(3), 171-175. Retrieved from http://www.jstor.org/stable/10.2307/20297847

Freud, Sigmund. (1901). *The psychopathology of everyday life.* London: Hogarth.

Horn, Laurence. (1972). *On the semantic properties of the logical operators in English.* Bloomington: IULC.

Levinson, Stephen. (1983). *Pragmatics.* Cambridge University Press.

Peckham, Aaron. (2005). *Urban dictionary: Fularious street slang defined.* Riverside, NJ: Andrews McMeel Publishing.

Percelay, James, Dweck, Stephen, & Ivey, Monteria. (1994). *Snaps : The original yo' mama joke book.* New York, NY: William Morrow Paperbacks.

Piddington, Ralph. (1933). *The psychology of laughter: A study in social adaptation.* London: Figurehead.

Raskin, Victor. (1985). *Semantic mechanisms of humor.* Dordrecht: Reidel.

Ross, Alison. (1998). *The language of humor.* London: Routledge.

Smuts, Aaron. (2009, April 12). *Humor.* Retrieved from http://www.iep.utm.edu/humor/

Valderrama, Wilmer. (Director) (2006). In Minerd, D. (Executive Producer), *Yo Momma: Atlanta.* Atlanta: MTV. Retrieved from http://www.mtv.com/shows/yo_momma/atlanta/video.

Knock Knock! Who's There? A Linguistic Analysis of the Structure and Application of Knock Knock Jokes
Amy Burbee

This 2013 paper offers a taxonomic approach to a genre of verbal folklore, at the intersection of humanities and social science. The relevance of folklore to therapeutics and to artificial intelligence, and of those disciplines to folklore and to one another is inspiring.

Abstract

Knock-knock jokes fall into two major classes. In Class I jokes, the teller repeats the setup prompt in the punch line, and these often involve phonological processes to reach the intended meaning of the punch line. The most common phonological processes that occur involve changing a single feature in a phoneme, like the voicing of a consonant or tongue height of a vowel. Fewer jokes involve inserting or deleting phonemes to create the intended meaning of the punch line. Class II jokes subvert the normal form and include a response by the joke teller to the setup phrase combined with "who." Often these jokes exploit social stereotypes or a structure that demonstrates superiority of the joke teller over the hearer to create humor.

Introduction:

Knock-knock jokes offer interesting examples of restricted wordplay. While most knock-knock jokes fall into a very limiting frame as speech acts, they offer speakers a chance at linguistic manipulation nonetheless. With applications to computer science, speech and language therapy, and education, these pieces of children's folklore offer an interesting subject to examine linguistically.

Most of the linguistic research on knock-knock jokes has been conducted by computer scientists investigating artificial intelligence and computational humor. In attempts to create robots and computer systems that demonstrate humor generation and participation, knock-knock jokes offer a predictable form with which programmers can experiment.

Taylor and Mazlack utilize knock-knock jokes that manipulate phonology in the punch line to teach humor to a computer. They constructed a similarity table for all encountered phonemes which the computer used to create punch line possibilities by replacing one phoneme in the prompt word. Once all these possibilities were compiled, word pairs were sorted to exclude nonsense utterances. The computer was then able to employ these similarities to distinguish legitimate knock-knock jokes from non-jokes. This study opened the door for other researchers to analyze linguistic aspects of knock-knock jokes in computer humor. Researchers, Mihalecea and Strapparava especially, expound on these methods.

Researchers of language acquisition and development have also used knock-knock jokes to measure children's mastery of language, and ability to understand dual meanings and language complexities. Freeman looked especially into the retelling of knock-knock jokes, which aspects were included, left out, or replaced, by children in different age groups (1998). Marcy Zipke suggests that riddles like knock-knock jokes can be used to teach metalinguistic awareness. She analyzes the dual interpretations of the key phrases and how these help children's mastery of language.

Some believe that the knock-knock joke in the form known today was originated by the radio host Fred Allen, who on December 30, 1936 conducted a series of fake interviews which included interviewing the man who supposedly invented this joke fad on April Fool's Day (Hample, 2001). Evidence for the joke form reaching back at least this far was found in a letter, penned in 1936 by a steward on the Nahlin steamship, which contained a knock-knock joke about King Edward III who was a passenger aboard.

Knock knock
Who's there?

Edward Rex.
Edward Rex who?
Edward Rex (wrecks) the coronation.
        —("Wallis Simpson", 2010)

However, perhaps the oldest example of knock-knock joke humor can be seen in Shakespeare's *Macbeth* Act II Scene 3 where a porter utters a series of "knock-knock jokes" to himself in response to an offstage knocking sound (Pollack, 2011). Though they do not follow the exact form and do not require two participants, they pose interesting similarity:

> [*Knocking within*]
>
> Knock, knock, knock! Who's there, i' the name of Beelzebub? Here's a farmer, that hanged himself on the expectation of plenty: come in time; have napkins enow about you; here you'll sweat for't.
>
> [*Knocking within*]
>
> Knock, knock! Who's there, in the other devil's name? Faith, here's an equivocator, that could swear in both the scales against either scale; who committed treason enough for God's sake, yet could not equivocate to heaven: O, come in, equivocator.
>
> [*Knocking within*]
>
> Knock, knock, knock! Who's there? Faith, here's an English tailor come hither, for stealing out of a French hose: come in, tailor; here you may roast your goose.
>
> [*Knocking within*]
>
> Knock, knock; never at quiet! What are you? But this place is too cold for hell. I'll devil-porter it no further: I had thought to have let in some of all professions that go the primrose way to the everlasting bonfire.

Methodology:

My data was gathered from the children's book *Knock Knock Jokes* compiled under the pseudonym Ima Laffin. Some other jokes came from online joke sites, as well as a famous post on Twitter, and from a TV show. The jokes collected were first categorized into two separate classes. Then, I analyzed Class I jokes to determine what type of phonological changes if any were occurring within the joke. Class II jokes were separated into those which required extra pragmatic knowledge and those which demonstrated the superiority theory to add to the humor.

Data and Discussion:

Consider the general frame of a knock-knock joke:

Line 1 (S): *Knock Knock* [the intro]
Line 2 (H): *Who's there?* [the scripted reply]
Line 3 (S): */name or other word* [the setup]
Line 4 (H): *<Line 3> who?* [the response]
Line 5 (S): [the punch line]

This knock-knock frame is crafted to mimic a real-life scenario in which a visitor is knocking at a door. Line 3 in the real-life situation, devoid of humor, would be the knocker's first name, "Amy," and the response in Line 4 would be, "Amy who?" Here the listener is asking for further identification, like a last name, "Amy Burbee."

Most knock-knock jokes follow this frame. The major variation comes in Line 5, the punch line. There are two classes into which these variations could fall. In the first, called Class I, the punch line includes a repeat of the setup from Line 3 as the first part of a larger sentence or phrase. This class more closely mimics the real-life scenario where the name given in Line 3 is repeated with more information added. For example,

Knock knock
Who's there?
Philip
Philip who?
Philip my glass, please!
              —(Laffin, 2004, p. 9)

On the other hand, the punch line could contain a reaction to Line 4 (the setup word combined with "who"). These jokes comprise Class II, where Line 3 is not quoted again in the punch line. For example,

Knock knock
Who's there?
Boo
Boo who?
Don't cry! It's only a joke.
              —(Laffin, 2004, p. 4)

When Class I knock-knock jokes are told orally, the joke-teller repeats the setup word in the punch line phrase with exact phonological imitation of its normal features. When conveyed in print, the same spelling of the Line 3 word is copied in the punch line. In some cases, the phonological pattern of the word from Line 3 maps exactly onto the intended meaning of the punch line phrase. For example,

> Knock knock
> Who's there?
> Michael /maɪkəl/
> Michael-esterol /maɪkələstɛrɔl/ is too high for this!
> *My cholesterol is too high for this!*
> —(Laffin, 2004, p. 14)

For some Class I jokes, the sequence of the phonemes stays the same between the setup word and the same word in the punch line, but the stress pattern must be altered to make the punch line phrase make sense, as in the example below.

> Knock knock
> Who's there?
> Isabel /ˈɪz ə bɛlˌ/
> Isabel who?
> Isabel necessary on a bicycle?
> *Is a bell /ɪzˌ ə ˈbɛl/ necessary on a bicycle?.*
> —(Laffin, 2004, p. 17)

For other Class I jokes, phonological processing is necessary to discover the meaning of the second utterance, as in the example below. Some researchers make these a type of their own, apart from the exact matches above, but here they are combined into one class (Taylor & Mazlack, 2004). For these jokes, there is a mismatch. The intended meaning of the punch line requires a different phonological pattern than the one given by the word it repeats, so there are different types of phonological changes that must be made to reach the intended meaning.

> Knock knock
> Who's there?
> Doris /dorɪs/
> Doris who?
> Doris open, come on in.
> *Door is /dorɪz/ open, come on in..*
> —(Laffin, 2004, p. 18)

Phonemes must be added to the setup, in some knock-knock jokes, to understand the funny punch line phrase. Consider this example:

> Knock knock
> Who's there?
> Peas /piz/
> Peas who?
> Peas to meet you!
> *Pleased* /plizd/ *to meet you!*.
>   —(Laffin, 2004, p. 7)

To reach the intended meaning of the punch line (in italics above), the two phonemes /l/ and /d/ have to be inserted by the hearer of the joke into the syllable /piz/ uttered by the joke teller in the punch line. The voiced alveolar liquid /l/ is inserted as a second consonant into the onset of the syllable, and the voiced alveolar stop /d/ is added at the end of the coda, creating the syllable /plizd/ which carries the intended meaning.

In the same way, phonemes can be deleted from the setup to create the intended meaning of the punch line. In the joke below, the two unstressed mid-central vowels, /ə/, must be deleted from the setup word /gərɪlə/ to obtain the meaning of the punch line phrase with the word /grɪl/.

> Knock knock
> Who's there?
> Gorilla /gərɪlə/
> Gorilla who?
> Gorilla me a sandwich please.
> *Grill* /grɪl/ *me a sandwich please..*
>   —(Laffin, 2004, p. 17)

Punch lines that require adding or deleting phonemes were the least common type of Class I jokes found in the data assembled. Jokes that require merely changing one distinctive feature of a phoneme to reach the intended meaning of the punch line were much more common. This results perhaps from the smaller amount of mental processing required to change a single feature of a phoneme than to add or subtract them, making the underlying phrase intended by the punch line easier to access.

Most knock-knock jokes of this form contain a monosyllabic word (usually a name) as the setup. Often the change to a single feature of a consonant happens within the coda of the syllable. This could result from an attempt by the joke teller to make the beginning of the uttered punch line match the beginning of intended underlying meaning of the punch line, to make this meaning more accessible to the hearer.

One of the most common phonological processes in the data collected is a change in the voicing of a phoneme to create meaning in the punch line, while manner and place of this phoneme stay the same. For instance, in the first example below, the voiced velar stop /g/ which makes up the coda of the syllable /pɪg/ has to be devoiced in the punch line, to express /pɪk/ with a voiceless velar stop in the coda. In the second example, the voiceless labiodental fricative /f/ has to be voiced to reach the intended meaning /liv/ with a voiced labiodental fricative in the coda.

> Knock knock
> Who's there?
> Pig /pɪg/
> Pig who?
> Pig up your feet and go see!
> *Pick /pɪk/ up your feet and go see!.*
> —(Laffin, 2004, p. 17)

> Knock knock
> Who's there?
> Leaf /lif/
> Leaf who?
> Leaf me alone!
> *Leave /liv/ me alone!.*
> —(Laffin, 2004, p. 18)

Changes in a distinctive feature of vowels were found often within Class I jokes as well. In the examples below, the change between the setup word and the intended meaning of the punch line occurs with the vowel, in the nucleus of the syllable. For the first example below, /luk/ containing the rounded high back vowel /u/ becomes /ʊ/ the rounded mid-high back vowel. The only difference between the two is tongue height.

> Knock knock
> Who's there?
> Luke /luk/
> Luke who?
> Luke through the keyhole and find out
> *Look /lʊk/ through the keyhole and find out.*
> —(Laffin, 2004, p. 11)

It seems that the most effective, and most commonly used, phonological changes in knock-knock joke humor of this class are those that require the least amount of mental work to access the intended meaning in the punch line, allowing the hearer to catch the meaning more quickly. However, "perfect" knock-knock jokes, with exact matches between the setup and the punch line were more difficult to find, perhaps because they are so hard to create. A joke changing a vowel feature or the voicing of a consonant seems to be easier to craft and provides an easier jump for the hearer than inserting or deleting entire phonemes.

In my analysis of knock-knock joke data, overall Class I jokes were much more common than Class II jokes. Because Class I jokes occur more frequently as examples of the genre, they exhibit what has become the expected pattern for knock-knock jokes. Class II jokes derive their humor, not from phonological variation, but from subverting the expectations of the listener. In the punch line, the joke teller offers an alternative interpretation of the response (line 4) than the one expected by the hearer. Consider the example below:

> Knock knock
> Who's there?
> Repeat
> Repeat who?
> Who! Who! Who!.
> —(Laffin, 2004, p. 6)

Here, the joke teller is intentionally misleading the hearer to expect a punch line containing the word repeat, which is the normal outcome of the knock-knock joke frame, rather than a reaction to what the hearer has said. The surprise interpretation of the response (line 4) by the joke teller leads to the humor, as explained by Incongruity theory (Ross 1998).

Class II jokes also allow social and political statements to be integrated into the knock-knock joke form more easily because the punch line is less constrained; there is not the obligation to repeat a word in close phonology within the punch line, as in Class I. For example, I found this joke which had been tweeted during the 2012 U.S. presidential election:

> Knock Knock.
> Who's there?
> WORLD'S BIGGEST LIAR!
> World's Biggest Liar Who?
> MITT ROMNEY!
> —(RB Blair, 2012)

Because of the looser form of these jokes, some derive their humor from joking about other social groups and playing on stereotypes, which results in humor, as Ross explains as her Superiority Theory, by "releasing anxiety about oneself through the denigration of others" (1998). For example, for the humor to be understood in the joke below, pragmatic knowledge about the common stereotypes of Russians and KGB officers is required. The humor results from a play on these stereotypes:

Knock Knock
Who's There?
KGB.
KGB Wh-.
SLAP* Ve vill azk ze qvestionz.
                —(Kaling, 2009)

Other Class II jokes create this play by making the joke teller seem superior to the joke hearer. For instance, the joke below creates humor by suggesting that the joke teller has a grasp of English grammar superior to that of the hearer, even though the hearer's response was correctly following the joke's accepted frame.

Knock knock
Who's there?
To
To who?
No, it should be "to whom"
                —("Knock Knock, Who's there? Grammar Police!",
2011)

One interesting manipulation of this speech act frame is seen in the joke below. This joke derives its humor from duping the hearer into following along with the automatic routine until he or she is stuck and the joke teller has demonstrated his or her superiority.

S: I know a great knock-knock joke.
H: Ok, tell me.
S: All right. You start.
H: Ok, knock, knock!
S: Who's there?
H: . . .
                —(eHow, 2000)

This joke also demonstrates the rigidity of the knock-knock joke form. The form is so automatic for the hearer in this example that he or she jumps right in without realizing the trick. This type of manipulation and role reversal would not work with most other joke forms.

Future Research:

There are several other research avenues that could be explored within knock-knock jokes. One area to consider is a discussion of how morphology plays out within knock-knock joke punch lines. For example, some jokes split the setup word into two separate words to form the punch line, while others insert the setup into a larger word in the punch line. An analysis of how word boundaries are created and exploited to add to the humor would be interesting. Also, it would be interesting to conduct participation studies to examine which class of knock-knock jokes hearers of different ages found funnier and whether, within Class I, jokes with exact phonology, close phonology, or more drastic changes between the setup and the punch line are viewed as more humorous.

References

*Chafe, Wallace. (2007). *The importance of not being earnest.* Amsterdam: John Benjamins Publishing Company.

Chomsky, Noam, & Halle, Morris. (1968). *The sound pattern of English.* New York: Harper & Row.

eHow. (2000). How to tell a knock-knock joke. *eHow Hobbies.* Demand Media.

Freeman Davidson, Jane. (1998). Language and play: Natural partners. In Fromberg, Doris, & Iergen, Doris. (Eds.) *Play from birth to twelve and beyond: Contexts, meanings, and perspectives.*(175-183). New York: Routledge.

Hample, Stuart. (2001). *All the sincerity in Hollywood: Selections from the writings of Fred Allen.* Golden CO: Fulcrum Publishing.

*Hempelmann, Christian. (2008). *Computational humor: Beyond the pun? Primer of Humor Research.* Berlin: Mouton de Gruyter.

Kaling, Mindy. (Writer) & Kwapis, Ken. (Director). (2009, February 12). "Lecture Circuit: Part 2" [*The Office*]. Daniels, Greg. (Producer). Los Angeles, CA: NBC.

Knock Knock, Who's there? Grammar Police! [Web log comment]. (2011, March 17). Retrieved from http://knockknockjoke.com/.

Laffin, Ima. (2004) *Knock knock jokes.* Edina, MN: ABDO Publishing.

Mihalecea, Rada, & Strapparava, Carlo. (2005). Making computers laugh: Investigations in automatic humor recognition. *Proceedings of the Human Language Technology Conference on Empirical Methods in Natural Language Processing*, 531-538.

Mihalecea, Rada, & Strapparava, Carlo. (2006). Technologies that make you smile: Adding humor to text-based applications. *Interactive Entertainment*, 33-39.

Niven, Felicia. (2011). *Weird science jokes to tickle your funny bone*. Berkeley Heights, NJ: Enslow Publishers.

Pollack, John. (2011). *The pun also rises*. New York, NY: Gotham Books.

RB Blair. (2012, November 3). Knock knock . . . Mitt Romney. [Twitter post] Retrieved from: https://twitter.com/TuxcedoCat/status/264898601656930307.

Richter, Gregory. (2013). *Senior seminar in linguistics: Linguistics of humor*. Kirksville, MO: Truman State University Printing Services.

Ross, Alison. (1998). *The language of humor*. Florence, KY: Routledge.

Shakespeare, William. (2011). *Macbeth*. Hartford: Simon & Brown.

*Sherzer, Joel. (2002). *Speech play and verbal art*. Austin, TX: University of Texas Press, 127.

*Shlien, R., & Wachs, A. (2000). Knock knock. Who's there? Cancer! *Psychology Today, 33*, 30-32.

*Summerfelt, H., Lippman, L., & Hyman, I. E. (2010). The effect of humor on memory: constrained by the pun. *Journal Of General Psychology, 137*(4), 376-394.

Taylor, Julia, & Mazlack, Lawrence. (2004). Computationally recognizing wordplay in jokes. *Electrical & Computer Engineering and Computer Science*, University of Cincinnati

Tibbalis, Geoff. (2011). *The mammoth book of really silly jokes*. Philadelphia: Running Press

Wallis Simpson 'not good looking'. (2010, November 1). *The Telegraph*. Retrieved from http://www.telegraph.co.uk/news/uknews/8100378/-Wallis-Simpson-not-good-looking.html

Zipke, Marcy. (2008). Teaching metalinguistic awareness and reading comprehension with riddles. *The Reading Teacher, 62*(2), 128-137.

Appendix: Jokes

Class I:

Knock knock
Lettuce
Lettuce who?
Lettuce in and I'll tell you
—(Laffin, 2004, p. 3)

Knock knock
Who's there?
Barb
Barb who?
Barbecue
—(Laffin, 2004, p. 10)

Knock knock
Who's there?
Amos
Amos who?
A mosquito bit me
—(Laffin, 2004, p. 14)

Knock knock
Who's there?
Dewey
Dewey who?
Dewey have to keep telling knock knock jokes?
—(Laffin, 2004, p. 22)

Knock knock
Who's there?
Wire
Wire who?
Wire you asking?
—(Laffin, 2004, p. 21)

Knock knock
Who's there?
Isabel
Isabel who?

Isabel necessary on a bicycle?
—(Laffin, 2004, p. 17)

Knock knock
Who's there?
Water
Water who?
Water we waiting for?
—(Laffin, 2004, p. 5)

Knock knock
Who's there?
Abby
Abby who?
A bee stung me on the nose!
—(Laffin, 2004, p. 8)

Knock knock
Who's there?
Scott
Scott who?
Scott nothing to do with you!
—(Tibbalis, 2011, p.255)

Knock knock
Who's there?
Peas
Peas who?
Peas to meet you!
—(Laffin, 2004, p. 7)

Knock knock
Who's there?
Gorilla
Gorilla who?
Gorilla me a sandwich please.
—(Laffin, 2004, p. 17)

Knock knock
Who's there?
Police
Police who?

Police stop telling these awful knock
knock jokes!
—(Laffin, 2004, p. 22)

Knock knock
Who's there?
Amy
Amy who?
Amy-fraid I've forgotten
—(Laffin, 2004, p. 6)

Knock knock
Who's there?
Dot
Dot who?
Dot's for me to know and you to find
out.
—(Laffin, 2004, p. 9)

Knock knock
Who's there?
Candace
Candace who?
Candace be the last knock knock
joke?
—(Laffin, 2004, p. 22)

Knock knock
Who's there?
Pig
Pig who?
Pig up your feet and go see!
—(Laffin, 2004, p. 17)

Knock knock
Who's there?
Pudding
Pudding who?
Pudding your shoes on before your
pants is silly
—(Laffin, 2004, p.18)

Knock knock
Who's there?
Doris

Doris who?
Doris open, come on in.
—(Laffin, 2004, p. 18)

Knock knock
Who's there?
Leaf
Leaf who?
Leaf me alone!
—(Laffin, 2004, p. 18)

Knock knock
Who's there?
Luke
Luke who?
Luke through the keyhole and find
out
—(Laffin, 2004, p. 11)

Knock knock
Who's there?
Kent
Kent who?
Kent you tell by my voice?
—(Laffin, 2004, p. 10)

Knock knock
Who's there?
Philip
Philip who?
Philip my glass, please!
—(Laffin, 2004, p. 9)

Knock knock
Who's there?
Ray
Ray who?
Ray-drops keep falling on my
head...
—(Tibbalis, 2011, p.250)

Knock knock
Who's there?
Dishwasher
Dishwasher who?

Dishwasher way I spoke before I had
false teeth!
—(Laffin, 2004, p. 12)

Class II:

Knock knock
Who's there?
Little old lady
Little old lady who?
I didn't know you could yodel!
—(Laffin, 2004, p. 4)

Knock knock
Who's there?
Want
Want who?
Good! Now try counting to three
—(Laffin, 2004, p. 5)

Knock knock
Who's there?
Boo
Boo who?
Don't cry! It's only a joke.
—(Laffin, 2004, p. 5)

Knock knock
Who's there?
Yah
Yah who?
Did I just hear a cowboy?
—(Laffin, 2004, p. 21)

Knock knock
Who's there?
Tank
Tank who?
You're welcome!
—(Laffin, 2004, p. 6)

Knock knock
Who's there?

Repeat
Repeat who?
Who! Who! Who!
—(Laffin, 2004, p. 6)

Knock knock
Who's there?
Oink oink
Oink oink who?
Make up your mind if we are speaking pig or owl.
—(Laffin, 2004, p.15)

Knock Knock
Who's There?
Broccoli
Broccoli Who?
Broccoli doesn't have a last name, silly.
—(Niven, 2011, p.11)

Knock Knock
Who's There?
KGB.
KGB Wh-.
SLAP* Ve vill azk ze qvestionz.
—(Kaling, 2009)

Knock Knock.
Who's there?
WORLD'S BIGGEST LIAR!
World's Biggest Liar Who?
MITT ROMNEY!
—(RB Blair, 2012)

Knock knock
Who's there?
To
To who?
No, it should be "to whom"
—("Knock Knock, Who's there? Grammar Police!", 2011)

Other

I know a great knock-knock joke.
Ok, tell me.
All right. You start.
Ok, knock, knock!
Who's there?
. . .
—(eHow, 2000)

"The Glittering Enchantments of Falsehood": Bluebeard in the Twentieth Century
Ian Crane

This 2017 example of literary folkloristics examines contemporary uses of one of the world's most widely distributed tale types. The mapping of themes invites the reader to test the scheme against further iterations of the Bluebeard story, and possible distant relatives, such as Orpheus and Euridice.

Despite its lack of name-recognition today, Bluebeard is a fairy tale that has played a significant if subtle role in much of Western culture. While the folktale has had some influence on musical history—for instance both Béla Bartók and Jacques Offenbach produced operatic works on the theme—the segment of art in which the theme of the Bluebeard story is most readily discerned is literature. Since the folktale of Bluebeard was first written down in France by Charles Perrault and in Germany by the Brothers Grimm, authors from Victorians like William Makepeace Thackeray and Charles Dickens to the present have used the narrative as a framework to develop literary works, particularly in short story form. With the arrival of the twentieth century and the vast expansion of literary movements, styles, and critical schools, the story of Bluebeard took on a new resonance for each generation of authors. While the Bluebeard tale type was subverted in myriad ways, the variation can be categorized into three umbrella macro-topics: the inversion of villainy, Bluebeard as manifestation of the oppressive patriarchy and capitalist society, and Bluebeard as guardian against the chaos of the unknown, against the darkness found in the aftermath of human catastrophe as well as inside the most obscure recesses of the human mind. This essay will examine how various modern authors have molded the Bluebeard tale type to fit their own thematic frameworks and what the adaptations say about both the authors and the times in which they lived.

In order to discuss how modern authors have subverted the Bluebeard trope, we must first explore the literary source from which more recent writers have gleaned their subject matter. The most prominent baseline text with the greatest influence over the cultural consciousness is also the earliest substantial written treatment of the tale, Charles Perrault's 1697 rendition in his collection *Histoires ou Contes du temps passé* (Grace 248). This is the telling which gives to many of the authors examined in this essay the primary narrative structure: the iconic azure facial hair, the airheaded female protagonist, and the *deus ex machina* of the protagonist's brothers arriving just before Bluebeard approaches to behead her. The most notable characteristic of the tale, and the characteristic most important to remember for comparison with other texts, is the presentation of the principle personages. Bluebeard is portrayed by Perrault as a man who, despite his elevated rank, is a cruel and despotic ruler of his household and his many wives. When his newest wife begs for forgiveness for her mistake, the narrator notes, "she would have melted a rock, so beautiful and sorrowful was she; but Bluebeard had a heart harder than any rock!" (Perrault). He is a man who is presented by Perrault as the unequivocal villain of the story.

The reason for this portrayal is, of course, his monstrous threat to decapitate his wife but also, on a more subtle level, the sadistic mind games that he plays with his wives. As one critic notes, "Bluebeard is the villain not only because he murders vengefully, but also because he imposes his arbitrary prohibition in the first place, in order to preserve his secret, and then provides the key" (Grace 249). This "arbitrary prohibition" is simply the verbal manifestation of Bluebeard's desperate need to control his wives. This need for control stems, in part, from what critic Nicholas Ruddick calls "unnatural masculinity," a phenomenon which he claims is represented physically by the beard itself. This explanation for Bluebeard's shocking behavior is supported amply by the primary source. It clears up some ambiguous moments in the text, for instance when the newest wife invites her friends and relatives to her chateau: "Her neighbors and good friends did not wait to be sent for by the newly married lady. They were impatient to see all the rich furniture of her house, and had not dared to come while her husband was there, because of his blue beard, which frightened them" (Perrault). Why would a blue beard alone frighten people? While it certainly would be an unusual fashion choice in the seventeenth century, the hue of the facial hair should not be cause for terror. The association of the blue beard with Ruddick's hypermasculinity gives these seemingly silly fears some validity and give Bluebeard's oppressive personality a physical form.

While unimpressive at first glance, the nameless new wife of Bluebeard is also painted with exacting strokes by Perrault. The fact that her name is omitted is particularly significant. As Ruddick contends, "The namelessness of the wife (in Perrault) emphasizes the ugly truth that once a woman has sworn the marriage vow to a monster like Bluebeard, she loses her identity and is reduced to a chattel (body) that he can dispose of as he wishes" (349). In addition to this Bluebeard-centered explanation, the namelessness of the female protagonist in Perrault's tale speaks volumes about the type of character she is; that type, it turns out, is none too flattering itself. For example, when Bluebeard invites his two would-be-brides and their mother to his estates for a visit, the youngest girl is quickly enchanted by his vast wealth, "In short, everything succeeded so well that the youngest daughter began to think that the man's beard was not so very blue after all, and that he was a mighty civil gentleman" (Perrault). This excerpt presents a protagonist who is so naïve that she allows herself to be completely taken in by wealth and flattery. The trope of the superficial and unthinking woman is thrown into still greater relief when the now wife of Bluebeard decides to enter the forbidden chamber. "Having come to the closet door, she made a stop for some time, thinking about her husband's orders, and considering what unhappiness might attend her if she was disobedient; but the temptation was so strong that she could not overcome it" (Perrault). This lack of self-control is characteristic of many early depictions of women in classical and biblical literature, for instance Eve and Pandora. By perpetuating the stereotypes of women as lacking in depth and forethought, Perrault displays not only Bluebeard as an unsympathetic character but his young wife as well.

Neither husband nor wife displays any character development throughout the story (as is often the case in fairy tales). Indeed, after her terrible ordeal, Bluebeard's wife doesn't suffer the slightest from unpleasant memories, "Bluebeard had no heirs, and so his wife became mistress of all his estate. She made use of one part of it to marry her sister Anne to a young gentleman who had loved her a long while; another part to buy captains' commissions for her brothers, and the rest to marry herself to a very worthy gentleman, who made her forget the ill time she had passed with Bluebeard" (Perrault). This proves that our young "heroine" has learned nothing from her first misadventure into the realm of marriage. Blue-beard's fortune allows her to smooth over the lives of both herself and her siblings in such a way that she was able "to forget the ill time she passed with Bluebeard." Not only has she learned nothing from her experiences but she has also forgotten that they even happened!

The baseline now established, it is easy to note that each of the twenti-eth century treatments of Bluebeard radically alters the thematic focus put forward by Perrault. One prominent thematic vein that runs through the modern retellings is the inversion of the original narrative, both in terms of personality and in terms of gender. This phenomenon is clearly present in Anatole France's 1909 story, "The Seven Wives of Bluebeard." In this version of the story, France cleverly frames his text as that of a literary scholar trying to clear the name of Bluebeard, a man he identifies with the name Montragoux; the narrator believes that "he (Charles Perrault) may, perhaps, have been prejudiced against his hero (Bluebeard)" (France 4). The narrator is impelled on his quest to rectify literary misrepresen-tation by certain supposedly "suspicious" elements in Perrault's tale; for example, "there was so great a desire to make me believe in the man's cruelty that it could not fail to make me doubt it" (France 5). Humor at the expense of dubious and obscure scholarship aside, this story functions as what one critic deems a critique of purely objective history, "History, as represented by the narrator, cannot isolate the true nature of things; it is limited to the interpretation of appearances, and appearances can be de-ceiving. Moreover, all interpretations are open to reinterpretation" (Levy 364). For Levy, Anatole France is critiquing those who would consider themselves infallible experts on what really happened in the past.

But how does France's critique of history connect to the Bluebeard tra-dition? The key lies, as usual, in the primary text. When France describes Bluebeard, he says, "Still, it is true that he did not please the ladies as much as he should have pleased them, built as he was, and wealthy. Shy-ness was the reason; shyness, not his beard" (France 10). The concept of a Bluebeard who is shy and not extroverted and vicious, as in Perrault, reveals a different vision of who this character can be. Later in the story, Montragoux gives his newest wife Jeanne the keys without any caveats, save his concern for her wellbeing (France 33). This is a depiction of an equitable relationship, sharply contrasted with the Perrault Bluebeard's ar-bitrary rule about not entering the cabinet which functioned as a symbolic gesture of control over his wife. Unfortunately, this newest wife is hardly deserving of such trust, as she and her family are described as "rakes," "rogues," spongers," and "owing everything" (France 22-23). This inver-sion of villainy, the swap of roles between husband and wife, displays the uncertain nature of what "good" and "evil" actually means when dealing with human beings, even when those human beings are fictional characters. Anatole France, by changing the roles of hero and villain within the Bluebeard framework, has raised questions about moral ambiguity. Can we really categorize certain characters as simply good or evil? As one critic notes, "The same facts can be used to build an image or destroy a reputation" (Levy 369). Perrault uses the facts to paint one picture and France uses them to paint another but it is simply a matter of presentation that can change the reader's expectations.

A more recent example of inversion within the Bluebeard tradition is in Margaret Atwood's 1983 story "Bluebeard's Egg." In this literary iteration of the Bluebeard tale, the inversion focuses not on ethical roles but instead on the reversal of gender roles in terms of who performs the function of both Bluebeard and his wife in the text. The story details the exploits of a Canadian housewife named Sally as she tries to navigate her marriage to a cardiologist named Ed who may or may not be a serial philanderer. A first glance, the story seems to be a standard Bluebeardesque narrative with a cold unfeeling husband and a naïve young wife. Ed is depicted at the beginning of the narrative as an unfeeling but controlling individual, even with regard to landscaping, "It was her idea to have a kind of terrace, built of old railroad ties, with wild flowers growing between them, but Edward says he likes it the way it is" (Atwood 131). Sally is portrayed as a curious wife desperate to uncover the truth about her husband, his past, and the intricacies of his heart.

This interpretation of Ed as a Bluebeard who preys on multiple women even while married is supported by many critics, for instance Ruddick, who notes, "Indeed, she (Sally) is so long the prey of self-deception that Ed's move on Marylynn may seem at first a kind of sensual protest against his wife's obtuseness, rather than what it later reveals itself to be, namely hard evidence of his hardheartedness" (352). While this reading has value, I find Atwood's use of the Bluebeard motif more nuanced than Ruddick suggests. When the text is examined in greater detail, Atwood raises doubts about Ed's role as a Bluebeard, or at least brings other possible interpretations to the table. While Ed's suspiciously flirtatious brush with Sally's friend Marylynn can be seen as a calculated bit of "hardheartedness" on Ed's part, it could also be read the opposite way as an act of carelessness. The narration has established throughout the story that Ed is simply not capable of self-deception. Sally even thinks at one point, "She thinks of moment after moment when this cleverness, this cunning, would've shown itself if it were there, but didn't. She has watched him so carefully" (Atwood 162). She has watched him "so carefully" and so has the reader; there is no hard evidence of Ruddick's "cunning" to be seen anywhere. Instead, a different dynamic comes into play. "Ed isn't the Bluebeard: Ed is the Egg" (Atwood 156) thinks Sally. The egg to which she refers performs essentially the same function as the bloody key in the Perrault version but stems from the later Grimm variant. So Ed is a blank canvas, a canvas that shows the guilt of someone who has metaphorically stained it with blood. If this is true, then Sally would fit into this framework as the naïve wife guilty of entering the forbidden chamber of Ed's mind. All she finds is emotionlessness and indifference towards her inside and, thus, her relationship with Ed, the egg, is irreparably stained with blood.

But if Ed isn't Bluebeard, who is? Atwood leaves several subtle hints along the way. Near the beginning of the story when describing the garden, the narrator notes that "Sally's blue scylla is in flower" (Atwood 131). This is an actual type of flower but it is typically spelled scilla. "Scylla" is the spelling used for the name of the terrible monster in Homer's *Odyssey* who snatches Greek sailors from their ships in order to devour them. Thus, in this brief clause, Sally is not only linked to a monster but a *blue* monster. Sally is the real Bluebeard in the story as well as the wife and doesn't even realize it herself. Throughout the entire story Sally's primary concern is that her husband Ed isn't in love with her. She worries that "Ed doesn't know what happened with these marriages, what went wrong… What if he wakes up one day and decides that she (Sally) isn't the true bride after all, but the false one?" (Atwood 134).The notion of Sally as a "false bride" is evocative; she is not only the young Perraultian wife but something more sinister. When "no changes she effects in herself seem to affect Ed one way or the other, or even to register with him" (Atwood 136), Sally begins to undergo a certain monstrous shift herself into cynicism. "'Trouble with your heart? Get it removed,' she thinks. 'Then you'll have no more problems'" (Atwood 138). She begins to realize that perhaps her feelings for Ed aren't so straightforward either, "Her heart looked so insubstantial, like a bag of gelatin, something that would melt, fade, disintegrate, if you squeezed it even a little" (Atwood 145). Sally's heart is "insubstantial," just like her marriage with Ed. She knows that if she digs any deeper into her own mind, as well as Ed's, she may find that there's no love there. Her "insubstantial" heart now begins to resemble that of a certain other hard-hearted spouse, Bluebeard himself. "She knows she thinks about Ed too much. She knows she should stop" (Atwood 151). Here Sally acts both as a Bluebeard who forbids entry into the forbidden chamber of the psyche by banning herself from thinking about Ed as well as the naïve young wife whose insatiable curiosity will not keep her out. She blankets her own anxieties by worrying about "Ed's" feelings, but really feels unsure about her own emotions.

Sally never fully opens the forbidden chamber of her psyche in the story, but the end hints that "This is something the story left out, Sally thinks: the egg is alive, and one day it will hatch. But what will come out of it?" (Atwood 164). This final line of the text works on multiple levels. Once Sally sees that Ed might be cheating with Marylynn, she cannot return to her former innocent attitude about Ed. In this reading the forbidden chamber is the knowledge that Ed is an adulterer and Sally functions as Bluebeard's newest wife, a victim of forbidden knowledge. The other, more subversive interpretation is that the forbidden chamber, the egg that will hatch, is Sally's own self-knowledge that she does not love Ed. She is the Bluebeard as well as the wife, the embodiment of gendered inversion within the Bluebeard framework, a woman who has "been with other men" and who objectifies her husband as a dolt and who "is in love with Ed because of his stupidity" (132) just as the traditional Bluebeard treated his wives like property who must obey his every word. When the egg hatches and the truth comes out, perhaps Sally will have to kill the marriage that couldn't fit her exacting expectations, just as Bluebeard killed the wives that couldn't meet his.

The second large grouping of twentieth century literature based on the Bluebeard folktale is the portrayal of Bluebeard as oppressor, a symbol of both an oppressive patriarchy and socioeconomic system. No text of this period addresses the topic more directly than Joyce Carol Oates' 1988 story, "Blue-Bearded Lover." The narrative is related in the stream of consciousness voice of one of Bluebeard's wives, but instead of succumbing to her curiosity and disobeying his command, she keeps her promise not to unlock the forbidden chamber despite the arbitrary and patronizing nature of his request. "'Why may I not enter it?' I asked... and he said, kissing my brow, 'Because I have forbidden it'" (Oates 185).

Due to its depiction of a downtrodden and unquestioning woman, "Blue-Bearded Lover" is a troubling text for many critics, and the ever-loquacious Ruddick has, of course, something to say on the subject: "Oates' story is not so much a critique of the patriarchy as of women's complicity in it" (Ruddick 351). While I do find this text subversive, I disagree with Ruddick's use of the word "complicity." Complicity implies that the woman plays an active role in propping up the patriarchy, an assertion with which I take issue. The female speaker of this story does not participate in the perpetuation of the patriarchy. Rather, she acts passively and lets her patriarchal husband control her, whether out of fear, ignorance, or even denial. Her comments about what she "learned" during her marriage—like,

"A man's passion is his triumph, I have learned. And to be the receptacle of a man's passion is a woman's triumph" (Oates 184)—cement the claim that this protagonist's denial of feminine agency stems not from her complicity with the patriarchy but from her own experiences as a recipient of patriarchal abuse. Even when she dares to dream of a better life, "of extraordinary beauty ... and magic and wonder" (Oates 186), she is quickly recalled to her patriarchal reality by her husband, under whose influence she seems almost brainwashed into submission: "And he kisses me, and seems to forgive me. And I will be bearing his child soon. The first of his many children" (Oates 186). This quote perfectly embodies the feminist message that Oates is trying to get across: a woman who is completely controlled, even in her own mind, by a controlling husband is so damaged by her toxic marriage that she feels she must ask her husband to "forgive" her for dreaming of "magic and wonder." Now the speaker of the story is reduced to character without distinct personality or agency, one whose only purpose in life is reduced to furthering the progeny of the very patriarchy that has enslaved her. This is thus not a story about women's complicity in the patriarchy, as Ruddick claims, but rather a disturbing portrait of a woman who is emotionally scarred by spousal abuse into denial.

While Oates' story focused on the plight of those oppressed by the patriarchy, feminism isn't the only ideology infused into twentieth century manifestations of the Bluebeard tale type. A critique on socioeconomic grounds was also a prominent strain found in such narratives, none more so than in Angela Carter's 1979 short story "The Bloody Chamber." The plot revolves around an innocent young girl who is seduced by and marries an extraordinarily wealthy Marquis. She moves to his castle with him only to find out that he is a sexually-perverted individual with too many medieval torture devices in his cellar for comfort. When the protagonist finds these torture devices and the bodies of previous wives in the eponymous chamber, she is confronted by her husband who threatens to decapitate her. He is stopped only at the last minute when the young girl's mother arrives and rescues her daughter.

While many facets of the story can de delved into, the presentation of the Bluebeard and wife characters and their place in the Bluebeard tradition is most illuminating. Carter's presentation of the Marquis as Bluebeard brings to light an element implicit but as yet unexplored at length by any other Bluebeard adaptation in this study: socioeconomic status. The Marquis, like all Bluebeards, is "rich as Croesus" (Carter 114). Unlike other twentieth century iterations of the story, however, Carter emphasizes the Marquis' wealth consistently throughout the story. While the narrative starts innocently enough with the Marquis using his money to buy his fiancée lilies and take her to the opera, as the plot moves forward his new wife realizes that her husband's money is also used to finance extensive collections of antique erotica and a castle filled with corpses and implements of torture.

The castle itself is an important aspect of the Marquis' character in that it symbolizes the decadence that his wealth has brought upon him. As one critic phrased it, "Perhaps the most intriguing is the manner in which this aesthete's paradise, this world of overexquisite taste, through its amorality, intensity, and excess, borders on the hellish and the hideous" (Lokke 10). Since the Marquis has lived such a stratified, elevated, and isolated existence, he is unable to form genuine human connections. That his wives are just objects to him, for instance, is clear when the couple's wedding night is described by the protagonist as the "Most pornographic of all confrontations. And so my purchaser unwrapped his bargain" (Carter 119). For the Marquis, sexual relationships are simply transactions without emotional connection. When he demands his wedding ring back from his wife before he is about to execute her, he says of the ring "It will serve me for a dozen more fiancées" (Carter 141). His cruelty is the result of centuries of decadence and sadism. For centuries his ancestors have terrorized the Breton peasantry by hunting human beings for sport or kidnapping women for their grotesque orgies. When seen through this lens, the Marquis in "The Bloody Chamber" makes more sense. He has been raised in an atmosphere where even the most perverted desires are immediately granted, and this glut of institutionalized wealth and power has, in turn, allowed generations of the Marquis' family to exploit the citizens of Brittany.

The portrayal of the Marquis' young bride is also influenced by socioeconomic factors. Because she is relatively poor, the protagonist of "The Bloody Chamber" (as well as her mother and nurse) is charmed by the wealth and power of the Marquis. When the women realize the horrible reality of their situation, both feel guilt for having been seduced by the Marquis. One critic explains, "Her (Carter's) rationale for the scene of maternal rescue is not to make the crude feminist point that modern women don't need to be saved by men, but to signify the mother's atonement for her guilt at her complicity in her daughter's betrayal" (Ruddick 354). The protagonist also feels guilty about her marriage, but her culpability stems from her enjoyment of the decadence in her new life. After describing the grotesqueness of her nuptial bed, the new Marquise is horrified to find that a part of her, the dark part that lies deep within everyone, was enjoying it: "When I had seen my flesh in his eyes, I was aghast to feel myself stirring" (Carter 119). Despite these seductions of both mother and daughter by wealth and decadence, the eventual defeat of the Marquis and the return to a humble lifestyle represent the reconciliation of the women to a life that is imperfect but filled with love, a life which stands in direct contrast with the protagonist's experience at the castle which is superficially perfect but dead underneath the veneer of luxury. In the words of one critic, "The marriage of wealth and power, standard goal for fairytale heroines, is rejected" (Renfroe 86). Unlike Perrault's wife, this Marquise is scarred by her experiences at Bluebeard's castle. However, this psychological pain she feels is well worth the price, since it means being rid of that terrible specter of socioeconomic abuse, the dreaded Marquis.

While inversion and oppression are both common themes in twentieth century Bluebeard stories, Kurt Vonnegut's 1987 novel *Bluebeard* brings an entirely new outlook to the ever-evolving picture of what Bluebeard can mean. In the novel, Vonnegut actually employs two Bluebeard figures, one a pastiche of Bluebeard and one a completely new form of Bluebeard. The parody of Bluebeard can be seen in the character of Dan Gregory, a famous hyperrealist popular artist who teaches protagonist Rabo Karabekian about the art world. The man fits many of the Perraultian criteria for a Bluebeard: he is abusive to women, in particular his girlfriend Marilee, as well as arbitrarily demanding of those in his household. The forbidden chamber for Dan is of course the Museum of Modern Art in New York City; he forbids both his girlfriend Marilee and Rabo from going there. Gregory's explosion of anger at finding Rabo and Marilee exiting the museum is where the parodic elements come into play, "'You parasites! You ingrates! You rotten-spoiled little kids!' seethed Dan Gregory. 'Your loving Papa asked just one thing of you as an expression of your loyalty: Never go into the Museum of Modern Art'" (Vonnegut 112). It is humorous how seemingly out of proportion his rage is compared to the trespass that the two young people make, but when Dan's character is taken into consideration the scene makes a lot more sense. Dan Gregory is a proponent of the strictest form of realism, a type of art that was slowly going out of fashion during the 1930's. This fear of irrelevance and cultural decay led Dan Gregory into the arms of the Italian fascist regime and to his demise but, despite his obviously problematic views, he was serving as a protector of what he believed to be humanity's heritage against the boogeyman of abstract art. He is an example of a pathetic Bluebeard, a Bluebeard doomed to fail in protecting those younger than him from his own forbidden chamber but who nevertheless persists in his mission until the bitter end.

Rabo Karabekian serves as a foil to Dan Gregory in terms of how he performs the function of Bluebeard in the novel. His forbidden chamber is the potato barn in his backyard and the secret inside, which he finally reveals to his friend Circe Berman, is a huge realist painting of the aftermath of World War II. When Rabo at first wants to keep the piece under lock and key, his friend begins to convince him otherwise. "When he finally reveals the contents of the mysterious structure to Circe Berman, she convinces him that he has at last reconciled body... with soul" (Kopper 583). While Karabekian has refused to put any "soul" into his other abstract expressionist paintings, he has finally done so with this work. The artist eventually relents, as he often does to the whims of Circe Berman, and agrees to have his enormous painting on display for the world to see. This is the antithesis of the oppressive Bluebeard; the artist has invited the general public into his once forbidden chamber. He describes the situation thusly: "'It isn't a painting at all! It's a tourist attraction! It's a World's Fair! It's a Disneyland!'" (Vonnegut 204). It creates a sort of amusement park of the horrors that humans can inflict on one another. As one critic puts it, "The horrors of his painting are now the raw material onto which others can project their own 'war stories,' the traumas that litter human experience" (Hertweck 145). While it may appear to Rabo Karabekian that hiding the horror and fear encountered in a postwar world is the only way to cope with the crises he encountered during World War II, he realizes that by revealing his painting to the world he is giving suffering people the tools to work through their own pain and confusion. This is the apotheosis of Bluebeard, when an incarnation of the character realizes that openness is better than oppression and that—unlike Dan Gregory, who was unable through fear to release control to others— it is the stronger decision to allow other people to make choices for themselves despite the consequences.

Despite the myriad variations on the Bluebeard theme throughout the twentieth century, the major works all tend to cluster into three overlapping thematic groups: inversion of the source narrative, commentary on oppression, and guardianship of knowledge, both beneficial knowledge and damning knowledge. These seemingly disparate stories remind us as readers that old stories cast long shadows and that a universal story like Bluebeard can be adapted by talented authors to express countless different themes and ideas. That is the mark of a narrative with lasting cultural power, and Bluebeard, certainly, will continue to inspire writers for centuries to come.

Works Cited

Atwood, Margaret. "Bluebeard's Egg." *Bluebeard's Egg*. Boston: Houghton Mifflin Company, 1986. Print.

Carter, Angela. "The Bloody Chamber." *Burning Your Boats: The Collected Short Stories*. New York: Penguin, 1995. Print.

France, Anatole. "The Seven Wives of Bluebeard." *The Seven Wives of Bluebeard*. New York: Books for Libraries Press, 1971. Print.

Grace, Sherrill E. "Courting Bluebeard with Bartók, Atwood, and Fowles: Modern Treatment of the Bluebeard Theme." *Journal of Modern Literature*, vol. 11, no. 2, 1984, pp. 245-262. JSTOR. Web. March 5, 2017.

Hertweck, Tom. "'Now it's the Women's Turn': The Art(s) of Reconciliation in Vonnegut's Bluebeard." *Hungarian Journal of English and American Studies*, vol. 17, no. 1, 2011, pp. 143-154. JSTOR. Web. March 5, 2017.

Kopper Jr., Edward A. "Abstract Expressionism in Vonnegut's Bluebeard." *Journal of Modern Literature*, vol. 7, no. 4, pp. 583-584. EBSCO. Web. March 5, 2017.

Levy, Diane Wolf. "History as Art: Ironic Parody in Anatole France's 'Les Sept Femmes de la Barbe-Blue.'" *Nineteenth-Century French Studies*, vol. 4, no. 3, 1976, pp. 361-370. JSTOR. Web. March 5, 2017.

Lokke, Kari E. "'Bluebeard' and 'The Bloody Chamber': The Grotesque of Self-Parody and Self-Assertion." *Frontiers: A Journal of Women's Studies*, vol. 10, no.1, 1988, pp. 7-12. JSTOR. Web. March 5, 2017.

Oates, Joyce Carol. "Blue-Bearded Lover." *The Assignation*. New York: The Echo Press, 1988. Print.

Perrault, Charles. "Bluebeard." *Histoire ou contes du temps passé*. University of Pittsburg, 2003. Web. March 5, 2017.

Renfroe, Cheryl. "Initiation and Disobedience: Liminal Experience in Angela Carter's 'The Bloody Chamber.'" *Marvels and Tale*, vol. 12, no. 1, 1998, pp. 82-94. JSTOR. Web. March 5, 2017.

Ruddick, Nicholas. "'Not So Very Blue, after All': Resisting the Temptation to Correct Charles Perrault's 'Bluebeard.'" *Journal of the Fantastic in the Arts*, vol. 15, no. 4 (60), 2004, pp. 346–357. JSTOR. Web. April 4, 2017.

Vonnegut, Kurt. *Bluebeard*. In *Novels 1987-1997*. Edited by Sidney Offit, Library of America, 2016. Print.

Folklore of Coming Out Stories: Self-Realization and Self-Revelation
L. N. Dunham

This 2018 paper applies structural and functional analyses to a field-collection of coming-out narratives; using Eleanor Wachs' Crime Victim Stories as a methodological example, the investigator tries to determine whether there is a standard way for experiencers to relate their stories.

Abstract

This study seeks to analyze the personal experience narratives of self-realization and self-revelation of members of marginalized sexual, romantic, and gender identities. We will refer to the folk group of such self-identified individuals collectively for our purposes as the LGBT community, but the identities of Lesbian, Gay, Bisexual, and Transgender should by no means be seen as exhaustive. "Gay" is also understood for our purposes as a blanket term for these identities in contexts in which the sources referenced here preferred it, particularly in the work of Goodwin (1989) and Liang (1997). The five informants were college students from the Midwest attending a social gathering specifically for members of the LGBT community and allies hosted by the local college Pride alliance. They were asked in interviews during or after the event to (1) define their identities, (2) talk about how they came to realize their identities, and (3) share whatever they consider their important coming out stories. Methodologies of collection did not change throughout the process. These narratives

are classified and examined through a folkloric lens to look for conservation and variation in structure and in comparison with related lore, and
to explore the functional purposes of sharing these stories with others. In
addition, this study will hopefully also help to expand the overall body
of LGBT folklore and increase understanding of the community. Further
studies may focus on variations within more specific sub-groups, and seek
a great number of narratives about their collection.

The body of academic work on the LGBT community as a folk group
is relatively small. This should by no means be assumed to mean that the
community has little folklore—although it is widely acknowledged that
defining the exact community and what constitutes folklore within it is no
easy task, there is certainly plenty of it. Rather the lack of collected lore
should be attributed to the quite-recent emergence of a distinct LGBT folk
group. This paper looks specifically at a selection of coming out narratives collected from five Midwestern college students to expand the lore
further. All informants were white and aged 18-22; three identified as
cisgender, one as transgender, one as gender non-conforming; three identified as gay, one identified as bisexual/pansexual, and one identified as
asexual and demiromantic. (For transcripts of their coming out narratives,
see Appendix.)

Literature Review

Goodwin (1989) provides a valuable insight into the overall folklore of
gay men as a community, focusing on verbal and nonverbal lore, humor,
drag, and crucially to this study, personal experience narratives. Weems'
(2005) case study focuses on LGBT people more generally and coming
out narratives more specifically, and gives more insight into the general
process and functions of coming out. The very recent *Qualia Encyclopedia
of Gay People* (Weems, Stewart, Goodwin, et al. 2011) is the most extensive
resource on overall LGBT folklore available and will also be considered;
note that despite its lack of publication by a university it is a peer-reviewed
source created by academics.

While not a folkloric study of the narrative, Liang's sociolinguistic analysis of coming out narratives was helpful as well. Finally, to compare
coming out stories to the much greater body of lore of personal experience narratives, specifically narratives of victims of urban crime, Wachs
(1988) is an invaluable source. This paper aims to combine these frameworks to look more extensively at both the structures and functions of the
coming out narrative, and to expand the especially low collection of these
narratives.

Classification

Before we can delve into a deeper analysis of the stories collected, we should establish the position of coming out narratives within the greater lore. That is, what constitutes a coming out narrative, and what disambiguates it from other personal experience narratives? Of interest are what does and does not qualify as a coming out narrative, what folk groups tell them, and how they are transmitted. In the following sections we will develop this definition of the coming out narrative: the retelling of one's first time revealing a marginalized sexual/romantic orientation or gender identity to a given person or group of people, generally to close friends within the LGBT community.

Defining the coming out narrative

The definition of a coming out story seems superficially simple; it is a story about one's coming out. The issue arises in exactly what qualifies as coming out. Weems (2011) describes the coming out narrative as "focusing on the moment of first disclosing one's sexual orientation." This collection, however, does not deal only with first revelations. While Weems does continue to accurately explain that "[the] initial disclosure is rarely the last," the article still focuses within its definition of the narrative type on those stories regarding the very first revelation of one's identity, rather than one's first revelation to a given group.

While Goodwin (1989) does not give a formal definition within his text, presumably since a reader of LGBT folklore would generally be familiar with the concept of coming out, he does include a broader range of lore in his discussions of the coming out narrative. He does this first within a larger focus on the process of gay acculturation, which he says crucially involves (1) self-identification, (2) inner association of oneself with the subculture, (3) first association with other members of the subculture, (4) gaining knowledge from other members, and (5) serving as a model or mentor for other members entering the subculture. He suggests that both self-identification and first association with the culture are forms of coming out which may appear in narratives along with the expected coming out to family, friends, and others (pp. 3-4).

Before his discussion of the narratives themselves, Goodwin adds that coming out "is a continuing process, [so] many people have more than one narrative about coming out" (p. 43). Liang also finds that both self-recognition and disclosure to others of homosexuality are parts of the metaphor of coming out, and that "coming out is a matter of a degree rather than of binary opposition" (1997, p. 291). That is, one is never fully out; it is a process, and this will be reflected within the quantity of narratives. She questions whether coming out has taken place if an addressee does not understand the message being sent, if someone unintentionally discloses their orientation, or if another intentionally discloses it—"outing them"—without their prior consent. She eventually defines coming out to others as "the successful and intentional communication by one individual of his gayness to another to whom such information has not previously been conveyed by the gay individual himself." This definition thus includes instances where the addressee might have guessed or heard through other means before the coming out (1997, p. 292).

These explicitly broader classifications of experiences of multiple first revelations to both oneself and to others qualifying as coming out are preferred and reflected by this study.

Folk group analysis

Notable is that the above definitions focus solely on sexual orientation as the defining characteristic of the relevant folk group. While it is true that no informants identified as heterosexual and all focused mainly on their respective sexual orientations, gender identities other than cisgender and varying romantic identities also came in to play. While the statement of these identities was certainly prompted by their inclusion in the questions asked before the interviews, their prevalence supports the idea that the scope of coming out has moved at least beyond sexual orientation. Weems (2011) does touch on this idea by expressing that coming out is "used in other social movements" in which it is "often associated with stigmatized identity or behavior." Folk groups he specifically mentions as ones which have appropriated the lore of coming out are "those who are HIV positive ... survivors of domestic or sexual violence, practitioners of BDSM... and Wiccan[s]." Whether or not members of these groups also share coming out narratives—revelations of their revelations—is not specified, and could be a point of further study.

The role of social movements in increasing the openness and comfort individuals experience with sharing previously taboo personal narrative stories is also displayed in Wachs (1988) when she notes the influence of the rise of women's rape and crisis centers on the level of comfort individuals feel with sharing rape stories (pp. xvii-xix). In the case of coming out narratives, they were certainly shared within the community before the gay rights movement was very large, but the movement helped move them into the mainstream.

The appropriation of the lore by other groups is probably not viewed as negative by members of the community when used in contexts of other stigmatized or marginalized "hidden" identities. Where friction may arise is when coming out is used to explain narratives based on less serious or more choice-based identities, such as being a fan of a widely disliked form of media, or indeed to some LGBT people, being a practitioner of BDSM. Weems' expanded folk group of individuals with potential coming out narratives could yield interesting analyses all their own, beyond the narrow focus of the previous lore on sexual orientation; but for our purposes we will not move beyond the mid-sized scope of the LGBT community.

Goodwin (1989) also makes a distinction between sexual orientation and community membership. In discussing gay men, he distinguishes homosexual men—those who desire and/or engage in same-sex sexual activities—from gay men, who "have identified themselves as gay, who consider their orientation to be an important … aspect of their lives, and who frequently interact with other gays *as gays*" (p. xii). Gay people then, in contrast to merely homosexual or bisexual ones, are those who have also gone through at least a few of Goodwin's stages of gay acculturation.

As in the 21st century homosexuality has gained more acceptance, these lines between orientation and community may have shifted; general openness about homosexual and gay issues may have brought more individuals into the gay subculture, while the mainstreaming of gay culture may have made it less unique. Analyses of those who engage in non-heterosexual activities but who do not identify with or interact with the subculture to see if they have similar lore—such analyses could yield interesting results, but are beyond the scope of this study. Liang does not touch separately on such individuals within her studies, but does seem to make less of a distinction (1997).

Variation in the lore is certainly expected from group to group within the LGBT community, but since all informants in this study are members of an organization specifically comprised of multiple identities with a focus on a collective fight for rights and acceptance, they might have more in common than, say, segregated gay and lesbian bars in a large coastal city where there are many more people around, and thus more ability to separate from an umbrella group without feeling isolated. Liang suggests some variations based on the race of individuals, noting that Asian American gay men focus more on coming out to others than to themselves, in contrast to European American gay men (1997). Studies of variation in narratives based on an informant's race, current or former religion, nationality, age, geographic location, etc. could yield very useful results as well.

Transmission of coming out narratives

The final aspect to be defined about coming out narratives is their mode of transmission. This particular study's approach to collecting the lore is probably a good example of what not to do when trying to study modes of transmission of personal experience narratives; three of five stories collected were during isolated and one-on-one interviews, two were with informants who were relative strangers to the interviewer. While Wachs (1988) noted that in studying urban crime stories "even strangers feel at ease revealing to one another the details of victimization" (p. 1), there is a starker contrast between coming out stories told in group settings or with friends (as with the first, second and fifth informants), and stories told to strangers, than Wachs claims there is in crime narratives.

Indeed the told-to-strangers narratives read more like the minimal narratives that Wachs identified in third-person accounts of crime victim narratives (p. 16), suggesting that there is a distance from the experience, and less vulnerability, when the teller is unsure whether they can trust their audience. Thus a fuller narrative seems to be spurred on by the presence of a more intimate and familiar group setting, which could be sought in future collecting to gain more natural data. Liang chose rap sessions, in which "Participation... [is] governed primarily by common experiences resulting from group membership rather than by acquaintanceship among participants" (1997, p. 298). This suggests that it is not intimacy so much as shared experiences and a sense of "safety in numbers" which was not present in this study, and which could yield more naturalistic results in a differently organized study.

Wachs does note that the reason her stories are so readily shared is that urbanites all share similar experiences with crime and can all relate—it might be that their stories would not be so readily shared with someone from a rural area. Likewise coming out stories are largely shared within the LGBT community—occasionally including allies, but likely not as naturalistically to a group exclusively of allies or of other non-LGBT individuals. Thus it was helpful in this study that the informant was a member of the folk group. Also of interest to a further study might be looking at conservation and variation between stories transmitted orally through natural or performative means in the case of coming out monologues and stories transmitted through the internet or non-verbal means. Only verbally transmitted stories are relevant to this study, however.

Structural Analysis

There are only a few notes on the structural aspects of coming out narratives within the folkloric literature. Goodwin (1989) notes that many narrators include "long introduction[s] ... to set the story within its proper biographical framework" (p. 43). Very specific biographical frameworks are included in the tales of the first, second, and fifth informants—the ones we deemed to have the most natural modes of transmission—so this seems to be conserved. He notes also how narrators may create "coherent narrative[s] containing several apparent digressions that in actuality are details essential to the plot" (p. 47). We see this employed in the first informant's seemingly irrelevant mention of her mother's occupation as an accountant which sets up the punchline, "'Dear, you know I'm doing taxes, right?'" The first informant in general seems to have a very structurally complex and well-practiced narrative.

We will categorize the types of shorter accounts based on to whom the disclosures were made. These are combined to form larger narratives, and we will discuss the observed orderings and obligation of inclusion thereof. Liang's classifications will also be considered. Organizing individual stories by narrative clause as Liang does could provide interesting structural analysis, but is omitted in favor of a focus on larger narrative patterns and on linguistic concerns.

Structure of larger narratives

Moving on from more stylistic features within the narratives, the "characters" included in the tales are largely limited to self, friends, and parents. Bystanders or strangers are generally given no focus compared to their prevalence in crime victim narratives, if they are indeed even possible characters in typical coming out scenarios. Wachs describes all of the characters in the stories she analyzed to be *dramatis personae*, "stock characters ... [whose] actions are presented without explanation since they are all well-known figures" (1988, p. 3). This seems to be preserved much more in stories about friends than those about parents; the stories about friends all read approximately the same—fairly mundane and accepting—while parents are given a much larger and more specific focus. Each character and some other common structural elements are discussed below.

Coming out to self

Discussions of self-realizations were present in each narrative, but this was prompted by the investigator and thus not necessarily required as a part of the narrative structure. The lore does suggest that it would be prevalent, however. Goodwin (1989) suggests that "Identity is usually established before sharing such experiences" (p. 42), and identity does indeed tend to be established in self-realization stories more directly than in

stories of revelations to others, which are able to use more general terminology. This establishment of identity within a self-realization story or as
a kind of introduction would of course be less necessary for the groups of
close friends among whom these stories might be more naturally shared,
but identity establishment would perhaps necessarily appear in Liang's rap
session style of sharing.

Liang views the self-acceptance of one's LGBT status as an act so culturally defiant that by conventional standards of conversation it "cannot [or
should not be able to] be incorporated into a tellable narrative" (p. 290).
But clearly it can be; clearly people incorporate these things into their identities effectively. She suggests that tellers of narratives are aware of the
expectation within the community that they base membership not only on
behaviors and preferences but on identities (see discussion of Folk group
analysis) and thus purposefully (but perhaps subconsciously) address both
aspects to demonstrate that they belong in the community. Once their
identity is firmly established by the story of coming out to themselves,
cultural conversational rules about defending implausible propositions allow them to continue to discuss coming out to others (1997, p. 295).

The self-realization story was especially long for the second informant,
a variation which may be common in asexual people and other groups
whose identities are less well understood by a given audience. If we assume that self-realization narratives are a natural way to establish identities within the larger narrative, it follows that a deeper explanation of
one's identity in order to bring the audience to terms might be very helpful. Liang also noted variations in length of self-realization stories between
European American and Asian American men, so racial divides and general Western and Eastern ideas about intensity of focus on emotions in
conversation may play a role as well. In particular Liang noted the greater
usage of "Metaphor ... inner speech ... and repetition" in the longer and
more emotionally charged European American narratives (1997, p. 300).

The inclusion of an explicit question about these narratives is perhaps
an element which could be omitted in future studies to gain more natural
data. It was included, however, in this particular study partially as a kind
of warm-up question to make the segments that followed more naturalistic,
and partially because it was simply of significant interest to the prime
investigator.

Coming out to friends

The only other kind of revelation consistent across the narratives of
all five informants is revelation to friends. The prevalence of this focus

may be particular to our narrow folk group of college-aged LGBT individuals. One might consider that their formative experiences with high school friends, who they are likely even still in contact with, would be fresher in their minds. Certainly a focus on revelation to friends would be expected in narratives of other age groups as well. These views may be reductive, however, so further studies of several different age groups would be helpful.

First coming out

First revelations do seem to have quite a bit of conservation, as discussed earlier in regards to Weems (2011). The second stories of the first and fifth informants after their prompted self-revelations were in fact explicitly stated to be their first times coming out, and this may be implied within the greater narrative of the second and third informants as well. All first revelations present seem to be to friends, or in the case of the third informant, to a first lover.

Coming out to parents

Although it is absent in one narrative, the narrative element which seems to be the climax of most coming out stories is the parental revelation. We might assume that this either has not occurred for the fourth informant or, since their family status is not known, that it may not be a possibility. It also may have been too personal for the informant. Indeed, this may perhaps be the most potentially traumatic event, even when one does not expect it to go badly, as one can make new friends but cannot nearly as easily replace a family. These stories tend to be the longest, most fleshed out, perhaps best remembered. They also appear to not infrequently be followed by an additional, more lighthearted story about coming out to friends, as for first and fifth informants.

Coming out to self through models/coming out to mentors

The fifth informant's revelation to a sibling, specifically here an older sibling, is classified separately from parents or other family as it seems to carry with it both the general nonchalant attitude towards coming out to friends and the emotional weight of coming out to family. Likewise their realizations based on learning of their brother's identity and that of one peer in their middle school are classified separately from family members or friends as something deeper seems to be going on, based not solely on familial relation or friendship but on mutual membership in the community.

Going back to the ideas of gay acculturation in Goodwin (1989), we consider the particular revelation to his sister to be some kind of a revelation to a mentor, leading to a reciprocal relationship of the revealer going through the fourth step of gaining more knowledge of the subculture while the other serves as a model for learning the ways of the subculture, the fifth step of acculturation. The informant's realizations based on their brother and a student at their middle school are based on their statuses as passive models for navigating the realization and revelation of their identities, indeed before an identity was even established, causing step four of acculturation to occur before step one. Both of the models in fact reappear in the later stories of coming out to friends, emphasizing even more their importance in the informant's eventual identification with the community.

Other mentors seem to have received brief mentions in narratives: consider the first informant's friend (an implied member of the community) whom she met at a roller derby, the next informant's singular asexual friend before college, the third informant's first boyfriend, and members of the fourth informant's organizations. All served as catalysts for their identifications with or cementers of their comfort within the community.

Coming out to institutions

The fourth informant's mentions of revelations to medical and other institutional professionals are interesting. This is likely a unique variation which may show some conservation among coming out narratives of transgender or gender non-confirming individuals, particularly those seeking physical transition. More specific studies would be needed to explore this element further.

Processual nature of coming out

Following the methodologies of Liang (1997), the common comments on current level of "outness" which allude to the processual nature of the process are here given a separate category as well, separate from a simple coda to other narratives, although only one of the three processual evaluations is perhaps a full narrative in itself.

Findings

The observed structure of larger narratives is as follows. The framework is based on the characterizations of both Wachs and Liang. Liang claims that at least two of the three larger categories (a) (b) and (c) must be present in a narrative, and our findings support this.

(a) Coming out to self.
1. Self-identification established, esp. when to strangers.
2. Variation in emotional focus and length based on sub-community membership, race, other factors
3. Realization through models, stage 4 of gay acculturation: not obligatory, may occur in (b)

(b) Coming out to others: (3) and (4) are not observed together and their order may be in free variation; (4) is placed second to relate its weight to that of parental revelations.

1. First coming out: not obligatory, usually to friends, always occurs first
2. Coming out to friends, nearly obligatory, can include multiple coming outs
3. Coming out to institutions: variation present in transgender narratives
4. Coming out to mentors: not obligatory
5. Coming out to parents: climax of most stories, nearly obligatory
6. Additional coming out to friends: occurs specifically after (5), can include multiple coming outs

(c) Processual nature of coming out
1. Evaluative note on current status
2. Categorization of degree of outness
3. Quick summary of ease, or of lack of other coming out experiences

Functional Analysis

The functions of the coming out narrative acknowledged in the previous literature are many. Goodwin (1989) stresses that they can "give people considering coming out examples of how to do so, how not to do so, and what to expect upon doing so." They signify a "rite of passage" and are "sometimes funny, sometimes sad, sometimes uplifting, [and] often poignant" (p. 43). This range of emotions and kinds of advice are certainly present in our collection. Goodwin notes also that the simple act of sharing the stories lets members of the community promote cohesion through "a sense of intimacy, a bond" that would not be as easily built otherwise (p. 43).

Weems (2011) touches on how coming out narratives are used by various social movements for "maximizing visibility and political power," mainly through prominent figures' revelations swaying public opinion. This focus is probably a bit too macro-sociological for our particular mode of transmission and folk group. Weems also suggests that the sharing of coming out narratives marks the community's search for tolerance and inclusion (2005, p. 254), which is more relevant to our study.

Most of the functions given by Wachs (1988) are too specific to urban crime stories to be relevant here, but a few are shared. She notes stories of surviving crimes, especially violent ones, as being testimonial to the urban individual's and community's resilience (p. 12). These survival stories ask for empathetic responses towards the victim teller while maintaining a distance from the trauma, and acceptance of the fact that no one victim can solve crime alone (pp. 13-14). Likewise, coming out narratives test the line between empathy and distance and are a form of group cohesion in the face of discrimination—and help lead the way to the tolerance and inclusion that Weems suggests they seek. She notes also the cautionary aspects of some tales, and functions of expressing anger in culturally sanctioned ways and of providing entertainment (pp. 61-62). For further analysis of which of these and other specific functions are present in our collection, we will consider the narrations transcribed in the Appendix one by one.

Informant 1 (Bisexual/pansexual Female)

As noted in our structural analysis, this informant appears to have a very well-developed and practiced narrative. Her parental revelation is clearly the climax which she was eager to relay to her audience; the ally in her audience particularly wanted to hear another story as well. Goodwin (1989) notes that coming out narratives are very frequently retold even among friends who have heard the same stories several times (p. 43). The function of the narrative, then, is clearly not that of some sort of one-time ritual. As with the process of coming out itself, the process of sharing coming narratives is a constant one.

It is clear from this informant's narrative in particular that providing entertainment and humor can be major functions in coming out narratives, as Wachs (1988) noted was true with crime victim stories as well. Goodwin (1989) focuses heavily on the prevalence of humor in gay folklore; indeed he feels that humor "is pervasive in the gay community" and that "Puns are common in gay conversations" (p. 13), the latter being a fact which this informant's final story reflects well with its play on the phrase, "playing for both teams." Goodwin puts forth the idea that the prevalence of humor in LGBT verbal folklore is the result of a long tradition of gay people using the ambiguous nature of puns and double entendres "as one way of identifying and communicating with one another without their homosexuality [etc.] becoming evident to straights" (p. 12).

The sending of ambiguous messages doubly allows the sender to deny the coded LGBT message if it is recognized by an outsider, while also allowing other non-openly LGBT people in a largely non-LGBT audience to subtly pick up on the intended message and find group cohesion. This necessarily oral nature of ambiguous messages in the past, Goodwin says, led to the development of especially good linguistic competence within the community, which has been preserved even now that LGBT topics are generally not so taboo. The wordplay acts as a way to patrol the boundaries of the community as well as a type of lore mentors teach newcomers to increase their gay acculturation and sense of community. The secretive ambiguity of these kinds of humor is certainly not necessary in the purely LGBT case of this and other coming out narratives when shared with other members of the community, but is instead a result of a vestigial function of gay humor used in non-gay contexts to help identity other members of the community.

The general message of Informant 1's narrative is that while coming out can be very stressful, it is often not a big deal, to such a degree that one might even become so comfortable that one forgets to tell some groups about one's identity, and there are no adverse effects. Thus the function of the narrative is one of kind reassurance, to acknowledge the weight and importance of coming out while stressing that it very often is received much better than one fears.

Informant 2 (Asexual Female)

Informant 2's self-realization narrative was noted in the structural analysis to be quite a bit longer than in the other narratives, a variation which was posited to have derived from her having an identity significantly different from her audience's. Thus one potential function of a coming out narrative is to inform an audience of outsiders about an unfamiliar identity or aspect of an identity; by going into great detail and opening up about one's personal experiences, a narrator can help an unfamiliar audience understand their perspectives and the perspectives of their sub-community.

The parental revelation in this narrative could be seen to have a few different functions. It could be seen as a cautionary tale towards others, stressing that coming out might not always be the best idea. Still, however, the narrator does not express any direct regret about coming out to her mother, only disappointment that it did not go as well as she planned.

More than providing any sort of message to the audience, however, the main function of sharing negative or even traumatic experiences may be more of a cathartic one for the narrator. Indeed talking with a group of friends about something one cannot even discuss properly with their own parents is often a very relieving experience. The catharsis could extend to audience members with similar experiences as well.

Functions for telling the narrative to a questionably "dissimilar" audience may include conveying a message, that the audience should maintain a positive outlook on the coming out process, for if the narrator can live through what seemed to be a worst case scenario, and be comfortable enough to discuss it now, then the audience should be able to do so as well. The narrative also may transmit messages to the audience that they should give more emotional support to the narrator and be careful in the future when discussing issues regarding parents or other groups with whom a narrator has had negative experiences.

Informant 3 (Gay Male)

The functions of this informant's short narrative are simultaneously positive but accepting of the troubles some people will have when a close friend or family member comes out. It conveys the message that not all people are going to take it as well as hoped; some will not be accepting at all, but in the end those that truly matter are likely to come around. The message is very nuanced.

Informant 4 (Gay Trans-gender)

This narrative's function seems perhaps significantly more advice-driven than the others. They give specific advice on how to go about choosing which groups to come out to rather than describe specific instances in which they did come out. They also suggest to transgender people that a willingness to be open and honest to medical professionals is, while awkward, a helpful step to take. Finally, they make it explicitly clear to those who may be new to the coming out process that it is indeed a *process*, and they need not, indeed probably could not—and *should* not—feel any need to come out to everyone they come in contact with.

Informant 5 (Gay Queer)

Most interesting in the narrative of Informant 5 is their mention of our previously defined models and mentors as defined through Goodwin's ideas of gay acculturation. The function of mentioning these specific narratives, concerning forms of guidance a narrator had in their relations to the community, is also a function of coming out stories overall: to provide a supportive and cohesive message, as Goodwin puts it, that "'You are not alone'" (1989, p. 48). The narrator was not alone, and in giving advice in this narrative, became a mentor themself.

The informant's long overarching narrative of their siblings' own struggles with their identities make the message of their parental revelation all the more satisfying: people can eventually change for the better when a loved one comes out; it may just take time. This ties in to Weems' (2005) ideas about coming out as striving towards tolerance and inclusion, ultimately gained in this case.

Findings

A full table of the functions noted is given below. An 'x' indicates that the function was a major function identified in the narrative, a ' ' that it was marginally observed.

Function	Inf. 1	Inf. 2	Inf. 3	Inf. 4	Inf. 5
Advice on how to come out	x	x	x		x
Cautionary tale		x			
Suggest evaluating trustworthiness of addressees				x	
Counsel nonchalant attitude towards coming out	x		x		
Suggest coming out is not always needed				x	x
Acceptance that some will not react positively		x	x		
Hope that some will change their minds		x			x
Openness towards medical professionals				x	
Entertainment	x				x
Through humor	x				
Group cohesion	x	x	x		x
Seek empathetic response		x			x
Search for tolerance/inclusion		x			
Express frustration		x			
Evaluation of processual nature of coming out				x	x
Wordplay as boundary patrolling		x			
Explain identity to others	x	x			
Through long self-realization story		x			
Catharsis		x			x
Acknowledge importance of previous models/mentors					x

Conclusions

We classified the coming out narrative for our purposes, in contrast to the narrow narrative-restrictive definition of Weems (2011) and the narrow group focus of Goodwin (2011) as the retelling of one's first time revealing a marginalized sexual/romantic orientation or gender identity to a given person or group of people, generally told to close friends within the LGBT community.

In our structural analysis, we confirmed conservation of the complex biographical frameworks and narrative structures that Goodwin (2011) noted in his collections, and we identified self-realization as a possibly prompted but still important establishment of precise identity. But we found only partial conservation of Weems' (2011) idea that first revelations are essential to the narrative. We identified instead parental revelation as the most essential and climactic element of the larger narrative, with an optional lighthearted story afterwards; and we discussed models and mentors as being—usually indirectly but sometimes directly— given focus. Finally we identified some structural features—a long self-realization or focus on coming out to institutions—that show variation in that they probably occur only in the narratives of some sub-communities. We produced a framework that describes the order of stories in larger coming out narratives.

In our functional analysis, we talked about the vestigial functions of gay humor in the coming out narrative, functions of counseling attitudes for new members of the community when sharing both positive and negative experiences, and of counseling attitudes towards coming out at all, and functions of mentioning mentors and becoming a mentor oneself. Other functions we noted were summarized in a table, and the particular narratives they were observed in were specified.

Further studies, which would also help expand the academic collections of coming out narratives, may focus on more precise sub-communities based on gender, sexual or romantic identity, or age, race, geographical area, etc. or on other communities which have appropriated the lore. Further studies might ask informants about modes of transmission (oral, performative, and non-orally through the internet) and reasons they feel they share their narratives; and they might go deeper into a structural analysis, and generally seek larger numbers of narratives to engage with the ideas in this study as well as with the previous literature.

References

Goodwin, J. P. (1989). *More man than you'll ever be: Gay folklore and acculturation in Middle America*. Bloomington, IN: Indiana University Press.

Liang, A. C. (1997). The creation of coherence in coming-out stories. In A. Livia and K. Hall (Eds.), *Queerly phrased: Language, Gender, and Sexuality* (pp. 287-309). New York, NY: Oxford University Press.

Wachs, E. (1988). *Crime victim stories: New York City's urban folklore.* Bloomington, IN: Indiana University Press.

Weems, M. (2005). Gay ritual: Outing, biking, and sewing. In M. Sims and M. Stephens (Eds.), *Living folklore: An Introduction to the Study of People and their Traditions* (pp. 245-254). Logan, UT: Utah State University.

Weems, M. (2011). Coming out. *Encyclopedia of Gay Folklife.* M. Weems, P. Stewart, J. P. Goodwin, et. al. (Eds.) Forthcoming.

Appendix: Stories Collected

Informants were asked before their interviews to (1) share their relevant sexual, romantic, and gender identities, (2) talk about when they first realized them, and then (3) talk about significant experiences in sharing them with others. No informants are identified by name and any identifying information has been redacted or altered.

Informant 1

The first two informants found it comfortable to share their stories in a group setting along with a third friend, an LGBT ally. The other members of the group especially wanted to hear the coming out story of the first to speak, and she was eager to tell it.

(a) Coming out to self.

She began by describing her slow self-realizations based on her "list" of people to whom she felt attraction.

Inf. 1: Umm so, I identify as bisexual, or pansexual, but like, they're like the same thing... In my mind, I identify with both of them... equally, whichever one makes the best pun at the time. [laughter] Uhh, but I usually use bisexual just 'cause it's, honestly it's easier to explain, more people know what it is.

Umm, so, I was straight for most of my life, like I really didn't have any crushes on girls or anything. And then when I was ... in high school

I had this concept of "The List" [laughter] of like.... And I, I'm sure this is a thing, but like, I thought I was so special for making— I, like, had a breakthrough, that every single person, no matter what their sexual orientation, has at least one person of the ... gender that doesn't align with your sexual orientation, that you would totally get with if you could. And it was mostly celebrities, like you know—I don't know—Jennifer Lawrence for me. Or like I said, like a straight guy would have like David Beckham or something. But... and then the list got really big. And then I was like, Okay, there's something, something not exactly straight about this. Umm, which is me most of my life. [laughter] Umm, so that was a thing.

(b1) First coming out.

The informant continued to tell about her first ever time coming out to another person, her best friend.

Inf. 1: Umm, the first time, the very first time I came out, umm, was on my seventeenth birthday. Umm, and, this is, so beautiful. I was, umm, in Forest Park—are you from St. Louis?

Int.: St. Charles.

Inf. 1: Okay, so I was in Forest Park and we were doing, me and my best friend Greg were doing paddle boats, and we got in the middle of, umm, this is so dramatic [laughter], we got in the middle of umm the lake, like the Grand Basin, with the, you know with the picturesque, the Art Hill, the thing and all the fountains around. And I was like, "Greg I like girls, did you know that?" [lots of laughter] So that was the first time and he was like, "Yeah, okay, cool, it's chill."

(b5) Coming out to parents.

The first informant went on to give her quintessential coming out story, the story of coming out to her mother, which the other listeners were eager to hear. It seems to have probably been "performed" before, given the cadence of it.

Inf. 1: Okay, the story, here's my story. Umm, I feel like I'm building up too much, it's not actually that great. So, umm, I had been thinking for a while.... This was [gives exact date]; I know this 'cause my cousin's birthday was on [the day before]. And my cousin, umm, for her birthday I spent the night at her house and the next day, umm her Quidditch team was gonna play the half time show at a roller derby. [laughter] Which was just perfect, and beautiful umm—[aside] that's where I met my friend Josie—anyway, so we were at the roller derby and I was like, Wow, there are a lot of lesbians here. Which I, sort of expected, but, Wow, that lady is married to a lady. [laughter] That's cool, I should probably tell my parents. [laughter]

Umm, and actually my dad was out of town. So I had to come out to my mom, just my mom, which was, kinda, whatever. Umm, so I got home, it was like midnight, and I had a headache, and I was just like.... For a while I had been thinking, I could just *say* it. Like, 'cause I had thought— I'm sorry, I'm bad at telling stories—I had thought that, you know, I don't have to come out, like, on principle it shouldn't be a thing, I shouldn't have to tell my parents. I should just, you know, start dating a girl and then if they have questions they'll ask. Umm, but, no it, it had been causing me a lot of stress, like I felt kinda sick when I was around my parents 'cause I couldn't say something, because that would be coming out and that would be so dramatic and I, it was giving me a lot of stress. So for the last couple weeks before that I had been thinking, like it's dinner I could just say, "I like girls." And that would be it. But I just like ... too stressful.

So my mom, is an accountant. And, around tax time, the entire kitchen table is full of tax forms, it's intense. She's very, she's very organized, she gets very into it, I mean, we can only ask her questions if she like, [laughter] if something is on fire or bleeding. Umm, so I'm sitting there and, I like get myself a glass of water. And the whole time I'm thinking, I could just say it, I could just say it. "Mom, I like girls. Mom I like girls, I'm, I like girls, I like girls." And I'm just repeating it over and over in my head. And I finally am about to say it and she's like, "Dear, can you get this thing from the printer?" [laughter] And so it's like, the tension is building! "Mom, I like girls. Mom I like girls." And I'm like going to the printer, I'm getting this piece of paper, I'm just like, thinking, "Mom, I like girls. I like girls, Mom." And so I'm drinking my glass of water and I say, "I like girls." And she says, "What?" [laughter] And I said, "I like girls. And boys. I'm bisexual." And she says, "Okay. Are you okay?" [laughter] "Have we, have we done everything to make you feel, comfortable?" And it was very, I felt very relieved 'cause she said that. And I said, "Yeah." And she said, "Dear, you know I'm doing taxes, right?" [lots of laughter] And that's my story. "Dear, you know I'm doing taxes, right?"

(b6) Additional coming out to friends.

She followed her essential story to discuss her coming out, or lack thereof, to other friends. Additionally, the ally had heard of another especially good coming out anecdote from the first informant and asked if she might repeat it.

Inf. 1: Umm, so that, that's that. And I like, forgot to come out to my best friends, which was interesting. I like, was texting the one, 'cause like, it just felt so natural to me, to like you know to talk about girls I liked to my best friends. And then they like talked to each other and they were like, "Did, did she tell you anything?" "No? Did she just like, forget to come out to us?" And then I texted them like, "I just came out to my mom!" And they were like, "Okay." [laughter] "Now I get it." Yeah, that's pretty much it.

Ally: [pause] Were you the one with the story where you were telling, your like one friend in your group of friends that like didn't know? Was that you?

Inf. 1: Oh yeah, yeah that was fun. I'm, I made a pun when I came out to my friends. 'Cause we were playing charades, and somebody was like, "We have an uneven number so I'll play for both teams." And I said, "Really, if anyone should be playing for both teams here, it should be me." And that's how I came out to my friends.

Informant 2

(a) Coming out to self.

After a brief break, the second informant began her story, an expansive look at her realization of her own asexuality in comparison to her dealings with her friends and other peers while growing up.

Inf. 2: So I identify as asexual, and … erm, maybe demiromantic, I'm thinking maybe aromantic, ehh. Umm, and, the asexual part, I kind of didn't actually realize there was anything like, uhh…. I would just never have crushes, and other people would be like, "This boy, oh my god." And I'd be like, Okay cool, you're cool. And so for the longest time I was like, whatever. A lot of my friends also didn't really make a big deal out of like, boys and such, so I didn't really like realize it until I was older—I don't really know how old.

But after a while people would be like, "So who's your crush?" and I'd be like, "Well, I don't have one." And they never believed me, and it was really annoying. So I would start making up crushes [laughter] and just like pick a random dude and be like, "I have a crush on so-and-so." And they'd be like, "Oh my God, really?" And I'd be like, "Mmhmm, totally have a crush on him." And usually they would be like, "Cool," and then continue their conversations, and didn't really ask me to do anything.

And so, one time though, I was friends with a guy. And I'm like [a] really affectionate friend, I just like hugging people and so [on] and so forth. So he was the only guy friend I had. So people just automatically assumed that I had a crush on him. And I definitely liked him, like he was a nice person and I enjoyed his company; we played video games together. And I was in like eighth grade and he asked me out and I was like, [pause, laughter] "Sure?" But basically, we didn't go on dates, we just played video games together [laughter] and there was no change; he just said he was my boyfriend. And he asked me to kiss him once, and I was like, "No." And we were together for until like halfway through freshman year because I was like sick on Valentine's Day and he left me chocolate in my like, locker—which I still haven't figured out how he got my locker combination. [laughter]

But, that's my one and only experience with a person and I never, "fell in love." And so I did figure out that I probably was asexual pretty quickly into high school, but I never really thought about aromanticism until fairly recently when I was like, What is it like to fall in love? And I got all philosophical and [cray]. [laughter] But yeah, so that was me coming out to myself, for the most part.

(b2) Coming out to friends.

The informant's revelations to friends were fairly nonchalant.

Inf. 2: Umm, and I've only ever come out to friends and my mother. So, most of the stories with my friends it was kind of like, "Guys, I'm asexual." And they were like, "Cool." [chuckle] Or a couple of them were like, "What is that?" And I explained and they were like, "Cool." Most of them already knew what it was because most of them were in like GSA and we actually had days where we explained in the Gay Straight Alliance what stuff was. And that's where I made my one asexual friend that I ever had until I came here [to college].

(b5) Coming out to parents.

The informant then talked about a formative coming out experience with her mother.

Inf. 2: But the not so fun story is when I came out to my mom. And I told her that I was asexual and she was like, "[I have] no idea what that means." So I tried to explain it to her and she was like, "Okay." And I did it at an opportune time because I needed to leave for dance class [laughter] so, I left for dance class and she never gave me a reply. And when I come back home, I see her on the internet researching it. So I was like, Oh, [clap] good, [clap] this'll end well. She'll like, get all this information and she'll know what it is and.... Then, we had a very deep and meaningful conversation—to her—in which basically she said, "You just haven't finished growing up yet,"

LD: Mmmmm...

Inf. 2: "And, someday, in college or somewhere, you're gonna fall in love with a guy." And I was like, "Tsk, sure, Mom."

Then she gave me this story about how she thought she was never gonna get married and have kids, and then she did obviously since I exist. And I was like, Cool, Mom. But like, you had boyfriends. I've seen them. [laughter] They're in your high school year book. You've pointed out pictures of you dancing and stuff in your high school yearbook, you've had boyfriends.

So like, that's not the same story—unless it is, and she just, is denying it herself but I don't think so. Umm, and, so, I brought it up exactly once after that and she kind of just, brushed it off. And that was … fun.

(c) Processual nature of coming out.

She ends with a comment on her coming out since, alluding to the processual nature of the process.

Inf. 1: But yeah, all my friends have been cool. And the people I meet here [at college] are all, awesome for the most part. So that's good.

That's my story. It's kind of sad. Sorry.

Informant 3

The third informant had a one-on-one interview. His is brief but still indicative.

(a) Coming out to self

This informant's self-realization directly led to his first relationship.

Inf. 3: So I identify as a gay male. And I first realized that when I started having feelings for another man. I had never thought about having those kinds of feelings for anyone, but it turns out the first time I did it happened to be with another man. And so I had to come to terms with that directly through falling in love with someone else.

(b5) Coming out to parents.

He next discussed coming out to his parents and grandparents, essentially equitable experiences.

Inf. 3: And eventually we did end up dating and that's when I had to come out to my mom because she, as a mother typically does, knew that something was going on. And she was completely accepting, as was my dad when he found out. But when I told my grandparents they … tried to accept it, but it was really hard for them to love that aspect of me at first.

After a while it became very natural to them and they decided that, since it was part of me they should still love it.

(b6) Additional coming out to friends.

He concluded with a quick note on coming out to friends. It is coded as additional due to its position and the implication that he had already come out to at least one friend, his lover.

Inf. 3: And coming out to friends has not been a big deal, although some have left before. But ... not everyone can be as accepting as Prism or as other groups on campus are.

Notably, a number of other members present at the event declined to be interviewed because, while they said that they would be happy to help out, they felt their stories were "not very exciting."

Informant 4

The fourth informant was interviewed the day after the Prism event, and discussed degrees of out-ness to various organizations and institutions as well as to friends.

(a) Coming out to self.

The informant did not expand much on the details of self-realization beyond providing a very basic biographical framework.

Inf. 4: I identify as gay and also as transgender. I came to realize that I was gay five years ago, but I had early indications of that before that point. And as far as the transgender part of my identity, I realized that about a year and a half ago.

(b2) Coming out to friends / (c) Processual nature of coming out.

They talk of the kind of trust it required to come out to friends.

Inf. 4: How I came to show that to others ... was through a gradual process of learning which people I could trust and that weren't obviously going to betray that confidence. And that's been a difficult process, and so for that reason I haven't come out to very many people except for close friends in my circle and also, obviously from the organizations that I'm involved in, such as Prism or Trans + Tuesdays.

(b3) Coming out to institutions.

Unlike other informants, this informant discusses coming out to people other than friends and family, specifically institutions.

Inf. 4: Although, I have had reason to come out to other people that I'm not socially involved with as well, such as doctors I work with, or other agencies I work with formally, just because of the questions they ask and because, even though it's somewhat awkward, I'd rather be honest and be able to have them help me better than not. And in most cases that's been met very professionally and it hasn't really made any difference, so that's ultimately good.

(c) Processual nature of coming out.

The informant further classified their degree of "outness" and reasons behind it.

Inf. 4: And so, if you were going to sum my identity up in one word, I would say that I'm partially out, partially open to the people around. I'm not entirely closed off to it but yet I don't feel comfortable nor really feel a need to be completely out to most people that I'm around, just because I don't feel like it's a really necessary part of myself to share with most people that I'm around.

Informant 5

The fifth informant, a close friend of the prime investigator, was interviewed in their private residence two days after the event.

(a) Coming out to self.

The informant operates on a very specific and long timeline.

Inf. 5: So I identify as gay, and queer—mostly interchangeably, gender is weird and all—and … and uhh, I'd say I started to, you know, realize that in myself starting around sixth grade. It took like, all of middle school to accept it and [to] the beginning of high school to start, you know, revealing it to other people. And then by the end of high school I was, fairly out, you know, to some weird degrees with some people, but, yeah.

(b1) First coming out.

Interestingly, the informant's first revelation was to not a close friend, but an acquaintance.

Inf. 5: Umm, the first person I ever came out to was umm… my freshman year of high school a girl asked me to the homecoming dance and I wrote her this like, ridiculously sappy letter, you know explaining like, "Oh, I'm sorry I, don't want to date you…. I'm gay." [laughter] You know, that stuff. Umm, and I mean, she was cool about that. Umm, we're not really [close] friends now but that was, cool.

(a3) Coming out to self through models.

The next section of their story went back to elaborate on their self-realizations.

Inf. 5: And umm, actually though, back on like, realizing it in myself. Umm, you know it [was] really rough at first, I remember like this site that I found online, something about like reparative therapy, and I was like, wanting that—and it was, really gross, a really weird part of my life to look back into. Umm, but like, around late middle school I learned that my brother was gay too, and, umm, didn't tell him immediately for whatever reason. But, that kind of, seeing someone else really close to me do it helped me. Umm, there was like, exactly one out gay guy in my middle school but, his existence helped me. I think a lot of people have those people in their youths.

(b2) Coming out to friends.

For quite a time they discuss coming out to various groups of friends.

Inf. 5: Umm, so yeah, the second person I came out to was like my best friend, in a text on like New Year's Day as my resolution. And then, I actually came out to my brother and two friends in a park like over spring break, like, the friends were talking about how my brother was gay and they were like, "Oh, so [name], when are you gonna come out?" And I was like, "Okay, right now." [laughter]

And umm, I don't know, I sort of got less out of that coming out than I had wanted, like less support. They were kind of like, "Oh, that makes sense; I had already guessed." Which like, is fine but it's…. You want like, more explicit support sometimes. Or you know, more…. You know it's a big deal to you so you want someone to take it as a big deal, so, then, like….

The only other significant coming out to people my age, umm, like was shortly after that at a set crew. And umm, I don't know, some girl asked me like, "Hey so since your brother's gay do you ever think that, like, you could be too?" And I was like, "Well I am bi." 'Cause, that's what I identified [as] at the time. And, what I don't totally unidentify with now.

Umm, and they were really, they were, a lot more, you know, what I was wanting out of it, I guess, the drama. The one guy who had been out in high school, or in middle school, was in that group, and he was really great, you know. We're not, huge friends now but he's ... important to my story.

And then like, I didn't really have other times I came out in high school. I think it was on my Facebook for a bit, you know for like, certain people. I had like set the privacy restrictions how I wanted them to be. So, people knew; I just didn't really talk about it. I didn't go on like, any dates except for one my senior year.

(b4) Coming out to a mentor.

They then discuss coming out to their older sister.

Inf. 5: But umm, my junior or senior year, I'm not really sure which, umm—my entire coming out story is kind of like built around my siblings because, fun fact, my sister is gay too—umm, I'd sort of heard from my brother that she might've identified as asexual at some time. Umm, and maybe she still does to some degree, I don't know. But umm, she had a tweet that was like, "Ugh, straight people." [laughter] And I sent her an e-mail and I was like, "I don't disagree with this but, are you like, saying what I think you're saying? Because I don't, strictly speaking, know that." And she was like, "I kind of knew you because I saw it on Facebook, but, yeah, we should talk about this and be cool, and...."

And she was just, so great, she's, a wonderful person. Umm, we talk about like, you know deep feelings and media and politics and theory and, a lot of stuff all the time now. And we're like, several years apart but it's really cool, like.... She was glad that I'd figured it out so young 'cause she didn't, which maybe that was like a generational thing too, you know, having things like Tumblr around, umm, to help people like really realize things earlier.

(b5) Coming out to parents.

The final major part of their story involved coming out to their parents and their status with their parents since.

Inf. 5: And then umm, actually it wasn't until the week before college that any part of my identity had been umm, even sort of discussed with my parents, like.... Like that caused me a lot of pain; umm, freshman year in high school was a really, dark time struggling with that, and—but you know, the rest of high school I was more chill about it; I just didn't, mention it because, you know, it didn't come up. And then umm, the year before, or the week before, I umm went to college, umm, my mom had just had surgery. So, I think she had been really like, you know introspective about life, you know, the things that matter I guess. And she was just like, "You know, your dad and I have been thinking for some time now that you might be gay." And, I don't even know exactly what she said, but it was something along the lines of, you know, "We're okay with that."

And that was really great, 'cause, when they first came out, or found out about my brother, they were not [accepting], so, they've come a long way. And she was just like, "We just want to make sure that, you know, when you're at college you be careful." And I don't really know if she was, warning me about non-gay people who might wanna hurt me or like the crazy gay people 'cause, my parents are conservative, but, I don't know…. It was supportive, it was … it was their way of, you know, coming to terms with it. And we still haven't addressed it, but I'm like, in an almost year-long relationship and they don't know about that to my knowledge. Umm, but I'm sure they can guess, you know. We'll talk about it, when we talk about it.

(b6) Additional coming out to friends.

Before finishing, they recalled one last story about coming out since coming to college.

Inf. 5: [laughter] Umm, coming out to my first college roommate was fun because, umm, he was just like, "So you know before we go into this year, I just wanna address what our sexualities are because that's some-thing that might matter, and I just want you to know that I'm really chill with it. So, what are you?" And I was like, "I'm pretty gay." [laughter] And he thought that was pretty fun. And then umm, one of my suitemates was pan and my roommate eventually came out too. We had one straight guy in the room, so that was fun. But yeah.

(c) Processual nature of coming out.

Their coda is a note on their current level of outness and status/need for future coming out experiences.

Inf. 5: I haven't really had to come out to other people in college. Here it's almost expected. [laughter] Yeah. So yeah, that is my story.

Memes and Humor: A Linguistic Analysis
Brandon Eychaner

This 2013 paper applies the tools of cognitive science to memes, a type of folklore unknown prior to the world wide web (but not unprecendented – see Dundes' work on xerographic lore).An example of genuinely empirical folklore: an experiment is conducted.

Abstract

In recent years, the internet has come to be one of the most powerful social media tools. By utilizing web services like Facebook, Twitter, Reddit, or hundreds of other websites designed for streamlined information sharing, ideas can spread to thousands of people in a matter of minutes. One of the most popular forms of humor on the internet is memes. Humor is associated with memory formation and is an important part of social behavior, widely cited as one of the defining characteristics of being human. This paper seeks to explore several topics, including a possible cognitive model of humor, the linguistic features of a specific meme paradigm, and an integration between the cognitive models of humor and the study of meme humor.

Introduction

Humor has only rarely been dealt with in the field of cognitive linguistics. Because cognitive linguistics is a relatively new branch of linguistics, the tools and methods for studying and understanding the cognitive models of language are not as well-developed as those in other fields of linguistics, and as such, the topic of humor has only begun to undergo inspection. Linguistics as a whole has, however, dealt extensively with other creative language use like metaphor, story-telling, lying, and sarcasm, though where these creative uses of language cross over into humor, there has not been much research. Within the past few years, however, several researchers have put forth various models for thinking about humor in a cognitive linguistic context, in addition to the recent availability of brain-imaging research dealing with humor appreciation. The most popular theory among these is the incongruity-resolution (IR) model.

The IR model of humor is widely used, but not well-defined; various researchers will define it in different ways. Widely cited is Raskin (1985), who quotes Beattie (1776, p. 155), a Scottish poet, in his definition of incongruity: "Laughter arises from the view of two or more inconsistent, unsuitable, or incongruous parts or circumstances, considered as united in one complex object or assemblage, or as acquiring a sort of mutual relation from the peculiar manner in which the mind takes notice of them." Suls (1972) defines it somewhat differently for the purpose of his two-stage model of humor: "Incongruity of the joke's ending refers to how much the punchline violates the recipient's expectations" (92), quoted in Ritchie (1999). Raskin's (1985) Semantic Script Theory of Humor (SSTH) posited that a text that could be interpreted in multiple ways was represented by various "scripts," and when two or more of these scripts interact in a specific manner, the text is humorous. Originally, it was not intended as an IR model (Ritchie, 2009), but was later extended by the General Theory of Verbal Humor (GTVH) (Attardo & Raskin, 1991), which contained more IR-related elements. Ritchie (1999) provides disambiguation for some terms associated with IR models, including "incongruity" itself, and what an "interpretation" (or "script" as Raskin [1985] might have it) is. Also heavily stressed in cognitive models of humor is Suls' (1972) two-stage model **(Figure 1)** of humor appreciation.

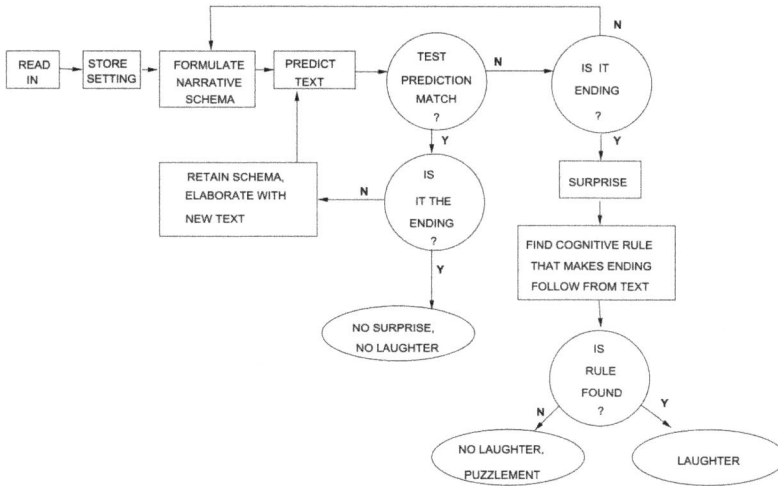

Figure 1 (provided by Ritchie, 1999)

The two steps in this model include "surprise," in which the audience reaches a point in the joke that does not obviously follow from previous parts of the joke (the IR equivalent to incongruity), and "coherence," which is the resolution of the incongruity. Suls' two-stage model applies specifically to cartoons and other related humor and assumes a punchline, rather than a set-up, that causes incongruity which is consistent with meme humor and is thus apt for analyzing the humor associated with memes. The two-stage model also assumes a loosely defined "cognitive rule" which is used to make sense of the punchline in the context of the set-up. Suls' two-stage model, in combination with a general definition of IR, will be used to evaluate the humor of memes in the current research. More important, however, is a model which is not entirely theoretical, and a discussion of the current research on the neural correlates of humor is warranted.

Cognitive Research in Humor

Coulson & Kutas (2001) make an attempt at measuring the cognitive processes related to coherence after surprise by recording event-related potentials in adult subjects. They assume a "frame shifting" mechanism, meaning that subjects are required to shift between two interpretations of a set-up during the coherence phase of joke comprehension. This may be equivalent to Raskin's (1985) "scripts," in that they represent various

interpretations of a text; the important difference is that scripts are semantic interpretations, while frames are cognitive mechanisms represent-
ing spaces in memory that allow the audience to make sense of a joke.
Coulson & Kutas provide this example:

> (1) I let my accountant do my taxes because it saves time: last
> spring, it saved me 10 years.

A SSTH analysis would provide two scripts for (1): one in which *time*
refers to time in general; and one in which *time* refers to jail time. A
two-stage approach identifies the surprise as instead coming from *years* in
the punchline, with the two cognitive frames eventually being resolved by
some cognitive rule. The first frame provides what seems to be the most
obvious interpretation before the punchline; namely, that the interpretation of *time* should be equivalent to the first SSTH script provided above.
Once the punchline is delivered, another frame is called upon in which
the audience understands that one can do taxes incorrectly, break the law,
and subsequently serve a jail sentence. When the surprise of the punchline
has been dispelled and the frame switch has occurred, this is the point at
which humor is appreciated in this model.

Timing

The point at which Coulson & Kutas (2001) posit this frame shifting
to occur is during a sustained negative ERP, 500-900 ms after final word
onset, as opposed to other joke-related ERPs that occurred at various other
times. *[ERPs – event-related brain potentials — are patterned voltage changes
in the on-going EEG that are time-locked to classes of specific processing events.
Most commonly these events involve the onset of stimuli, but they can also
include the execution of a motor response – ed]*

Jokes also elicited a positive ERP over the frontal areas bilaterally,
generally associated with working memory (Goldman-Rakic & Friedman,
1991; Salmon *et al.*, 1996; MacLeod, Buckner, Miezin, Petersen, & Raichle,
1998; Visser, Jefferies, & Ralph, 2010).

Neuroanatomy

Pivotal to the study of jokes is ambiguity resolution, which has been
shown to occur in several areas in the brain. Namely, they are the pars tri-
angularis, ventral and dorsal pars opercularis, and pars orbitalis (all generally associated with Broca's area) for semantic ambiguity, and additionally
the planum temporale (superior posterior temporal gyrus, or Wernicke's
area) for syntactic ambiguity (Price 2010). Additional studies have shown
the right homologue to Wernicke's area is key in the resolution of semantic

ambiguity as well (Harpaz, Levkovitz, & Lavidor, 2009), and it follows that damage to the right hemisphere, and especially in pre-motor areas associated with working memory and the Wernicke's area homologue, would contribute to difficulty in humor appreciation, a phenomenon which has been corroborated by multiple lesion studies; *viz.* Zaidel, Kasher, Soroker, & Batori (2002), Shammi & Stuss (1999), Bryan (1988), and Marinkovic *et al.* (2011). Various problems associated with right frontal lobe lesions suggest that humor is not simply a linguistic phenomenon. Subjects that have experienced detriments to their social functions like emotion recognition also show problems in understanding jokes. Thus, a cognitive model of humor must go beyond the scope of linguistics to account for behavioral differences, emotional recognition, self-awareness, and other related complex facets of human behavior and psychology.

Additionally, some lesions cause patients to exhibit an inability to recognize the incongruity in jokes, while others can recognize, but not resolve, the incongruity. Bihrle, Brownell, & Powelson (1986) find in a left-hemisphere lesion study, only recognition of incongruity is affected, while resolution may still take place unaffected in the right hemisphere, suggesting that humor is a multi-stage process in which humor appreciation is not dependent on a conscious understanding of the incongruity associated with jokes. Moran *et al.* (2004) further investigate the neural correlates of incongruity detection and resolution using fMRI on subjects watching *Seinfeld* and *The Simpsons*. This study is different from the others in that it uses data gathered from subjects being exposed to verbal humor over a period of time which is not encapsulated in a single image or traditional set-up-and-punchline joke. In spite of the unique format of the study they find that incongruity detection occurs (as might be expected from previous data) in Wernicke's and Broca's areas, exhibiting left-lateralization, while the resolution and subsequent appreciation activate similar areas bilaterally (areas consistent with the aforementioned studies). Interestingly, the authors also find that insular cortex (usually cited as the neural basis for strong emotions [Fiol, Leppik, Mireles, & Maxwell, 1988; Phillips *et al.*, 1997]) is broadly activated during the appreciation stage. These findings are corroborated in a 2012 study by Chan, *et al.*, in which the authors find three separate significant stages of neural activity; incongruity detection, resolution, and emotional response.

In other words, (verbal) humor is made up of at least two separate facets: linguistic incongruity-resolution; and an affective element. This affective element (see Moran *et al.*, 2004) is a term used to account for the degree to which individuals find jokes funny in the context of past experiences, personal knowledge, and other related factors. Due to the cognitive complexity of humor, it is arguably necessary that a very general term exist for extraneous processes involved in humor which are not readily categorized. It is, however, important to understand how these affective elements interact with humor on a cognitive level for several reasons.

Human memory seems to have several distinct neural substrates which function both independently and together, depending on the type of memory being formed or recalled (phonetic, spatial, working, motor, long-term, short-term memory, etc.) (Schmidt, 2002; Zurowski, *et al.*, 2002). Emotion, and subsequently humor, have been known to positively affect one's ability to recall information (Lippman & Dunn 2000; Schmidt 2002; Summerfelt, Lippman, & Hyman, 2010). Two of these neural substrates – the amygdala and hippocampal complex – function together when emotional pathways are utilized simultaneously with memory formation (Phelps, 2004). This is perhaps the reason why humor, which elicits an emotional response, aids in memory formation. Understanding this interaction between humor and memory has several possible implications for education, or for understanding the complex relationship between human cognition and language.

The brain imaging data applied to the two-stage model, then, gives a clearer, more complete way to understand how cognitive linguistics provides a functional model for humor appreciation. A more concise delineation of the humor appreciation process is as follows, in accordance with Suls' (1972) proposed model (Fig. 1).

Narrative Schemata

As the set-up is delivered, the audience stores the information in working memory and retrieves relevant long-term memory to develop a "narrative schema," or frame. Within that frame, the audience will predict information which has not yet been given by the joke. If the prediction fails to match the information in the joke, and the joke has ended, the audience experiences surprise at the incongruity. At this point, a cognitive rule (corresponding to the ambiguity-resolution cognitive processes) is looked for, and if one can be found which resolves the incongruity, a frame switch occurs. The frame switch elicits a reinterpretation of the set-up of the joke, and, in the right affective context (not accounted for by Suls in his model), laughter occurs. If no rule can be found, the joke ends in confusion and non-humor. Subsequently, extending this model further into cognitive processes, the emotions elicited from the joke may interact with the neural substrates responsible for specific types of memory, until these effects have ceased.

Memes

Memes set up their own linguistic context (that is, idiosyncratic symbolic systems), which is readily observed in the image rather than in the language included within the meme. Because of this, rather than having a genre of jokes associated with a phrase (ex., "Knock, knock...") or a specific linguistic structure, the meme genre is dependent on the image on which the joke is written. It may be argued that the images are a paralinguistic feature of that genre, or that the image serves as a complete contextual background on which the joke is based. Two main types of memes and a third, hybrid type, are the subject of the current study. Conventionally, a blue background is associated with the "Socially Awkward Penguin" (Awk. P.), a red background is associated instead with the "Socially Awesome Penguin," (Aws. P.) and the hybrid type uses both red and blue backgrounds (see **Illustration 1**) called the "Socially Awesome Awkward Penguin" (SAAP). All three types include an image of a penguin in the center of a square using the background color schema as part of the set-up and punchline. Notice that in the Awkward paradigm, the penguin is facing left, while it faces right in the Awesome paradigm, and is split in two halves facing different directions in the hybrid type.

Socially Awkward Penguin   Socially Awesome Penguin   Socially Awesome/Awkward Penguin

Illustration 1

An "awkward" scenario is one which demonstrates a situation in which the subject lacks common social knowledge or is in some way acting inappropriately in a social context. An "awesome" scenario, on the other hand, includes some behavior which is potentially rewarding or positive, or in some cases a potentially awkward behavior, but which ends in an unexpectedly positive outcome. However, the background scheme seems more important as a semiotic system than the central image itself. Without the penguin image itself, an identical background scheme may still invoke the same joke paradigm, assuming that the reader has background knowledge on the meaning of the original meme structure **(Ill. 2)**. Without contextual knowledge, however, the red and blue backgrounds mean nothing. Thus, social media play a key role in the propagation and definition of the proprietary semiotic system in these memes.

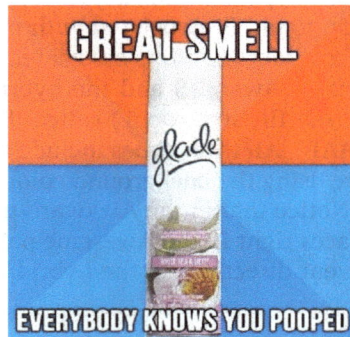

Illustration 2

As with many other types of humorous media and jokes, these memes include a set-up and a punchline. In the case of the Awk. P., the setup is either neutral or positive with respect to social behavior, but ends in a punchline which is unfavorable or inappropriate **(Ill. 1)**. The Aws. P. meme incorporates either favorable, neutral, or unfavorable social behavior with a favorable outcome or punchline. The SAAP begins with a positive situation and ends with an unfavorable reaction. Due to the structure of each meme, a different amount of incongruity arises between the set-ups and punchlines, which may affect the degree to which they are seen as humorous. There are several rules which memes generally follow, depending on the type of meme as well as the topic of that meme. The penguin meme can be characterized by some nonstandard uses of English which potentially contribute to the humor (perhaps through an incongruity between the expectation of correct grammar and blatant violation of these grammar rules). Namely these errors are simple deletions; deletions of pronouns, overt subjects, and determiners are very common. The most noticeable of these is the lack of pronominal use in the set-up. Among the most popular one hundred of each variation of the penguin meme collected from their respective dedicated websites, only seven contained overt subjects in the set-up, three of which were due to a quotation mechanism.

(2) Set-up: "I like your accent, where are you from?"
Punch line: Talking to a deaf person.

A total of thirty out of the three-hundred images contained an overt subject in the setup but did not include a determiner.

(3) Teacher displays lost jacket in front of class.
Didn't like it anyway.

This rule is less common in the punchline. Out of the three-hundred images, twenty-two punchlines included an overt subject, and ten more had subjects without determiners. As a general rule, however, determiners and overt subjects are not required in either part of the joke, and it is assumed, unless otherwise specified, that the subject of each part of a given joke is the penguin, which represents some anonymous person or one with which the audience may identify. In fact, only one image contained an overt subject that referred to the penguin.

(4) Tissues at front of class.
I'll just wipe my nose on my sleeves for 80 minutes.

However, this may simply be considered bad style. (4) may be more appropriately in style if changed to something like (4a):

(4a) Tissues at front of class.
Wipe nose on sleeve for 80 minutes.

Because of the limited space available for text in the image, as well as the humor associated with the ungrammaticality and shortness of the meme's linguistic style, overt subjects are considered extraneous. Also evident in (3) and (4) and in a majority of other memes, noun phrases are not required to have determiners where they might otherwise, in prescriptive standard English, be required: ((3): *[a] lost jacket, of [the] class;*

(4): of [the] class). As such, in meme language, a complete (singular) noun phrase does not require a determiner, and sentences do not require an overtly marked subject at all. The lack of grammatical sentences and abundance of sentence fragments in the penguin meme may be responsible for some of the humor associated with it, due to the aforementioned incongruity which ungrammatical sentences may cause, which must be resolved by the audience.

Experiment

Introduction

When the incongruity-resolution model is applied to the penguin meme, there are several things that may contribute to the overall humor associated with and within each type. **Table 1** provides the elements present in the current research and associated definitions. Examples are included in **Table 2**, which categorizes the 30 memes used in the present research and notes the number of grammatical deletions present and type of each example. The text of each meme is provided in the **Appendix**.

Table 1

Elements Affecting Humor Type of Joke	Definition
Physical	Involves violence or physical striking, or accidents
Courtship	Involves courtship behavior (no sexual activity)
Self-deprecating	Involves self-deprecation of the subject or negative emotional reaction
Inappropriate Behavior	Involves behavior which is uncalled for, accidental, or inappropriate to the situation
Disability-related	Involves a subject (main or otherwise) with a disability
Boasting	Involves a subject acting boastfully
Number of Deletions	Includes lack of overt subject, missing copula and aux. verbs, and lack of determiners
Type of Meme	
Socially Awkward	See Ill.1
Socially Awesome	See Ill.1
Socially Awesome/Awkward	See Ill.1

Table 2

Type of Meme	Appendix #	# Deletions	Type of Joke
Socially Awkward	3	3	Inappropriate Behavior
	5	0	Self-deprecating
	7	4	Inappropriate Behavior
	10	4	Disability
	13	1	Disability
	15	1	Inappropriate Behavior
	18	2	Inappropriate Behavior
	23	1	Inappropriate Behavior
	25	2	Inappropriate Behavior
	28	0	Inappropriate Behavior
Socially Awesome	1	2	Boasting
	11	1	Inappropriate Behavior
	14	3	Boasting
	16	1	Inappropriate Behavior
	17	3	Inappropriate Behavior
	19	3	Boasting
	26	4	Boasting
	27	3	Boasting
	29	0	Inappropriate Behavior
	30	2	Boasting
Socially Awesome/Awkward	2	4	Courtship
	4	4	Physical
	6	2	Inappropriate Behavior
	8	2	Self-deprecating
	9	1	Physical
	12	2	Self-deprecating
	20	3	Inappropriate Behavior
	21	1	Courtship
	22	2	Self-deprecating
	24	3	Inappropriate Behavior

In this experiment it is assumed that different degrees of incongruity exist according to the meme type. Due to the important nature of the background and semiotic system provided therein, each meme provides a different expectation and frame in the set-up and punchline. The Awk. P. provides a neutral or positive set-up and creates the expectation that something will go wrong. By default, the audience should theoretically predict a neutral punchline in all cases; that is, they will predict something that follows logically from the set-up according to common social practice. The background, then, serves to facilitate the frame-shifting process by providing a pragmatic context with which to match the disambiguating cognitive rule. The Aws. P. generally provides an awesome set-up and an awesome punchline. Here, there is less of an incongruity to resolve. There are less inappropriate behaviors that challenge preconceived notions of what an acceptable reaction to the behavior in the set-up might be, and thus, should theoretically be significantly less humorous than the Awk. P. The SAAP, however, should be significantly more humorous than the Awk. P. due to the larger amount of incongruity present. With an awesome set-up, the audience is looking to expect a punchline which is not difficult to understand in the context of the original set-up. When the punchline is delivered and instead is awkward or inappropriate, a greater amount of incongruity is created and a frame-shift is necessary to resolve the incongruity, theoretically making the SAAP more humorous on average. The present study seeks to test whether there is a significant difference between the perceived humorousness of each type of meme as a whole.

Methods

In this experiment, 10 random images were taken from the top 100 memes of each type under inspection (Awk. P., Aws. P., and SAAP) for 30 total images. The 30 images were presented to two groups ($n_1 = 28, n_2 = 27, n = 55$) and the order of presentation was randomized for both groups. Subjects were asked to subjectively rate the humor of each image on a scale from 1 to 10 (1 being not humorous, and 10 being extremely humorous). Each image was presented for 15 seconds on a projector. All subjects were college-aged, though gender was not controlled for. The size of each image was also not controlled for; however, the majority of the images were the same size (27 out of 30 presented at 300 x 300 pixels, and 3 out of 30 presented at 200 x 200 and subsequently zoomed to 140% size, effectively 280 x 280 pixels). Images were also controlled for the number of deletions (no statistically significant differences were present between the three types), but not for text length.

Results

Using two-sample t-tests, the average humorousness of each type was evaluated and compared against the other types. In accordance with the hypothesis, the Awk. P. was found to be rated as significantly more humorous than the Aws. P. ($p < .00$) (Fig. 2), and the SAAP was found to be rated as significantly more humorous than the Awk. P. ($p = .02$) (Fig. 3). There was no significant correlation between average humorousness and the number of deletions present in each image.

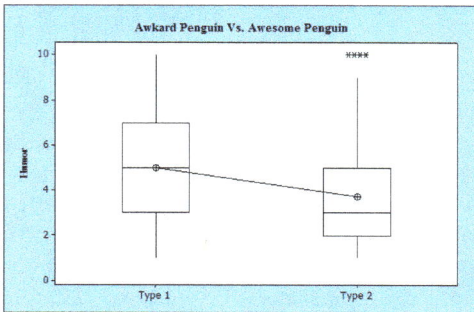

**Two-Sample t-Test
  and CI: Awk.P., Aws.P.**
Two-sample T for Awk.P. vs Aws.P.

```
        N Mean  StDev  SE   Mean
Awk.P. 550  4.99  2.38  0.10
Aws.P. 550  3.73  2.7   0.088
```

Difference = mu (Awk.P.)-mu(Aws.P.)
Estimate for difference: 1.267
95% C1 for difference: (1.003, 1.531)
T-Test of difference = 0 (vs not =):
T-Value = 9.43; P-Value = 0.0; DF = 1076

Figure 2

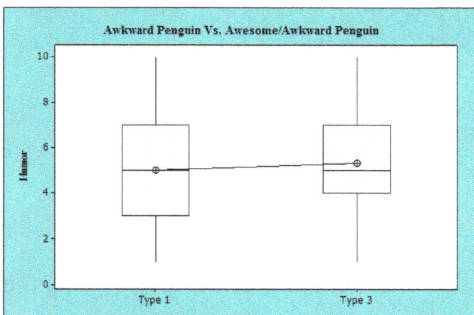

**Two-Sample t-Test
  and CI: Awk.P., SAAP**
Two-sample T for Awk.P. vs SAAP

```
        N Mean  StDev  SE   Mean
Awk.P. 550  4.99  2.38  0.10
SAAP. 550  5.32  2.28  0.097
```

Difference = mu (Awk.P.)-mu(SAAP)
Estimate for difference: -0.327
95% C1 for difference: (-0.603m -0,051)
T-Test of difference = 0 (vs not =):
T-Value = -2.33;　　　　　P-Value = 0.02;
DF = 1096

Figure 3

Discussion

The results seem to indicate a significant relationship between the type of meme and the average subjective humor associated with each type. The least humorous type seems to be the Aws. P., followed by the Awk. P., with the SAAP being rated consistently more humorous than the other types. The findings seem to support that hypothesis based on the IR model of humor. However, there are several factors which may have inadvertently affected the results. Gender was not accounted for, and many of the images assume a male subject (see Appendix examples 2, 4, 8, 9, 11, 15, 20, 21, and 29) with only one assuming a female subject (see Appendix example 6), if we are to assume the penguin is heterosexual. Naturally the gender and sexuality of a subject are things to consider when the joke itself is gendered.

Additionally, memes that elicited any laughter may have been rated as higher on average than they would have otherwise, due to the fact that individuals who are alone suppress laughter (Devereux & Ginsburg, 2001). Since humor appreciation is affected by social circumstances, collective laughter may have affected how some subjects rated the humorousness of various images, skewing the data higher for those images which elicited laughter. Joke type was not controlled for (physical, courtship, etc); nor was joke length. The type of humor present in each image and the amount of time required to read the text on each image may have affected the degree to which subjects found them humorous. Further study would benefit from controlling for all the aforementioned categories; subject gender, image text length, joke type, and group vs. individual rating tasks.

Conclusion

Humor remains one of the more enigmatic topics in psychology and linguistics. Due to the recent surge in brain-imaging studies, however, the elucidation of the neural pathways and cognitive mechanisms associated with humor is now becoming a possibility. As more data becomes available, previous theories of humor, such as the two-stage model posited by Suls (1972) and the GTVH by Attardo & Raskin (1991) can be integrated into our current understanding of these processes and edited accordingly for applicability purposes. Despite being a relatively new field of study, cognitive linguistics remains a powerful tool for functionally analyzing language, and further study of humor within the framework of cognitive linguistics may provide an invaluable approach to integrating the cognitive processes associated with language to other facets of human behavior.

References

Attardo, S. & Raskin, V. (1991). Script theory revis(it)ed: joke similarity and joke representation model. *Humor: International Journal of Humor Research, 4*(3), 293-347.

Bihrle, A. M., Brownell, H. H., Powelson, J. A., & Gardner, H. (1986). Comprehension of humorous and nonhumorous materials by left and right brain-damaged patients. *Brain and Cognition, 5*(4), 399-411.

Bryan, K. L. (1988). Assessment of language disorders after right hemisphere damage.*International Journal of Language & Communication Disorders, 23*(2), 111-125.

Chan, Y. C., Chou, T. L., Chen, H. C., Yeh, Y. C., Lavallee, J. P., Liang, K. C., & Chang, K. E. (2012). Towards a neural circuit model of verbal humor processing: An fMRI study of the neural substrates of incongruity detection and resolution. *Neuroimage, 66*, 169-176.

Coulson, S., & Kutas, M. (2001). Getting it: Human event-related brain response to jokes in good and poor comprehenders. *Neuroscience Letters, 316*(2), 71-74.

Devereux, P. G., & Ginsburg, G. P. (2001). Sociality effects on the production of laughter. *The Journal of General Psychology, 128*(2), 227-240.

Fiol, M. E., Leppik, I. E., Mireles, R., & Maxwell, R. (1988). Ictus emeticus and the insular cortex. *Epilepsy Research, 2*(2), 127-131.

Goldman-Rakic, P. S., & Friedman, H. R. (1991). The circuitry of working memory revealed by anatomy and metabolic imaging. *Frontal Lobe Function and Dysfunction*, 72-91.

Harpaz, Y., Levkovitz, Y., & Lavidor, M. (2009). Lexical ambiguity resolution in Wernicke's area and its right homologue. *Cortex, 45*(9), 1097–103.

Lippman, L. G., & Dunn, M. L. (2000). Contextual connections within puns: effects on perceived humor and memory. *The Journal of General Psychology, 127* (2), 185-197.

MacLeod, A. K., Buckner, R. L., Miezin, F. M., Petersen, S. E., & Raichle, M. E. (1998). Right anterior prefrontal cortex activation during semantic monitoring and working memory. *Neuroimage, 7*(1), 41-48.

Marinkovic, K., Baldwin, S., Courtney, M. G., Witzel, T., Dale, A. M., & Halgren, E. (2011). Right hemisphere has the last laugh: neural dynamics of joke appreciation. *Cognitive, Affective, & Behavioral Neuroscience, 11*(1), 113-130.

Moran, J. M., Wig, G. S., Adams Jr, R. B., Janata, P., & Kelley, W. M. (2004). Neural correlates of humor detection and appreciation. *Neuroimage, 21*(3), 1055-1060.

Phelps, E. A. (2004). Human emotion and memory: interactions of the amygdala and hippocampal complex. *Current Opinion in Neurobiology, 14*(2), 198-202.

Phillips, M. L., Young, A. W., Senior, C., Brammer, M., Andrew, C., Calder, A. J., ... & David, A. S. (1997). A specific neural substrate for perceiving facial expressions of disgust. *Nature, 389*, 495-498.

Price, C. J. (2010). The anatomy of language: a review of 100 fMRI studies published in 2009. *Annals of the New York Academy of Sciences, 1191*, 62-88.

Raskin, V. (1985). *Semantic Mechanisms of Humor.* Springer.

Ritchie, G. (1999). Developing the incongruity resolution theory. *AISB Symposium: Artificial Intelligence and Creative Language: Stories and Humor.* Univ. of Sussex, 69-75.

Ritchie, G. (2009). Variants of incongruity resolution. *Journal of Literary Theory, 3*(2), 313-332.

Salmon, E., Van der Linden, M., Collette, F., Delfiore, G., Maquet, P., Degueldre, C., ... & Franck, G. (1996). Regional brain activity during working memory tasks. *Brain, 119*(5), 1617-1625.

Schmidt, S. R. (2002). The humour effect: Differential processing and privileged retrieval. *Memory, 10*(2), 127-138.

Shammi, P., & Stuss, D. T. (1999). Humour appreciation: a role of the right frontal lobe. *Brain, 122*(4), 657-666.

Summerfelt, H., Lippman, L., & Hyman Jr, I. E. (2010). The effect of humor on memory: Constrained by the pun. *The Journal of General Psychology, 137*(4), 376-394.

Visser, M., Jefferies, E., & Ralph, M. L. (2010). Semantic processing in the anterior temporal lobes: a meta-analysis of the functional neuroimaging literature. *Journal of Cognitive Neuroscience, 22*(6), 1083-1094.

Zaidel, E., Kasher, A., Soroker, N., & Batori, G. (2002). Effects of right and left hemisphere damage on performance of the "Right Hemisphere Communication Battery". *Brain and Language, 80*(3), 510-535.

Zurowski, B., Gostomzyk, J., Grön, G., Weller, R., Schirrmeister, H., Neumeier, B., ... & Walter, H. (2002). Dissociating a common working memory network from different neural substrates of phonological and spatial stimulus processing. *Neuroimage, 15*(1), 45.

Appendix

Text of memes used in the study:

#	SET-UP	PUNCH LINE
1	Slept through a final	Set the curve
2	Hits on cute cashier girl	Credit card declined
3	Professor asks rhetorical question	Raises hand
4	Cute girl at concert gestures for a high five after song	Aims incorrectly and smacks her in the face
5	Come to front of the auditorium to get your award	Oh God No
6	Cute guy opens door for you	Panic and open other door
7	Waiter reaches for menu after ordering	Shakes hand
8	Getting married	Can't come up with 4 groomsmen
9	Catch a cute girl's eye	With your elbow
10	Came out of handicap stall	Guy in wheelchair is waiting
11	Forget to zip your pants	On purpose
12	Never forgets a face	Never remembers a name
13	I like your accent, where are you from	Talking to a deaf person
14	Friend zone	Never heard of it
15	Cute girl asks how old I am	"Level 23"
16	Called the police	to join my party
17	Fart in class	Proll into most epic beatbox ever
18	Tries to hold back a sneeze in class	Farts

19	Finish test first	Walk out like you own the place
20	Holds door for girl	To Men's Room
21	Compliment a girl on her freckles	Acne
22	Dresses up fancy for a Christmas party	Wins Ugly Sweater Contest
23	Homeless guy tells me to get home safe	"Thanks, You too!"
24	Gives lost stranger directions	Realizes later that they were wrong
25	Tries to take just sweatshirt off in class	Nope, everything
26	Cell phone goes off while walking into a room	Theme music
27	Forgets ending to joke	Comes up with a better one
28	"Okay, Class, find a partner"	Oh God No
29	You have a boyfriend?	What about a 'Man'friend?
30	Meet the most interesting man in the world	Get bored

Folk History from Down on the Farm in Shelby County
Holly Simpson Fling

This classic entry in family- and oral- history won the 2010 Dolph and Becky Schroeder Prize, the Missouri Folklore Society's highest honor for folklore scholarship by a student. Weaving together interview, archival work and onsite investigations, it is a reflective narrative of the investigation itself – the questions, the detective work, the reconstruction of other people's reasoning.

I grew up on a farm in Shelby County, Missouri, during the 1970s and 1980s. At that time, cable television was not available outside of the city limits, and no one had yet considered the possibility of owning technology, such as personal computers or VCRs. Instead, we relied on our imaginations and storytelling for entertainment. My father, who was born in 1921, was an animated storyteller, and we spent many evenings riding in the farm truck through the countryside and listening to him tell his tales. He was not the only storyteller around, though; several of our elderly neighbors enjoyed nothing more than trading tales with my father beneath the big maple tree in our backyard.

Given that my father and these other storytellers are all gone now, it has been more than twenty-five years since I have heard them tell their tales, but I still hold many of these stories in my memory, some more fragmented than others. While these oral accounts were certainly fun to listen to as a child, as I grew older, I realized that they had likely been embellished; but, in *Folkloristics*, Robert A. Georges and Michael Owen Jones argue, "In addition to being historical phenomenon themselves—whether conceptualized as survivals, continuities, or revivals—examples of folklore also frequently serve as sources of historical information" (84). "When used as historical sources," they go on to explain, "folklore examples enable researchers to reconstruct past events and to supplement, corroborate, and challenge or correct existing historical records and interpretations" (84). As oral histories that have been passed down by word of mouth, then, I realized that these stories needed to be recorded before they became missing pieces of times past.

Even as Georges and Jones acknowledge that not every oral tradition is historical truth (85), they point to William Lynwood Montell's work. In the absence of historical records due to fire, Montell gathered and analyzed historical traditions of local people to reconstruct the history of Coe Ridge Colony, an African American settlement in Cumberland County, Kentucky. In *The Saga of Coe Ridge: A Study in Oral History*, Montell finds that "no historian who is aware of the ways of the people on a local level, especially in rural areas where ties to the land are strong, will question the importance played by oral traditions in the lives of the people" (xvii). Furthermore, he insists, "Accuracy of local historical legends is not the most important question to be faced by the person who gathers and analyzes them, but rather the essential fact is that these folk narratives are believed by the people who perpetuate them" (xvii). Regardless of the level of historical truth, then, Montell works "to preserve for the generations to come a bit of the area's history which otherwise might one day be erased from the memories of the local people" (13). Like Montell, I, too, am working toward a preservation of the past: of my father's past, my own past, and my son's past. The past belongs to those who lived it, to those who remember it, and to those who will someday read about it, so it is of utmost importance to preserve it for the interest of the future generation. My father was born and raised in Shelby County, where he lived practically his entire life, so all of his tales revolved around this area of Missouri. In fact, many were based upon our family farm. I have chosen to recall from memory and to do further research on six specific tales that he and the other storytellers used to recount about local sites or landmarks and events that took place at these locations: the Honey Trail; the old cemetery; the men in Blue and Gray at Walkersville; the brick factory at Walkersville; the Brick House and its associated burials (including the physical and narrative traces of slave times), and the big rock from Salt River. I have chosen these particular stories because they fascinated me most as a child, and, for that reason, they stand out more clearly in my mind than other tales.

The Old Cemetery

The remains of what my father referred to as the Honey Trail run alongside the North Fork of Salt River and past an old cemetery that is surrounded by an iron fence and hidden in the woods on the west side of our family farm. My father often told me that our farm was made up of what had once been several farms; in fact, while working in the field, he would occasionally unearth artifacts with his plow, relics that had once belonged to these families, and even remnants of those who had lived on this land before the settlers. From arrow heads to keys and door knobs, my father's plow was an archeological tool that unearthed bits of the past. Once, he even uncovered a gold ring, which had likely belonged to one of the original settlers of Shelby County.

The Shelby County Historical Society Museum in Shelbina holds maps that identify the names of those who first purchased land in Shelby County. Other maps at this museum show ownership of the land during specific years, such as 1878 and 1902. Some of these original settlers, I discovered, lived Back West, as my father called that section of our farm, and they had been buried in a cemetery in the woods beside Salt River. I began my research on this cemetery by studying the names of these original settlers, particularly those who had settled on the west side of my family's farm in the Salt River Township. At the museum, I also found census records dating back to 1840. These records noted who lived in the homes, including family members, servants, and enslaved Africans.

Following my visit to the museum, I read through my family's farm abstract, which is essentially an archive of legal documents, such as land patents, wills, and court proceedings, which records any action having to do with the farm. True to my father's word, I found the abstract to be comprised of several abstracts, showing that our farm was, as he had said, originally several separate farms.

The earliest abstract, dated 20 October 1835, lists Peter Roff as the landowner. According to an account I found archived at the museum, which was written by Nicolas Watkins, one of Shelby County's first settlers, Peter Roff had actually settled on this land in November 1832. Watkins reports that when he and Roff, along with other men, first arrived in Shelby County in 1832, they did not find any other white settlers to the west of where they settled on Salt River.

Between my study of the museum maps and the farm abstract, by the time I visited the cemetery, I was already familiar with most of the names on the gravestones; for example, the farm abstract includes William Coard's land patent, as well as a copy of his will, so I already had a sense of this family's history when I came upon Coard's gravestone in this cemetery, along with those of his wife, Frances, and his daughter, Hester. The Coards had settled in Shelby County by 1838, as their land patent is dated 1 September of that year. This cemetery also contains three other gravestones, all of which date from the 1850s to the 1860s and belong to the children of L. and T.J. Duncan. The Duncan family is not mentioned in our farm abstract, but the museum's map of the original land purchasers shows a Levin Duncan to have settled a farm adjacent to William Coard's farm in 1848.

The Honey Trail

While this farmland that once belonged to the Coard family is now uninhabited and secluded from traffic, this was not always the case. According to my father, people used to drive their horse-drawn wagons north into Iowa in search of honey, and the trail they followed crossed our farm and forded the river near where the cemetery now hides among the trees. In its overgrown state, the trail only becomes visible about forty feet into the woods, but it does still exist. According to *A History of Monroe & Shelby Counties, Missouri*, prior to 1836 the only roads running north and south in these two counties were called the "Bee roads" (660-61), and there were only two of these roads, both of which were "little better than trails" (661). These Bee trails ran through the central and eastern parts of Shelby County, and they were made by the settlers of the counties to the south, as they traveled north every fall in search of honey (661). The Callaway trail, "the route commonly pursued by the honey hunters of Callaway County" (661), ran north of Shelbyville. As our farm is south and west of Shelbyville, I knew this trail could not be the trail from my father's story. The Boone trail, however, which was "made by the bee hunters from Boone County," is documented as having "crossed Salt River above Walkersville" (661). Since our family farm is located on Salt River above Walkersville, it seems likely that my father's Honey Trail is a surviving part of this Boone Trail.

The points at which these trails crossed streams were known as Bee fords, and, indeed, *A History* makes note of the Bee ford of Salt river [sic] (661), which should be where the trail crosses Salt River on the western side of our farm. Although most of my research suggested my father's stories about the Honey Trail to be accurate, *The Western Historical Manuscript Collection-Columbia* claims that Clark County, Missouri, just to the east of Scotland County, "was the terminus of the old 'Bee Roads' of pioneer days" ("Collection"); thus, while these trails did lead north, they may not have reached as far north as Iowa, as my father had claimed.

The Blue and the Gray

Aside from my father, one of my favorite storytellers was our neighbor

Melvin Snell. Before Melvin passed away in 1982, he recalled his grand-mother's claims to having seen, as a child, the injured and dead soldiers in both the Blue and the Gray laid out in the front yard of a house that sat on a hill near Walkersville. I do not recall if Melvin ever stated ex-actly how many men were seen by his grandmother, so I hoped to find this information in my research. To begin studying this oral account, I searched for evidence of a dispute near Walkersville during the Civil War. In *Civil War Day by Day: An Almanac 1861-1865*, E.B. Long and Barbara Long, note "a skirmish near Walkersville" on 2 April 1862 (192). My great-grandmother's copy of the 1911 *General History of Shelby County, Missouri* contains further information about this conflict: on this date, a Union cav-alry officer, Col. H. S. Lipscomb, of the Eleventh Missouri State Militia, and a Captain Wilmont, with the help of thirteen other men and a wagon, were transporting supplies from Shelbina to Shelbyville (86). Approxi-mately one mile downriver from Walkersville, Confederate "Tom Stacy, with sixteen of his band, bushwhacked the party, killing two militia men named Long and Thomas Herbst and a prominent and worthy citizen of the county named Lilburn Hale" (86). The number of men involved in the skirmish and the violence that led to these three reported deaths suggests that, if the dates corresponded to Melvin's grandmother's childhood years, this may have been the occurrence from Melvin's story.

Next, then, I began to look for evidence of Melvin's grandmother's iden-tity and whereabouts during the Civil War. Although I did not know her maiden name, I knew that his Grandmother Wiggins had supposedly once lived on an eighty-acre section of our farm, the same section on which my mother's house now sits. According to an 1878 map at the museum, J.H. Wiggins did own this particular piece of land, and in the *General History*,I found that, on 8 December 1870, John Wiggins was married to a Martha Cadwell of Shelby County. One of this couple's four children, Allie, had later married Elwood Snell (489). Allie Wiggins Snell would have been Melvin's mother, and her mother, Martha Cadwell Wiggins, would have been Melvin's grandmother. As Martha was married in 1870 and gave birth to four children following her marriage, she would have likely been a young girl in 1862, during the time of the Walkersville skirmish.

Because only three men were killed in this skirmish, Martha's claim of seeing soldiers in both blue and gray seems questionable. Still, if the two deceased Union soldiers were wearing their blue uniforms, and if the citi-zen were dressed in gray—and even black and brown can look gray when dirty—then she very well could have seen what she described. Also, these men would have included not only the dead but also the injured, which may have increased the number of bodies in the yard. Although there does not seem to be any existing information on injuries received during this minor Civil War event, injuries were common in the Missouri wilderness and perhaps merited little or no attention. And, as this incident took place during the Civil War, historical displacement could help to explain how two militiamen and one citizen came to be described as the men in the Blue and the Gray: in *From Memory to History* Barbara Allen and William Lynwood Montell explain how original actors of historical events become displaced through orally communicated history. Even chief actors, they argue, "may be displaced by... better known or locally more prominent figure[s]" (36-37). Melvin's grandmother's story may have been shaped through a child's perception from the beginning, and, as it was orally passed down over 148 years, it may have been altered by family members to emphasize Walkersville as a Civil War battlesite. But, even if Martha Cadwell Wiggins's memories were altered, the evidence suggests that her story is an example of true folk history.

The Brick Factory

Not only did Melvin's grandmother likely witness an important moment in the making of our nation but according to another of his stories, she also had a hand in the building of a local town. As he told it, Martha Cadwell Wiggins had handled almost every brick that built Shelbina, and most of Shelbina's downtown buildings date back to the 1880s and 1890s.[1] Melvin's intriguing claim seems hyperbolic, but it might indicate a connection between his grandmother's family and the owners of a brick plant. Local folklore does point to the past existence of a brick factory at Walkersville. Because Walkersville was once the largest town in Shelby County, as my father always said, land that is now associated with Shelbyville or Shelbina was, at that time, referred to as "the Walkersville area."

While there does not appear to be information available as to where the brickwork for downtown Shelbina was made, according to *A History*, in September 1881, a two-story brick building was constructed in Shelbyville with brickwork by William Moore (839), and, one of the museum's maps shows that several Moore families had settled farms near Walkersville between 1838 and 1839. The Township 56 and Township 57 maps from 1878 and 1902 also list William Cadwell as a land owner in the Walkersville area, but on the opposite side of the river from the Moore farms. This area of the county is rich in clay; thus, it is possible that the brick factory did exist at Walkersville, and since William Moore was known for

---

[1]Since I wrote this paper in 2010, most of Shelbina's downtown buildings were destroyed by fire.

brickwork, he may have been the owner of this factory. Although Melvin's grandmother would have been married by the time these buildings were constructed, she may have been connected to the Moore family, especially since her father owned land nearby. Without more information, it may be impossible to know the exactness of Melvin's story, but the evidence does point to the possibility that it is at least rooted in truth.

The Brick House

Located only a mile north of Walkersville, the Brick House had allegedly been constructed from clay on our family farm, and my father loved to tell the folk history of this house. Although several houses had once stood on our farm, as they had been long vacated with their wooden frames left susceptible to the elements, most of these homes had disappeared by the time I was born; however, one large house remained: the Brick House, as it was known by Shelby County residents.

Exactly when the Brick House was built, no one knew for sure, but in the 21 November 1894 edition of the *Shelbina Democrat* I found a list of "Farms for Sale," including an advertisement for George Roff's farm. George Roff was the son of Peter Roff, whose land patent for 154.63 acres, dated 20 October 1835, is now part of our farm abstract. By the time George put the farm up for sale in 1894, he had expanded his father's original land patent to 235 acres. In the ad, he boasts that the land is "[o]ne of the most desirable farms in the county" and asks $36.00 per acre. He also describes the farm as including a six-year-old, eight-room house and a "large frame barn." Considering the date on the newspaper and this description, it appears that the Brick House was built in 1888. By the late 1970s, this once beautiful home had developed large holes in its exterior walls. In its crumbling state, my father was afraid that this empty house might pose a threat to the teenagers who were known to trespass on the farm. For fear of an accident, then, he had the house demolished in the summer of 1980, but its history still stands through the oral accounts that he heard when he returned home from the Second World War to work on what was then *his* father's farm.

When World War II began, my father was attending college in Kirksville, Missouri, at Northeast Missouri State Teachers College, now Truman State University. After returning home from serving his country, he went home to Shelby County to work on what is now our family farm, but, at that time, was owned by his father, Dr. Samuel L. Simpson. My father worked on the farm alongside Luke, an elderly African-American man who had been born on the farm and worked there throughout his life. As they worked together, Luke told my father what he referred to as "just old stories." But

Luke's old stories, as it turned out, were tales that had been orally passed down to him over the years.

One of these stories involved the construction of the Brick House. As the tale goes, the house was built for the Roff family by formerly enslaved men and women. Luke was under the impression that these people who worked to build the Brick House had formed the bricks out of clay they dug from the farm, and then baked these bricks in kilns that they fashioned underground. A nearby hickory grove provided the wood that fired the kilns; as Luke told my father, and as my father explained to me, hickory would have been a good choice because it burns very hot. It is also true that the soil in the location where these bricks were supposedly molded contains a high percentage of yellow clay; in fact, this section of the farm is just to the south of what has always been known as the Clay Knob.

Luke recalled hearing that the construction of the house was financed by a man who suffered debility from leg damage yet lived in a south-facing room at the top of the house where he kept his money in a box beneath his bed. Indeed, records from the Circuit Court and Probate Court at the Shelby County Courthouse confirm that a man named Jonathan Roff made frequent loans at high interest rates to various members of the community, including his brothers, George Roff and Thomas Roff. The 1880 census identifies Jonathan as living with George and George's eleven-year-old son, also named George. This record describes Jonathan as asthmatic, confirming that, even though the census says nothing about a leg ailment, his health was, indeed, poor. Jonathan Roff died in 1889, only one year after the house was completed, but it is possible that he loaned his brother the money to construct the home in which they lived together during this last year of his life.

Burials: Traces of Enslaved People

The formerly-enslaved workers who, according to Luke, built the Brick House may have been with the Roff family since before emancipation. Unlike Schedule One of the 1860 Census, which lists free inhabitants, Schedule Two lists the enslaved inhabitants of Shelby County. Rather than including names of those enslaved, it recognizes the owners and the number, ages, sex, and color of the enslaved people. In this particular year, Peter Roff held six enslaved people: one fifty-seven-year-old black female; one thirty-six-year-old mulatto male; one twenty-six-year-old black female; one twenty-year-old mulatto male; one six-year-old mulatto female; and one one-year-old mulatto male (2).

After these men and women were legally freed, they were said to have remained on the farm, which may not have been an unusual situation. In the 1913 *A History of Northeast Missouri*, Walter Williams argues, "Most of the masters in Missouri at least, treated their slaves humanely, and were kind and considerate" (638-39). Many claims similar to this one have been disputed and discredited, but Williams may be at least partially correct when he adds that "some of the colored people refused to leave their old masters, and nearly all held their former owners in great respect, and continued to look to them for help in time of trouble" (639). The fact is, from lynching and Jim Crow to socioeconomic barriers, white people continued to oppress black people following slavery, so in their "refusal" to leave the Roff farm, these men and women may not have had a choice other than to stay or die.

When these formerly-enslaved men and women passed away, they were buried in the same cemetery as the Roff family, just to the south of the Brick House. When a road was later built through this cemetery, however, only the white bodies and a few gravestones were moved while the black bodies were left behind. An affidavit included in the farm abstract refers to a 17 February 1913 deed concerning a ½-acre strip of land that was transferred from Richard S. Hooper and Emma E. Hooper to William T. Coard for the purpose of developing a road. While we do not know the exact whereabouts of the gravestones that were supposedly moved, the current Roff Cemetery does contain two bases that are both missing their stones and one unmarked stone, so these may have been the stones from the black graves in the original cemetery.

From Brett Rogers' research on "Improvisation and Tradition: Grave Art in Black Missouri," it seems that it would not be unexpected if the stones over the black graves had always been unmarked. Rogers points out that graves in black cemeteries are often marked with whatever may have been on hand at the time: pipes, concrete blocks, bricks, carved pieces of wood, or even rocks. Many of the gravestones in Rogers' work bear some sort of markings, whether carved or painted, so whoever moved these stones likely knew that they marked the graves of formerly-enslaved Africans.

In Roy Neff's collected cemetery records from 1964, he confirms, "Roff Cemetery is located about 4 1/8 miles north and west of Shelbina, Mo. on the Simpson Farm Where the old Brick House is located [sic]. . . . The burial place was only a short distance south of the house," he writes, but when "a road was put thru the burial place... most of the bodies were moved to the present site, where the large stone marks the place for all of the names found." Of course, by "most of the bodies," Neff means the named white bodies. While Neff confirms, "[S]laves made the brick for the house on the farm that the house is located on," he fails to acknowledge that these people had been freed by the time the house was built; however, Roff's advertisement in the *Shelbina Democrat* verifies that the Brick House was built twenty-three years after the end of the Civil War.

When Neff visited the Roff Cemetery, he found "[t]he present stone ... about ¼ mile south of the house in a pasture, now in fragments." Although this likely would have been true in 1964, during the early 1980s, my mother spent hours jamming metal rods into the ground until she had uncovered all of the stone fragments. She then reconstructed the Roff family's cemetery, restoring a piece of the farm's history. Eight members of the Roff family are buried near this large stone: Peter; his first wife, Sarah; his second wife, Nancy; his sons, Jonathon and Robert; his daughter-in-law, Julia, who was the first wife of George; George and Julia's son, George; and Thomas's first wife, Mary. Peter Roff's daughter Caroline's first husband, William Harding, rests under a separate stone. And, following my father's death in 1993, we buried his cremated remains on the farm in the Roff Cemetery, just as he had always requested.

My father's family had always been under the impression that Luke was related to these people who lived and worked on the farm, and whose bodies supposedly remain beneath the road. Since Luke told my father that he had been born on the farm, it is possible, then, that Luke's "old stories" were actually tales from his family's folklore.

The Big Rock

One of these stories involved a seven-foot-tall black woman and a large, flat rock that served for years as a doorstep to the Brick House. This woman allegedly died after she carried the rock from where it rested on a bluff overlooking Salt River up to the Brick House, which set about a mile north of the river.

At some point, the name Robert Ryburn was carved into the face of this rock. In the farm abstract, I found a 14 September 1908 deed stating that Edward Ryburn had purchased the land just south of Peter Roff's original farm. Edward Ryburn and his wife Amanda only owned the Brick House for five and a half years, as they sold their land on 12 March 1914; but that was long enough for their son, Robert Ryburn, to leave his mark on the land. Before tearing down the Brick House, my parents had this rock moved to their own home. It took three large men with pry bars to load the rock onto the rear of a tractor with a three-point hitch hay fork, but to this day the big rock from the river continues to serve as a step, both a metaphorical step through time and a tangible stepping stone to the door of my childhood home.

The use of large river rocks as doorsteps must have been a common practice during the nineteenth and early-twentieth centuries, as, at my childhood home, another of these large rocks sits on the opposite side of the patio from the Ryburn rock. The second rock came from the northwest corner of our farm, where it had once been used as a step up into another farmhouse. This rock bears the initials C.C., so I set out to look for persons with those initials who had lived near the spot where this house had once been. A 1902 edition of a Shelby County atlas identifies C.W. Coard as the owner of 123 acres on the northwest section of our farm. From the farm abstract, I learned that C.W. Coard had purchased this section of the farm on 20 November 1897. While C.C.'s identity cannot be proven, the initials do match the name of C.W. Coard, who at one time owned the land from which this rock was taken.

Over time, as some people move away, and others pass away, knowledge of the past risks becoming lost, perhaps forever. The only surviving picture of the Brick House known by my family hangs on my mother's dining room wall.[2] This picture was taken in 1917 and shows five people sitting on the lawn, but only two of these people are identified on the back of the picture: Emma Ida Bunting Rozholtz and Bonnie Dean Bunting Muller. According to the farm abstract, on 1 March 1920, John A. Bunting and his wife, Adelia A., purchased a section of the farm; but it was not the section on which the Brick House stood, so the Bunting children must have been visitors on the day that this picture was taken. In addition to this picture, my mother's dining room also contains a doorstop and two pieces of furniture, a walnut corner cupboard and a walnut mantle, all of which were taken from the Brick House before it was demolished.

Relics from the past, such as furniture, written records, gravestones, and names carved into rocks all serve as reminders of people who once existed; but oral accounts, like those that have been passed down from Luke to my father, or from Martha Cadwell Wiggins to her grandson Melvin, can tell us more about history than these artifacts alone can say. Lost history may never be recovered, but by writing down everything I remember about the oral accounts I heard as a child, I can at least do my part to preserve the history of the early residents of Shelby County, Missouri.

---

[2]Since I wrote this paper, Robert Ryburn's descendants uncovered another picture of the Brick House with the words "Shelbina, MO" written on the back. Although they did not know where the house was located, they took the picture to The Shelby County Historical Society Museum in Shelbina, and the museum director happened to show me a photcopy of the image. On the Ryburns' next trip to Shelby County, they visited my family's farm, and we all traded information.

Works Cited

Allen, Barbara and William Lynwood Montell. *From Memory to History: Using Oral Sources in Local Historical Research.* American Association for State and Local History, 1981.

"Collection Inventories and Descriptions." *Western Historical Manuscript Collection-Columbia.* University of Missouri and the State Historical Society of Missouri.

"Farms for Sale." *Shelbina Democrat.* 21 Nov. 1894. Shelby County Historical Society Museum Archives.

General History of Shelby County, Missouri 1911. Henry Taylor, 1911.

Georges, Robert A. and Michael Owen Jones. *Folkloristics: An Introduction.* Indiana U.P., 1995.

History of Monroe & Shelby Counties, Missouri. National Historical Company, 1884. Library of Congress: Internet Archive: Ebooks and Texts Archive.

Long, E.B. and Barbara Long. *Civil War Day by Day: An Almanac 1861-1865.* Doubleday, 1971.

Montell, William Lynwood. *The Saga of Coe Ridge: A Study in Oral History.* U of Tennessee Press, 1970.

Neff, Roy. *Salt River Township: Roff, Cemetery.* 1964 Shelby County, Missouri Cemetery Records. Shelby County Historical Society Museum Archives.

"Original Land Purchasers." Map. Shelby County, Missouri, Township 57-N Range 11-W (5th PM). *Shelby County Atlas. 1833-38.* Shelby County Historical Society Museum Archives.

Roff, George and Thomas Roff, executors of Jonathon Roff Deceased. *Accounts and Vouchers for Settlement.Shelby County Circuit Court and Shelby County Probate Court. Shelby County Courthouse.14 May 1890-11 November 1891.* Shelby County Historical Society Museum Archives.

Rogers, Brett. "Improvisation and Tradition: Grave Art in Black Missouri." Oral presentation at Missouri Folklore Society Conference. Neosho, MO. 5 November, 2010.

"Section 7—Township 57—Range 10 No. 5." Abstract of Title. *Shelby County Abstract and Loan Co. (A Corporation).* Shelbyville, Missouri.n.d.

Simpson, James Lloyd. Oral Accounts recorded by Holly Simpson Fling.

Snell, Melvin. Oral Accounts recorded by Holly Simpson Fling.

"Township 56 & 57 North Range 10 West of the 5th Principal Median." Map. *Shelby County Atlas. 1878.* Shelby County Historical Society Museum.

"Township 57 & Part of 56 N. Range X W. of the 5th P.M." Map. *Shelby County Atlas. 1902.* Shelby County Historical Society Museum.

W. R. Strachan, Assistant Marshall. "Schedule 1.—Free Inhabitants in Salt River Township in the County of Shelby State of Missouri enumerated by me, on the 14th day of June 1860." P. 37 of *Post Office Shelbina.* Shelby County Historical Society Museum Archives.

—. "Schedule 2.—Slave Inhabitants in… the County of Shelby State of Missouri enumerated by me… June 1860." P. 2 of *Post Office Shelbina.* Shelby County Historical Society Museum Archives.

Wailes, [first name illegible], Enumerator. "Schedule 1.—Inhabitants in Salt River Township, in the County of Shelby, State of Missouri enumerated by me, on the 11th and 12th day of June, 1880." Shelby County Historical Society Museum Archives.

Watkins, Nicholas. "History of Shelby County." Shelby County Historical Society Museum Archives.

Williams, Walter. *A History of Northeast Missouri.* Chicago: Lewis Publishing, 1913. Google Books: American Libraries.

A Space for People Who Don't Have Space: An Oral History of the Aquadome
Wes Harbison

This 2013 study was prompted by the writer's curiosity about the earlier phases of a campus institution he was engaged with, and led him to interview the founding generation of the Aquadome. The Truman Index *announced its closing in an article of August 29, 2015, and then its re-opening in a Sept 27, 2018 piece.*

The Cochran Building, at 117-9 N Main, original home of the Aquadome. (photo Missouri Dept of Natural Resources, State Historic Preservation Office). The building was condemned after a September 2015 storm, and subsequently demolished, the Aquadome relocating to 121 S. Main.

Introduction

Behind Kirksville's Downtown Cinema 8 is an old storefront. Throughout its history, the building at 121 N. Main Street has been among other things a buggy store, a church, a pool hall, vacant, and most recently a do-it-yourself (DIY) music venue and community center named the Aquadome. Affectionately known to some as "the dome," the venue has hosted numerous music and art projects and has primarily been overseen by dedicated people from Truman State University (TSU) and the greater Kirksville community. Over the years, there have been two distinct Aquadome generations: one that is currently active, and the founding generation, which has been deeply lacking in documented historical detail. With that in mind, I have recorded an oral history about this venue in order to salvage these details before they fall out of reach, leaving only a few newspaper articles as the record of this creative outlet for Kirksville, Missouri.

This project is divided into several sections, the first of which focuses on currently available historic documentation regarding the Aquadome. This is summarized in order to establish basic information about the venue. From there, we will shift to the oral history I have recorded, comparing the first and second generations of the Aquadome. These comparisons will be divided into History, Organization, and Philosophy.

It is important here that I mention my place in this history. When I first came to TSU as a transfer student in the fall semester of 2011, I discovered the Aquadome on a bike ride through town. Since then, I have been volunteering at events and am currently a member of its executive board. Early in my time as a volunteer, I heard several stories about the "old Aquadome," a kind of mythical-sounding place once located in the same building, populated by the sort of artistic and free-spirited people that I could imagine existing, but not actually envision myself meeting in real life. After some research, it became clear that this earlier incarnation of the Aquadome had not been well-documented. However, artifacts seemed to always be popping up—a handbill, a flyer, old books, abandoned artwork—and I stayed interested. I am pleased to be as much a participant in this history as I am a recorder, but this has undoubtedly affected the ways I conducted research and interviews, and especially my interpretation of information. It seems difficult, if not impossible, to analyze something in which I am so involved without my opinions and experiences influencing the results. With that acknowledged, I have made my best attempts to remain as unbiased as possible in the construction of this project.

Documentary History

To begin, available information about the Aquadome comes predominantly from *The Index*, Truman State University's student-operated newspaper. There are four articles in particular that address pertinent historical information—some of which not only contradict what I learned in interviews, but occasionally each other. In "Artists' Haven in Financial Peril," the Aquadome is said to have originally opened in May of 2000, but "Student Plans to Re-open Venue" suggests 2001. Inconsistent information like this merits caution when citing these articles. However, because historical documentation is limited, I will lay out what information these articles provide for a basic backstory about the venue.

The Aquadome's history according to *The Index* reads that the business was started sometime between May of 2000 and 2001. It was a non-profit business run by a committee made up of TSU students, graduates, and community members, at least as of March 2003 (Dowell). Although a "committee," by definition, often consists of appointed members, another article states the structure was "set up as a collective, anyone could be involved in the decision-making process" which "operated by consensus." Nicole Rainey is quoted saying the Aquadome had "maybe an average of 10 to 15 people who run it" (Ponche).

In reference to the types of events held at the Aquadome, as well as the amenities of the building, the articles mention a variety of concerts (commonly referred to as "shows"), a carnival, bookbinding workshops, karate lessons, break dancing parties, weekly vegan dinners, a vegan potluck on Sundays, a zine library, studio art space, a collection of art supplies, a darkroom, and sound equipment.

As early as March 6, 2003, there were serious financial issues that left volunteers scrambling to raise money for the $400 rent. Although loans were occasionally made to support the venue, committee members often supplemented rental fee payments with their own money. Funds were also generated from renting the top floor to artists for studio space and musicians for practice space. However, in January of 2004, the Aquadome decided to close its doors, citing financial issues, a sparse roster of events, and a decline in volunteers.

Few comments throughout these articles are made with regard to the philosophy of the Aquadome. Nicole Rainey speaks of the venue as being both drug- and alcohol-free, specifically mentioning the presence of high school students and the desire to be inclusive toward them at the venue. She is also quoted saying, "what the community wants, the Aquadome is," suggesting the venue was designed to be flexible, although there is no elaboration on this in the article.

The second generation of the Aquadome, which is significantly more documented outside of *Index* articles, largely because of the Internet and social media, began in the summer of 2011, backed, at first, solely by Brie Vuagniaux, a TSU student. Inspired by what she knew of the first Aquadome, she began making improvements to the building with her own money that summer and started holding events during the fall semester, such as "The Down and Dirty Punk Folk Show" on Friday, August 26, featured in the *Index*'s "Unexpected Harmonies" article.

This article does fortunately make reference to some of the philosophy behind the present-day Aquadome. Vuagniaux is said to have hoped for a mixed audience, merging people from Kirksville and Moberly Area Community College with TSU students: "This is what it was about originally. We are trying to bridge the talent between the local community and the college. There are so many good things here. We want everyone to get to experience them. We're trying to develop a community in Kirksville."

Oral History

Beyond this, there is not much expansion on the ideology or history of the Aquadome. In search of greater depth than what appeared in these brief articles, I began conducting interviews. Of the four interviews I conducted, a majority of the information that appears in this study comes from my combined interview with Julia Davis, Nicky Rainey (mentioned above as Nicole), and Nick Kuntz on October 6, 2012. As volunteers and organizers from the first generation of the Aquadome, they offered much previously undocumented information. I had both planned and actually attempted to contact other members of the venue, but I either received no response or was limited in my search due to time constraints. Because I do not have information from other volunteers, it is important to note that Julia, Nicky, and Nick "all kind of had the same experience" at the Aquadome and were "removed" from some of the "tensions and things that came up."

In addition to the Julia-Nicky-Nick interview, I also conducted interviews with Brie Vuagniaux on October 7, 2012 and Hannah Copeland, the current president of the Aquadome, on October 21, 2012. Finally, on October 31, 2012, I interviewed Jim Jereb, an art professor at TSU who has taught Aquadome volunteers and attended Aquadome events during both generations. He provided interesting information about public opinion of the venue.

Beginning with a prehistory of the Aquadome, Julia, Nicky, and Nick laid out the events and people that led up to the formation of the venue.

Nicky: Morgan [Peckosh] grew up in Kirksville and had been hosting shows in Kirksville probably since he was in high school... and had this whole community of people. I mean... there was a punk scene in Macon in the 90s and there's a documentary about it.... There was a lot of stuff going on here.... And so when Morgan was in—I guess he went to Truman... he started or was part of this on-campus organization called Campus Music Collective where they would get money from... [the TSU Student Activities Board] SAB to host bands on campus....

Julia: They had a lot of shows for a while—before the Aquadome opened up—in Kirk Memorial, in the old gym in there... They had a lot of shows in there and I guess they wanted their own space.

The three questioned the date of the Aquadome's founding, at first saying 2000, but then allowing that it might have been earlier, settling on sometime within the 1999-2000 school year. They listed the founders of the venue as Morgan Peckosh, Ben Garrett, Amanda Bunyard, Amelia [Self?], and Jesse Pasley. Julia, Nicky, and Nick came to the venue early in their college careers, just after the September 11, 2001 attacks on the World Trade Center.

Nicky: It was a wild time... in American History.... [9/11] was very shocking.... And the US immediately went to war in Afghanistan, which, for people of a certain political mindset, was very deeply disturbing. And also the homeland security thing started escalating and that was very troubling. And so I think all of that fed into our drive to keep the Aquadome open.... And the music reflected that feeling too, I think—the punk music at that time.

The music Nicky mentions, although not always punk, was a major part of what the Aquadome did. Nick reminisced about bands from Plan-It-X, an influential DIY folk and punk record label, playing at the Aquadome, specifically mentioning This Bike is a Pipe Bomb and Soophie Nun Squad. Julia brought up metal band Fat Day more than once as a memorable music experience.

Julia: They were all older—they were professors. They were like physics professors... that went on tour in the summers, I guess.... It was like a tiny opera, it was like a tiny metal opera. [Laughs] They had a whole story. They had blowup animals that they would throw out into the audience.... The one [show] that I went to, it was about a Viking child that only had one horn on his helmet. And so they would throw out a sea creature blowup animal that was part of the story and the audience would interact with it. And they had these helmets that they had put buttons on and attached to musical instruments and so they could play their instruments by pushing the buttons on their helmets that also had horns that went along with the story.

Reflecting on the attendance at shows and the technological changes that became mainstream just as the first generation of the Aquadome came to a close, the three give some insight into the typical audience at events:

Nicky: Indie rock really changed when the Internet became more accessible. Now a lot more people are into indie rock and punk rock, because a lot more people have more access to more music.... [Back] then, if you wanted to know about hardcore punk bands... people would trade mix tapes.... So the shows, I would say the average attendance to the shows would be like 20 people.

Nick: No, I think the average is probably lower than that.... We had shows multiple times a week often, which would hurt. So then people didn't want to turn out to shows all the time.... Sometimes there'd be a ton of people and other times there would be stretches where... there would be the same 10 people there.

Julia: A lot of the time... I would feel obligated to go to a show, just so the band would have an audience. I'm not really into straightedge hardcore, but I've been to a lot of straightedge hardcore shows. [Laughs] I always felt like, oh, I learned how to dance to everything. Cause you just made it fun.

Non-music events, which are covered in the articles from *The Index*, are expanded upon in the interview. There were figure drawing classes, a haunted house, screen-printing teach-ins, political organizing, and film screenings—many of which were art films created by their friends or friends of friends; but they also screened feature films on occasion, such as 1927's *Metropolis*. The Tom Thumb Art Gallery, a TSU-student-founded traveling art show, was held at the Aquadome multiple times. The space was also rented out for events, such as a sorority dance, and used by groups such as Anti-Racist Action and the Lonely Minds Club as a meeting place. As

Nick put it, "The Aquadome was about having space for people who don't have space."

After roughly a four-year run, the Aquadome decided to close its doors in 2004, but not without celebration.

> Nicky: By the end, when we closed it down, the last couple of months were really hard for us and we were really sad, but we just couldn't do it anymore, we had no money.... So I made that zine [*The Aquadome: A Love Story*] and me and a few other people threw a pitiful goodbye potluck and nobody came. And it was just really sad. And Morgan Peckosh... was living in Columbia and heard that it was closing and from Columbia organized a huge event for its going away. And we held it in the whole upstairs and they turned the whole upstairs into a MX bike racing track and built jumps and stuff... and brought in punk bands.... And it was really well attended. And so there [were] punk bands playing and people riding MX bikes around in circles and people throwing flour everywhere and people getting drunk and dancing. So it was really beautiful and cathartic.... It was just a lovely way to end.... I was just so grateful for that.... It was a very big part of our lives.

After the Aquadome's final event, the building was emptied, the keys were returned to the landlord, and 121 N. Main Street was left to become whatever business came next. After a few years passed, the Aquadome's history resumed in summer of 2011 when Brie Vuagniaux came to the storefront with the intention of reopening the venue at what she saw as the perfect time.

> Brie: I had just gotten out of my English degree [at TSU] and I wanted to go into nursing. And I had at least a year and half of prerequisites for nursing.... And I had this great amount of time where I didn't just want to work, I wanted to be really busy and I wanted to be doing somethin' fun in town. And so I'd heard about this place called the Aquadome that used to exist ten years ago in this abandoned shitty building and, um, I took a stroll down here to follow the rumors and see what this building looked like because I thought starting a venue might be a good way to spend my time and I was all inspired by those people that used to be a part of it because they were the wildest, craziest people in town. I mean, these are the people that every one that you meet, you're like, "I want to know them really well."

She had also participated in Tom Thumb Art Gallery XV during April 2011, which was held in the then-former Aquadome, and she was inspired by her experience.

> Brie: I was like, I want to keep this place open all the time. I feel like Kirksville artsy kids could really use this.... You only have a few years in your life and it's very good to do this during college, it's like the prime time to really go off the grid and like live in an abandoned warehouse and make art all the time and be wild and anarchist and, you know, figure out what matters to you. Because once you have to start working and stuff, it's a lot harder to juggle that side of yourself with the rest of your responsibilities. So it's good to figure it out while you can and exploit it and then not look back. You know what I mean? [Laughs.]

Shortly after Brie had the new version of the Aquadome up and running, an executive board and volunteer roster were established. One of the earliest major issues dealt with at the new Aquadome was finding an identity for the business. When Brie first reopened the Aquadome, she envisioned "a very inclusive community center" that would host one or two small shows each week, provide a place for musicians to stay, and potentially have potlucks. Before she opened the space, however, a friend suggested a variation on that plan.

> Brie: I met Jillian [Burke] right before I opened it and she wanted to use the Aquadome as a Food Not Bombs place, so she could have that political potluck every couple weeks.... We sort of thought of it as like a community center... slash music venue for travelling bands. But then it was more like a music venue for bigger shows and a rental space is how we ended up using it.

Brie had also hoped for the venue to be "straightedge," meaning the space would have been drug and alcohol free like the first Aquadome.

> Brie: ...I thought that would be really neat. If people could go party elsewhere but then come here for just pure art.... Then we met with reality, remember? We were like... "Okay, what do the people want?"

During a short period when this policy was enforced, when flyers often read "Substance Free," I personally recall attendance dropping drastically.

Ironically, I never felt like these rules were enforced strictly, as I often saw at least a couple people drinking by the end of each night's performance, potentially because they simply didn't know about the rule.

The unclear identity, facilitated by different visions people had for the space, led to disorder and public confusion about what purpose the Aquadome served. One of the board members at the time was Hannah Copeland, a then-recent friend of Brie's who later became secretary and is currently serving as president. Reflecting back on this identity struggle, Hannah commented:

> Hannah: So, from early in September 2011 to maybe October, there was a lot of... turmoil about defining what the Aquadome was—if it was a community center or a music venue.... We decided... music brings people together—that's a global phenomenon and the Aquadome really harnesses that. And the community aspect of it can be incorporated into the music.... At this point, we went from defining and fighting over what the space was and... I feel like we just kind of realized that there really wasn't a point in fighting [laughs] and it really is just a music venue with art and people like it and it brings people together, so that's community.

After settling this identity issue, the members of the Aquadome began hosting events more regularly, scheduling more rentals, and continuing to improve the project. In the summer of 2012, they held an event called Work Week, a full week of scheduled cleaning, maintenance, and remodeling that generated good results.

> Hannah: I want so badly for people to feel comfortable in the space and we cleaned a lot. And now it looks great! That was a goal [of ours] and it came true.

The executive board is now in the process of better defining what volunteers and board members do at the Aquadome. The hope is that this will make the venue easier to pass down to new volunteers as older members move on. Finally, bringing this history to the present, a goal Hannah mentioned during our interview was to raise enough money to purchase a PA. In the recent past, most amplified events at the Aquadome used borrowed or rented sound systems. Since our interview, enough money was generated through donations and fundraising events and the PA was purchased, making the Aquadome more equipped than at any other time in its second generation.

Organization

With the historical events of the venue now set out, I think the specifics of Aquadome's organizational structure should be mentioned, as it is one of the more outstanding differences between each generation. Here, Julia, Nicky, and Nick discuss the consensus-based structure of the first generation.

> Nick: It was consensus-run, so there wasn't a board or anything. And whoever would contribute to the meetings was just whoever showed up, and anyone could show up. But mainly it was the same set of people.
>
> Nicky: So, consensus-based decision-making is like a Quaker thing but it's also an anarchist thing.... It's a decision-making process where you don't vote, where you have to discuss something until everyone agrees.
>
> Nick: Or you just decide you're okay with not agreeing.
>
> Nicky: So it's hard.
>
> Julia: And it can take forever.
>
> Nicky: And it did.

Contrasting this collective setup, the new Aquadome's organization and meetings are relatively structured, although there has been noteworthy variation in that structure throughout this generation's evolution. From the onset of the second generation, there was a board of executives used for decision-making. Earlier on however, it was very easy to be a member of the board. For example, I was invited to be on the board the first time I expressed interest in volunteering which was also the first time I had ever been to the Aquadome. Such a loose board arrangement meant that certain people did more than others and had more authority than others in a way that was essentially undefined. As time passed, however, there was an effort to make decisions more efficiently, resulting in a more refined organizational structure. Hannah mentioned that, earlier on, meetings could last a couple of hours, but are now often under an hour.

The system currently in place has five elected positions: president, vice-president, secretary, treasurer, and public relations. It is important to note that these positions are organizational and do not reflect a member's authority. Meetings are held once a week, with half an hour for board members to discuss specific financial issues or topics deemed too technical or boring for general volunteers. After those 30 minutes pass, the meeting opens up to the public.

In addition to the Aquadome's structure, a major component of its history has been its philosophical foundations—ideas that shaped what took place in each generation.

> Nicky: Part of the punk ethos at the time was not just about the music, but it was also about activism and social justice.... Also, there were a lot of artists that were sort of hanging around. So having a space was a way to facilitate artists having studio space, and also having a space where people could organize political stuff, and then a way for... people who were vegan and vegetarian who felt disenfranchised....

This line of thought ties into the comments about the September 11 attacks made earlier. With social unease on the mind of the volunteers, the old Aquadome seems to have been a sort of hub for the artistic and the political, with an emphasis on visual art and music.

The new Aquadome has made a shift away from this social issue-based motivation, but not entirely. As already stated, Brie was very influenced by what she knew about the first generation and seems to have taken this with her as she developed the venue. With these foundations and the mindset that the Aquadome should primarily be a community music venue, the current Aquadome operates in a way that is still very much DIY, but which is more like a non-profit business than a politically charged collective. When I mentioned the lack of political activity currently at the Aquadome, Nicky said, "It seems like it's a different kind of project now... something else... that more fits the needs of what your generation is interested in."

Bibliography

Dowell, Jesse Collin. "Artists' Haven in Financial Peril." *The Truman Index*, 6 March 2003.

O'Brien, John. "Unexpected Harmonies." *The Truman Index*. 31 August 2011.

Ponche, Kalen. "Aquadome Closed." *The Truman Index*. 28 Jan. 2004.

"The Aquadome." *The Aquadome*. [Zine] Kirksville, MO. Sept. 2012. Web.

Rainey, Nicole. *The Aquadome: A Love Story*. [Zine], Kirksville, MO. 2004.

Vickers, Nathan. "Student Plans to Re-open Venue." *The Truman Index*. 30 March 2011.

Interviews

Brie Vuagniaux (7 October, 2012)

Hannah Copeland (21 October, 2012)

Julia Davis, Nicky Rainey, and Nick Kuntz (21 October, 2012)

Appendix: The Aquadome: A Love Story

At the beginning of my interview with Julia, Nicky, and Nick, I was given several copies of the zine Nicky made upon the Aquadome's initial closing. The Aquadome: A Love Story is very much what its title suggests, with all the highs and lows that come packaged with that kind of relationship, presented through short entries from Aquadome volunteers. The zine doesn't cover any significant historical events that aren't mentioned elsewhere, but it provides a kind of snapshot of the feelings these volunteers and this group of friends felt. One entry in particular, written by co-founder Ben Garrett, touches on the imperfections that Julia, Nicky, and Nick managed to be uninvolved with, but arrives at the same appreciation the three express. He writes, "For all of its faults, or maybe even in part because of them, The Aquadome was the last place I could ever truly say that I belonged in and felt needed and loved and appreciated in, just for being me" (pg 2). The zine follows this essay.

One Final Note

It's worth mentioning that since the initial completion of this project in 2013, an additional source of information about the Aquadome's first run has been made known. Quite a few articles were published in *The Monitor*, Truman's alternative newspaper, regarding the Aquadome between 2000 and 2003. These are available online at: http://trumanmonitor.wordpress.com/archives/.

(joe Moccia)

FREE! Sponsored by CAMPUS MUSIC COLLEC FUNDS 41··

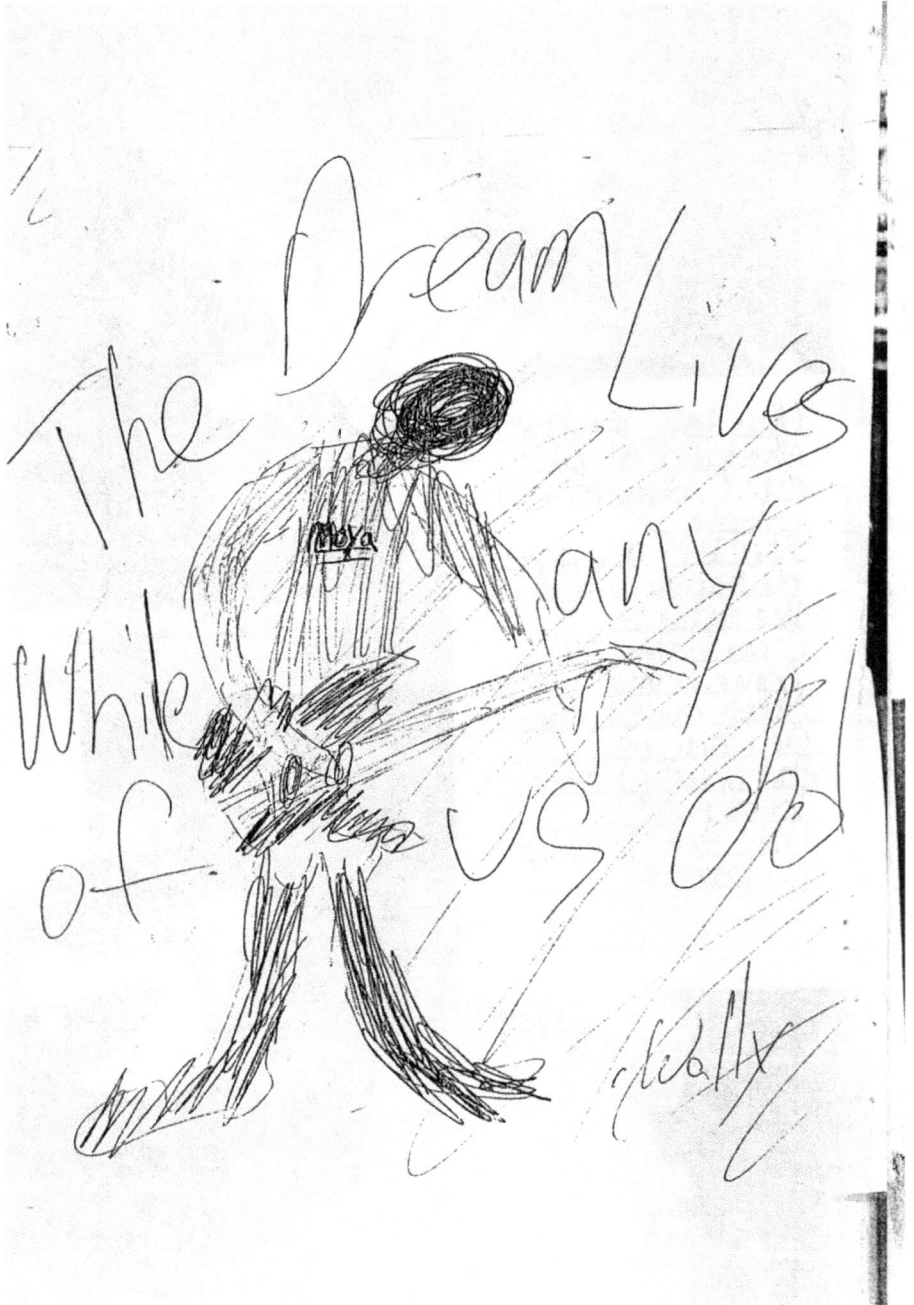

The Aquadome is my savior. I was a wayward, destitute child falling quickly into the blackness of the diploma awarding mental ward. I was without hope and certain that escape from my dark, tear-stained cell, my bed is like the straight jacket I wish my mom would have made me wear before all of the times I was hurt, was impossible. Physically, the Aquadome was as far from my prison as Barbara Dixon would let me wander, I wandered further, she could never know. Instead of the scheduled electroshock administered by the faculty of Truman, I could shock myself with the sounds of the Kirksville underground. Which reminds me, the Aquadome is the Underground Railroad and its music is fetter-releasing. I was led through the black tunnels by flames held by those who had freed themselves before; this freedom presents the possessor with seeming divine powers, light, eternal and pervasive, in the midst of the darkest of man's creations. I was just a child, I am still. But I am free of the dingy sweatshops and attempting to grow without scars and deformities considered so normal by Bill Gates and Ayn Rand.

In three days, the stone will be thrust aside and the Aquadome will be reborn and full of glory, screaming with joyous music and youthful chants for justice and love.

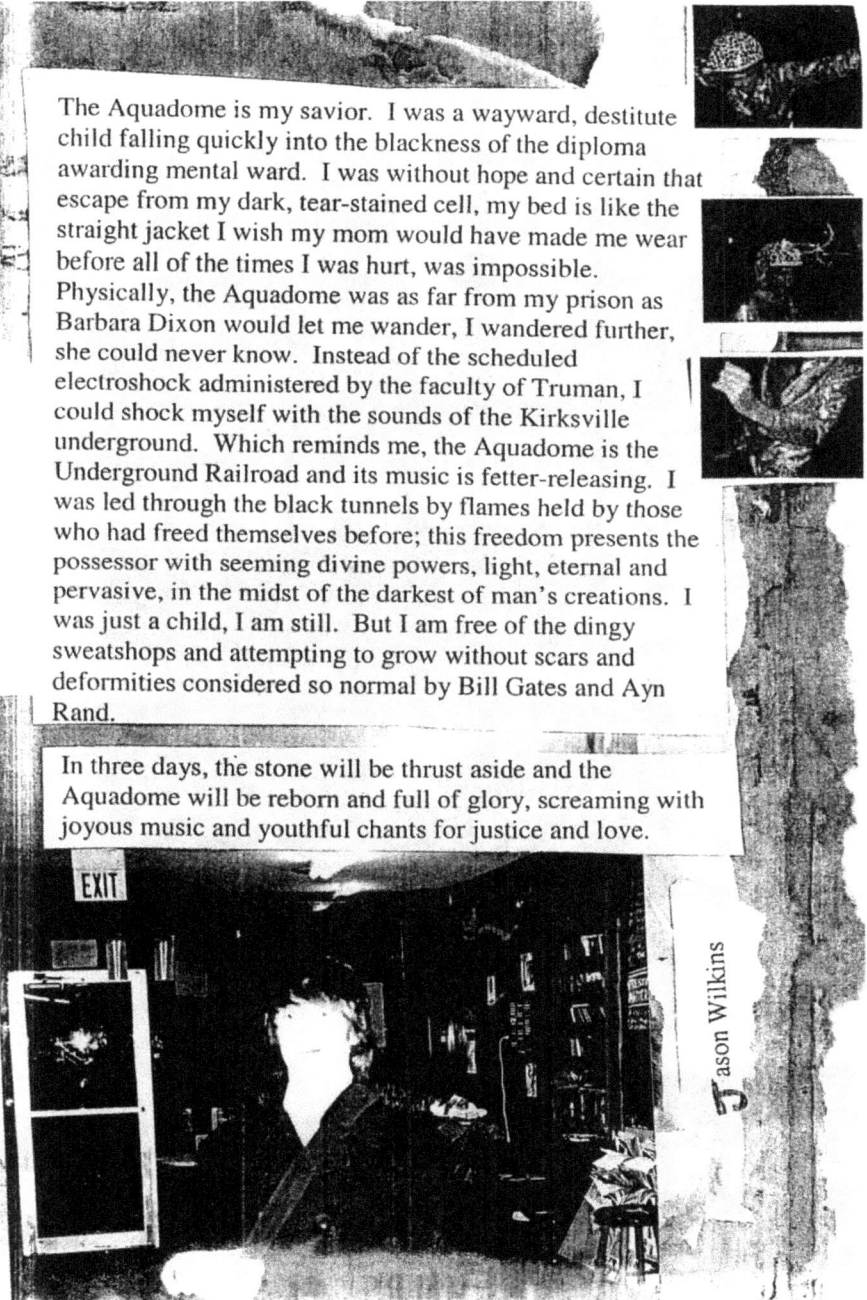

Jason Wilkins

The Lonely Minds Club   James Simms

It all started my second semester. I was drifting away from what few friends I had. Neither my friend Nicole, nor Tim was in my WACT class anymore, and I stopped hanging out with Tim altogether (his lackadaisical style didn't fit with my high-strung academic antics). I also felt myself growing more distant from my friend Eric. We saw each other Friday nights, but every visit we just got stoned and didn't talk too much.

Some weeks into the semester I decided there must be more highly intelligent, socially inept people on campus, and I was going to start a club, post fliers on campus, and stop having a sucky social life. I named it The Lonely Minds Club. (The irony in this name was that in all the people who participated, I was the only one who was lonely.) Nicole (as mentioned previously) told some people at the Aqua Dome about it and we started having meetings there.

Having meetings at the Aqua Dome turned out to be a shrewd idea, because it drew Aqua Dome regulars (who were unaware of the club's existence) into the mix. Among the list of people who took part were Todd, Amanda, Ben, and Afro Mike. Among the things discussed: the nature of randomness and pirate literature.

The Lonely Minds Club dissolved when its founder got sick and was forced to withdraw from school. Its demise was in congruence with its existence: every Tuesday at 9, you had no idea who you were going to meet, what you would talk about or even if the Aqua Dome was open. (As a postscript, I dropped in one Tuesday when a concert with a folk singer had been scheduled. As I am a huge heavy metal fan, it was somewhat awkward.)

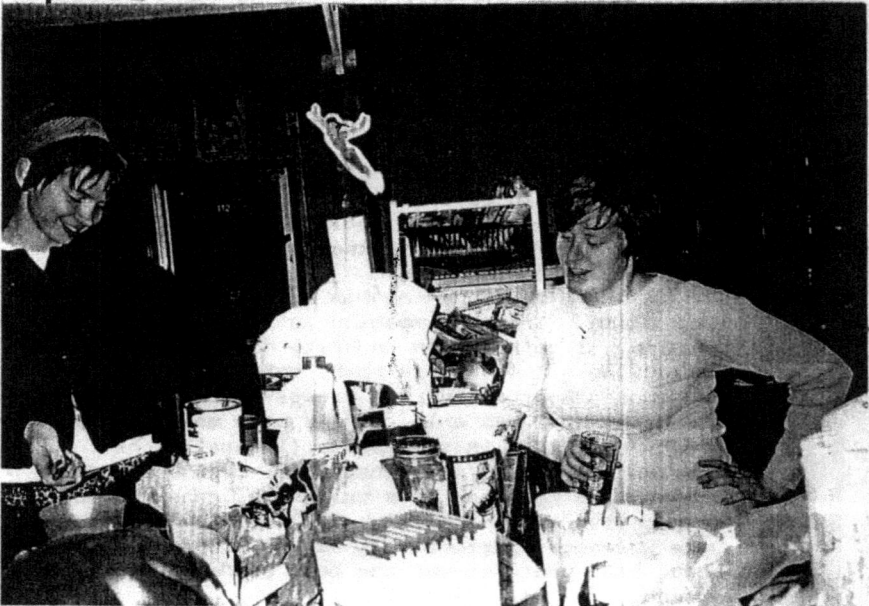

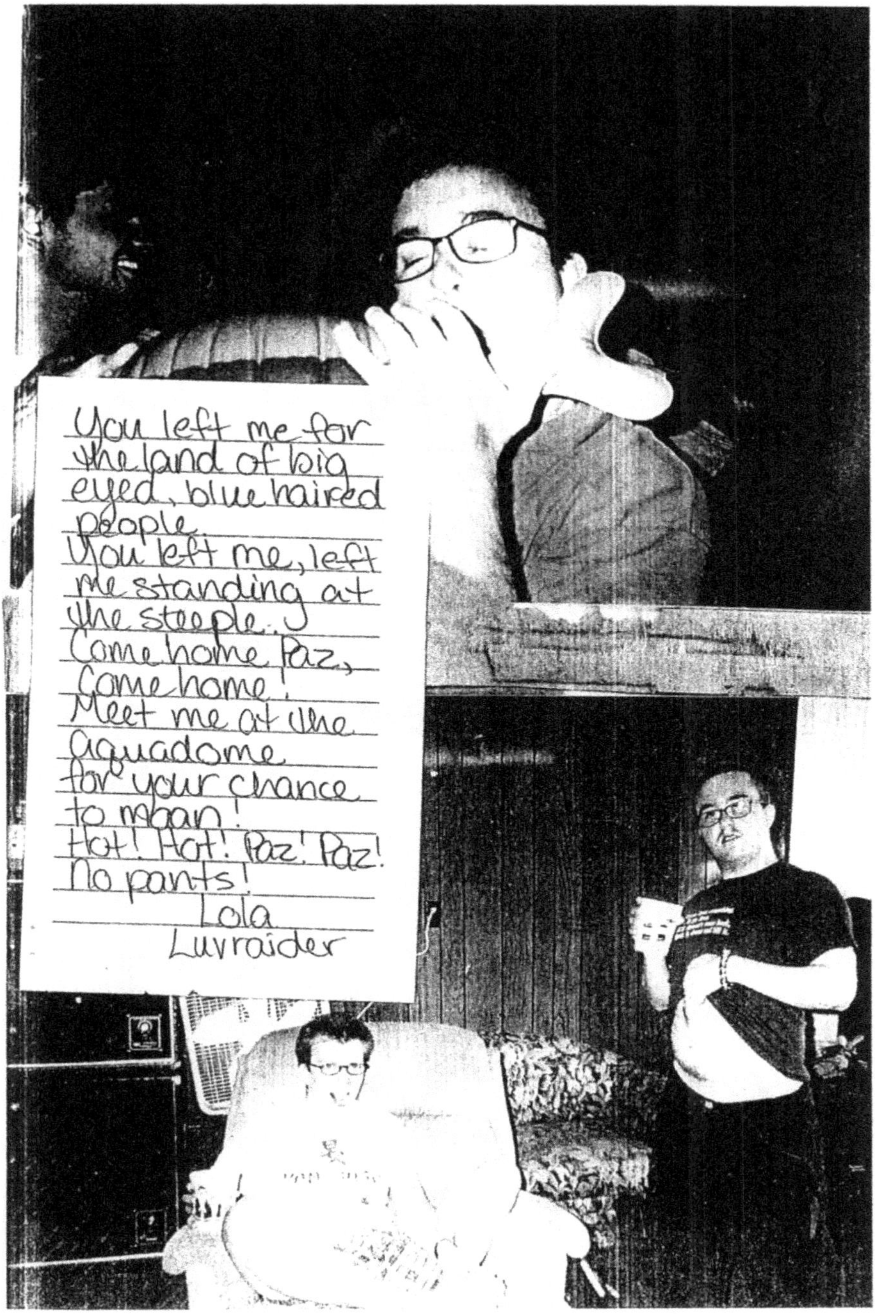
You left me for
the land of big
eyed, blue haired
people.
You left me, left
me standing at
the steeple.
Come home Paz,
Come home!
Meet me at the
aquadome
for your chance
to moan!
Hot! Hot! Paz! Paz!
No pants!
Lola
Luvraider

Dust to dust Aquadome

Sweet sad big space creates
whole parts of bodies and fluids,
parades of bodies strung
string to string making lines
across states, across oceans,
to Germany and further,
these pieces of something like hope
stretch out in anything can happen,
they smell a little like armpits
and feet and sudsy old food dishwater,
dusty cold feet carpet.
Something you could call open arms
and open hearts, sometimes
so wide open that white sharp ribs
and bones like bike frames spill
out like silver spray paint blood
into the street.
It was all anyone had, because
it made itself from everyone,
even the slim ladies in stiff shoes
walking by to the tanning booths,
sometimes in the lonely kid corner
by the darkroom at the late sunset
time, the sky was so bold
through the window that
even wood paneling was so
delicious, abstract things like freedom
came in and made sense
and punched open that space between
gut and spine that was so tight before.
The wide open refrigerator
pulsing white heart beat
with this sweat dancing
and pounding feet and arms
thumping pores slowly opening
with hot rhythms and the feeling
of humans being made of
skin and blood and hopes.
What remains is all the skin cells shed,
all the strands of hair, and the mud

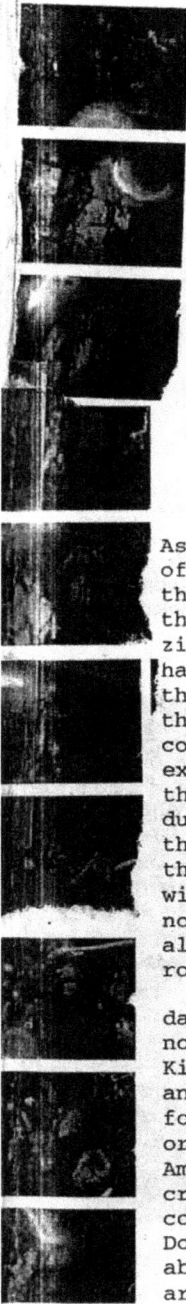

on shoes and under fingernails,
hands holding plates,
and voices warming up a room
too cheap for electric heat.   –Dana Kuhnline

This thing art pours out,
flicks up like thick paint and
laps at foundations of buildings,
it's inside pockets, and laced through
those certain evenings when it hurts
your chest to be alone,
the Aquadome.

love story, eric T.

As I was sitting in the quiet dark of the back seat
of Courtney's car late last night, riding home from
the Eleni Mandell show in Kansas City, I got to
thinking about what I would like to communicate in a
zine lamenting the Aquadome's closure. The car ride
had reached the point at which you begin to believe
that nothing at all exists in the darkness outside of
the car to the left, the right, behind. All that I
could see, and therefore understand or even believe,
existed ahead of us - the long gray road glowing in
the stubborn illumination of our headlights. It is
during such middle of the night road trip moments
that I find myself clinging, almost desperately, to
the sight of that glowing stretch of road. To be
without it would be to see nothing, understand
nothing, and, ultimately, believe nothing, hurtling
alone through seething darkness propelled by a
roaring mindless machine.
        For me the Aquadome was a bright light in a
dark place. It was something in the middle of
nothing. I do not mean to write dismissively of
Kirksville. I love this town, but in the Aquadome
and (more importantly) the creative, loving community
found there, I was able to find some meaning, some
order, some life in the middle (literally) of
America. The Dome was a haven for creation and
creators in the face of a culture of consumption,
competition, disposability, and homogeneity. The
Dome was never perfect. It was no Utopia. But for
about four years it was the best goddamn thing
around.

Dinner at the Aquadome
by Kathy Widitz

AQUADOME
sweet
Biscuits

2½ c Flour
¼ c sugar
2 t. baking
powder
¾ c. marg-
arine
1 C. soymilk

Mix!
bake @ 400°
12-18 min?

So, once upon a time, there were daily dinners at the Aquadome. For a brief span of time, people actually took turns cooking these dinners. One day it was my turn. Boy was I excited. I planned all the goodies I would cook- food that I liked, and I knew others would like as well. Somewhere along the line, I got paired up with another cook. Paid Paul. Now, Paid Paul also was very excited about cooking and had also planned what food he was going to introduce the Aquadome dinner eatin' community to. The day arrived and the cooking began. I started pounding out dough t make homemade Perogies. Paul was crackin' ope the cans of del Monte fruit to make his sauce for the noodle salad. Every once in awhile he'd ask me my opinion on how his creation was coming.

Should I add another can of peaches to the sauce? Or maybe this can of mixed fruit? I have no experience eating or creating noodles with fruit sauce, so my replies were mostly limited to, I have no idea, Paul and Sure. When the dinner was ready we had Potato Pergoies with buttery fried saurkraut and sweet bisquits a la Kathy and noodles with fruit sauce and mashed potatoes with peanut butter and celery a la Paid Paul.

I don't know what everyone else ate, but I know I didn't touch Paul's food, and he didn't touch mine

What I wore in the Aquadome, winter 2001,
2002:underwear to keep the bootie warm, long
underwear, knee high socks, pants, regular
socks, super warm quilted shoes, bra to keep
the boobies warm, undershirt, long sleeve
shirt, short sleeve shirt, gloves, hoodie,
sweatshirt with sleeves ripped off, hat,
sometimes a coat and if sitting down, a
blanket. ahhh those were the days.

Things I remember:
Ex-Mennonite Leon
Ted complaining about those crazy people who
forgot to put the Tuna in the Tuna Casserole
Band Practice with numb fingers
Dancing in the Streets during the Hazard Show
and with those Iowa Kids
Crazy good shows like Fat Day, Horse the band,
and Pine Hill Haints
How the dude from Horse the band was in luv
with Kristen
Eating some damn good food
Freezing my patootie off in the winter
Sweating all the winter fat off in the summer
Dancing on the Countertop
Every inch of the Dome covered in freshly
screenprinted posters
The reek that came outta the bathroom/light
room
How long meetings used to take
Logan and the chainsaw at the Haunted House
Roosters v. Robots and the time Ben almost died
The Eighties Prom
Fustration over not enough money
The Garage Sales
When Mikey broke the glass door

When Nick crashed into the wall
Eating fresh veggies from the garden
Building rooms in the upstairs outta anything
and everything
Standing in front of my peers at my Senior
Seminar Presentation discussing and watching us
crazy kids dance at the Zombie
Zombie show.
The feeling of Love and Community

THE AQUADOME (or, how I learned to rock)
by, Nikki B.

I have always been a very, **very** bad dancer.

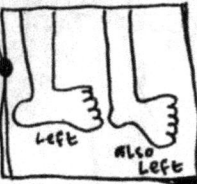

Left   also Left

You suck

criss cross'll make you jump! jump!

BY the age of 11 or 12, I stopped, completely, and learned how to rock out **very still**

at the aquadome, everyone danced kind of funny, and they wore rooster hats.

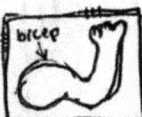
bicep
(very strong)

(booty)
(very shaky)

they also made tasty food & burned stuff, which I liked.

I met some of the people I love the most. ♡

and even though I am still a bad dancer, now — I never, ever stand still.

(never.)

I Will Deeply miss the Ana Dome. This is the only really good thing in this piece of shit town. the bad thing i can remember about this place is the time i got kicked in the balls by a lead singer

Seth L. McCoy

The summer before I moved to Kirksville I had been planning to move to New York City amongst other places. It's complicated why my choices of where to move where New York, Washington State, or Kirksville, Missouri. Regardless, I was torn. But, all summer long a little voice in my head just kept whispering *Kirksville, Kirksville.* And I didn't want to listen. In the end I decided to go because the feeling inside that something was waiting for me in Missouri was so strong. The truth is by the time my summer job ended I was really excited to make the move.

The first weekend I was in Kirksville, by yet another chance of fate, I found my way to The Aquadome. As soon as I rode past this little building on my bike (while everyone stared) the first thing I thought was, "Well, here are all my friends." And I'm pretty sure the only person I talked to all weekend long was this cute drummer from out of town who turned out to be a little crazy. It took two whole years for me to really believe I was a part of that community. Partly because I'm crazy and partly because everyone I met while living in Kirksville was crazy too. Well almost.

The only reason I found my way there so quickly was because of a small sign made out of cardboard and sharpie sitting on a table in the SUB. And that was just one of many yet to come and yet to be made with my own two hands.

That first weekend was full of anxious glances, awkward conversation, and flaming cardboard robots. The two years that followed went much the same way but also included lots of food, fighting, dancing, loving, hugging, crying, and general Rock 'n Roll. The Aquadome was almost always a place I felt at home, due mostly to spending my Bonus Bucks on bread, fruit and soy milk to bring to pot lucks.

Through much determination and desperation The Aquadome gave me a lot of good friends, good times, and great knowledge. I often find that measuring my love against the simultaneous hate for something or someone is a good guage of how successful and important it is. And if that's so The Aquadome is up there on my list. I've talked a lot of shit, and shouted out my frusterations but friends of mine across the world will tell you how much I've loved the 'dome as well.

So Blah. I'm trying to get out all the things out I'm thinking. But I'll explain it like this. I hated living in Kirksville. So I left. But last night at 11:30 p.m. I found myself buying a train ticket over the phone and frantically calling my friends in Kirksville so someone could pick me up at quarter to ten on a Saturday morning at the station in La Plata. Word.

Much love, and cinnamon rolls.

Oh, yeah and the thing that I love most is coming back to Kirksvi'' and seeing people I know wearing clothes I had forgotten I or owned.

Rock on.

"dear AQUADOME,"

The Aquadome is where I first played with 'Julie Andrews and the Front Porch Ramblers,' where I got to know my 1st real girlfriend, and where we began to plan our Long Distance Bicycle Tour (which we actually got to ride last summer).

The Aqua dome is where Doug Steward showed the film series portion for his Queer Theory class And I got to watch queerness unfold before me for an entire semester (every thursday Night).

The Aqua dome is where I use to watch the paint freeze onto my fingers in my studio space upstairs. 10$ a month which ment I didn't have to paint in my own (thing) bedroom.

The Aquadome is where I drew my 1st Nude model. Where I attended my 1st potluck, my 1st Critical Mass bicycle rides & my 1st Anti-war protest March.

Roll on: Forever in me & you! All my love, Katastrophe Louise.

Love story #1

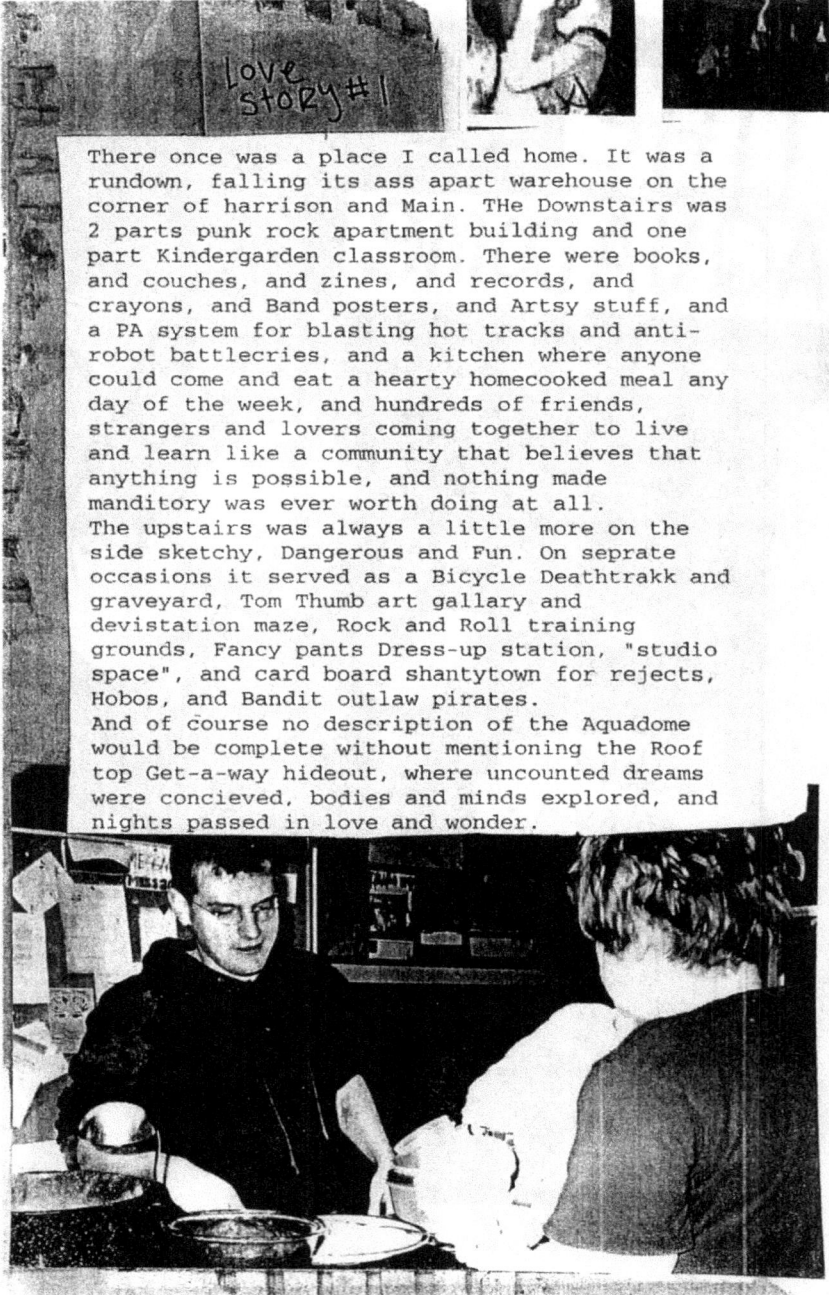

There once was a place I called home. It was a
rundown, falling its ass apart warehouse on the
corner of harrison and Main. THe Downstairs was
2 parts punk rock apartment building and one
part Kindergarden classroom. There were books,
and couches, and zines, and records, and
crayons, and Band posters, and Artsy stuff, and
a PA system for blasting hot tracks and anti-
robot battlecries, and a kitchen where anyone
could come and eat a hearty homecooked meal any
day of the week, and hundreds of friends,
strangers and lovers coming together to live
and learn like a community that believes that
anything is possible, and nothing made
manditory was ever worth doing at all.
The upstairs was always a little more on the
side sketchy, Dangerous and Fun. On seprate
occasions it served as a Bicycle Deathtrakk and
graveyard, Tom Thumb art gallary and
devistation maze, Rock and Roll training
grounds, Fancy pants Dress-up station, "studio
space", and card board shantytown for rejects,
Hobos, and Bandit outlaw pirates.
And of course no description of the Aquadome
would be complete without mentioning the Roof
top Get-a-way hideout, where uncounted dreams
were concieved, bodies and minds explored, and
nights passed in love and wonder.

The Dome was not always home for everyone. At times it was guilty of being Too dirty, smelly, unorganized, Intimidating, uncomfortible, exclusive, Fraudulent, inefficint, Sexist, Racists, classist, age-ist, able-ist, Heterosexists/normative, uncohesive, expensive, and just generally a pain in the ass, to be home to anybody. But for all of its faults, or maybe even inpart because of them, The Aquadome was the last place I could ever truely say that I belonged in and felt needed and loved and appreciated in, just for being me.
In the End, The Aquadome is really just a cheap, rundown, peice of shit building on the edge of downtown that is filled with junked and unfufilled dreams. But for almost a good four years it was a place where people who cared about eachother, art, music and world they

lived in, could go and share in thier experiences of life. Yeah, For me and my fucked up ways of looking at the world; the Aquadome was home. And although I think it's long past time to let the sinking ship drown, I don't know that I'll ever find another place in the world I will call home with the same innocence or conviction.

(Ben)

THE
AQUADOME

a love story.

Drag Lore in the Midwest
Scott Henson

In this 2010 paper, the investigator followed the folkloristic precept to seek out those whose stories are not told, and give them the chance to tell them, the marginalized, those who (with highly varying degrees of self-determination) lived at the fringe. In a time before well-established Institutional Review, the writer was deeply concerned with ethics, protecting the privacy, agency and dignity of informants.

The term "drag," in reference to a male performer wearing female clothing, is said to have originated in 1870s theatre slang to describe the performer's sensation that the long skirt she was wearing, which trailed behind her on the floor as she walked, was dragging. Others have suggested that the term comes to us through *polari*, or gay slang used through the 19th and 20th centuries, from the Yiddish word for "to wear", *trogn*; and a folk etymology emerged in the late-20th century suggesting that "drag" is an acronym for "DRessed As a Girl." While the mainstream culture has, no doubt, developed a large body of their own biased lore concerning drag queens, based on who they perceive these performing artists to be, it is more important, for the sake of pinning down the group identity of an often neglected and marginalized culture, to understand who they perceive themselves to be.

In any live entertainment genre in which constituent performers habitually share dressing rooms, network, and go about learning a craft from one another, a group culture emerges through social ritual and communication. With a rich variety of folk traditions, drag performers have built a mode of expression that transgresses gender norms in order to entertain general audiences and maintain group identity. Due to their insularity within a relatively rural, politically conservative geography, male drag performers in the Midwest, especially, have had an opportunity to develop a vivid folklore. The evidence of oral, material, and customary lore in Midwestern female impersonators is not only evident in front of the curtain, but in offstage rituals, as well. It should be noted that academics have also devoted many studies to "drag kings," or females who do male impersonation, in works such as *Female Masculinity* by Judith Halberstam, but data from this culture suggests a separate folk group, warranting separate study.

Fieldwork for this study involved using an online registry called "the Drag Queen Registry" to contact drag queens from Missouri, Illinois, Iowa, Indiana, Kentucky and Michigan. Through e-mail surveys, I asked the potential sources questions such as, "How did you come up with your stage-name?", "Did you have any mentors within the drag community?" and "What are some of the jokes and phrases you notice getting a lot of circulation in drag performances?" I received seven responses from the nearly 50 sources I e-mailed. These seven replies provided, often in entire paragraphs, a wealth of first-hand experience, and were the primary texts used in this study. (Full texts of each emailed response are appended, their grammar and spelling unedited, left as immediate, energetic, and transgressive of rules as they arrived in my in-box.) Data was also collected from prior anthropological research, however, as well as from various online resources for those doing female impersonation.

Understanding many of drag's folkways necessitates an understanding of its position within a larger culture. Although not all female impersonators are gay men, Newton says that drag performers often see themselves as a subculture within the larger queer culture, which, in turn, is a subculture within the larger heterosexual culture. One of the impersonators she interviewed said she felt that drag queens constitute a "society within a society within a society" (121). Even within the gay community, drag queens are given conflicting amounts of reverence. Moore says in interviewing gay men, she found that although relations between drag performers and the larger gay culture are currently in an upswing, many gay men still feel that drag's flaunting of connotatively feminine characteristics goes against the homosexual male's struggle to combat those connotations and stereotypes. Thus, according to many, drag culture should be segregated from gay culture in the public eye (108).

Interestingly, later in Moore's discussion of the interviews, she writes that drag queens also occupy a somewhat heroic position within gay culture. She writes that an overwhelming number of her informants reflected on female impersonators' role in the Stonewall Riots. On June 28, 1969, when police raided the Stonewall Inn, a bar that openly welcomed homosexuals in Greenwich Village NY, gay men and women fought back, inciting a riot and several subsequent protests. According to Thompson's chapter in *Out in Culture*, men who openly wore women's clothing at Stonewall "showed the most courage and sense during the action" (451). Not only that, but Moore's older informants said that in the days when gay bars were systematically raided, drag queens would retaliate while leathermen, "who make a literal fetish of machismo," would back down. "Drag queens are thus, in gay mythology given a macho interior," she writes (109).

Shared storytelling elements within the Midwestern drag culture also appear in the way that each informant has related the life experiences that ultimately led them to perform publicly in drag. That is, a very particular theme behind these decisions was repeatedly emphasized: a passion for performing and a lack of opportunity to play female characters in their area. A Springfield informant said, "I'm a Musical Theatre major in College (or was) and I started doing drag because I wanted to be able to play the characters I would normally not get to play because of the fact that I am a man" (Appx. E). A Kansas City informant said, "I remember I would ask my pawpaw to make me 'costumes' for my favorite characters in TV or in movies. They all happened to be, surprise surprise, female characters" (Appx. B). A variant telling of this origin story from a Kansas City informant suggests that doing drag provided not simply the female characters that normative stage performance lacked, but an additional assurance of stability:

"This was a way for me to develop a permanent character...it wouldn't be for just a few weeks of a production or on one weekend...this was for long term" (Appx. A). The emphasis of this narrative theme in recounting personal experiences could either be the product of a diffusion in storytelling technique among performers or independently occurring expressions which reveal the way that the folk group continues to attract new members. In other words, it's either a product of the folk group, an indirect way of explaining its preservation, or both.

It is important to note that none of my survey responses evidenced any desire, on the part of the female impersonator, to actually live as a woman or to ever become one. The act of drag performance seems to be a personal but temporary transgression of the imposed norms and codes that are placed on performers. For most, it's not a reflection of who they would like to be, but an exclamatory reaction to who they're told to be. A Terre Haute informant reports feeling "release" when doing drag, saying, "When I'm on stage, nobody knows a thing about me that they don't see in a 5 to 7 minute number. I can be anything and anybody I want to be" (Appx. G). An Indianapolis impersonator described the same sense of liberation in getting to be someone else, yielding this analogy: "It's like Halloween on a more regular basis" (Appx. F). A second narrative trend emerged in relating a decision to perform drag to these imposed norms by referencing a socially conservative childhood environment. One Missouri informant from my sample said that they grew up in a very conservative town, and one in Indianapolis acknowledged being a Southern Baptist minister's son (Appxs. B, G). These were among the first items of information given in explaining the compulsion to perform drag. Emphasizing this feature of their experience, at the outset of their explanation, helps performers to identify with one another's prior oppression and to unite the entire folk group under a shared transgression against a normative, conservative identity that each member was forced to accept at some point in the past.

Once the decision is made, a transition into the drag community requires performing at amateur nights until becoming more recognized and securing more permanent roles, said a Louisville, KY informant (Appx. D). There does exist a career-building master-apprentice relationship within the folk group, however. Many have referred to the community's "drag mothers," a term that exhibits some stability across my informants as meaning experienced members of the drag community who help a young performer to develop performance techniques and an onstage persona. They "take them under their wig, per say, [sic]" wrote one informant who said she didn't have a drag mother, herself (Appx. B). In fact, many of my informants did not claim to have drag mothers, yet, like one Springfield MO drag queen (Appx E), cited senior members of the community who helped them with specific costuming techniques and performance skills such as applying makeup, using hip pads and competing in pageants. Variants of the term "drag mother" are "drag mama" and "drag parent," a title which seems to be used when more than one mentor is involved in the development of an emerging performer (Appxs. A, D).

Drag mothers' and drag parents' influence can be seen in many elements of the rookie drag performer's career, sometimes including his or her stage name. One Kansas City drag queen said, "Most of the Queens I know have names that either they just made up on their own or their Drag Mother gave them" (Appx. B). This statement's fidelity across the sampling region is attested to by a Kentucky drag queen, Felicia D. Knightt, who described the origin of her first name, middle initial and last name: "Felicia comes from the movie 'Pricilla Queen of the Dessert'; D = diva and Knightt comes from one of the drag parents I have" (Appx. D). Should a drag queen decide to take an element of the drag parent's name, however, data shows that the adoption doesn't merely apply to the selection of a performer's last name. A drag queen from Kansas City, for instance, said that her middle name, "Kaye," comes from the last name of her "drag mama"

(Appx. A).

Aside from the adoption of the drag parent's name, there are a variety of self-naming practices that observe distinctive patterns within my sampling. Many, for instance, are alliterative: "Desire' Declyne," "Sassy Sassafras," and "Damania Douglas." Often, impersonators borrow names from female figures in pop culture and history. For instance, a Kansas City informant describes her last name this way, "Belmont–old money–richest woman in the south during the Civil War," and the aforementioned Louisville informant mentioned finding the name Felicia in the 1994 film, *Priscilla, Queen of the Desert.* The Kansas City informant from my sample described naming as a fun and often collaborative process between performers, while indicating yet another naming pattern: blatantly sexualized plays on words. "I will say that we have fun making up drag names such as Pat McCooter, Twila Twatlicker, Clamydia Jane, Tara Panties, and the list goes on…" (Appx. A). A few of these names seem like a subversion of names that otherwise would be relatively normative. "Pat" and "McCooter," for instance, seem to be likely candidates for 1950s sitcom fare, separately, which only become suggestive when combined. Each of the names mentioned are female-specific references. There are drag names, however, that are able to suggest the drag queen's masculinity. Gay-Mart.com suggests the "Amanda" template for aspiring drag performers, a few of which are currently in use by those in the field. For instance: "Amanda Playwith, Amanda Love, Anita Amanda Feelgood, etc."

These crafty reminders of a performer's masculinity underneath the drag manifest themselves not only in naming practices, but also in performance rituals and oral lore. Esther Newton's fieldwork with female impersonators from the Midwest shows us that common maneuvers to this end include pulling out a piece of breast padding and displaying it to the audience, removing a wig, or dropping one's vocal pitch suddenly. Newton also collected a phrasal way of relating this idea from an impersonator: "Have a ball. I have two" (122). Newton posits that reminding largely gay audiences of the performer's underlying physiological maleness allows the drag queen to appear safe to male homosexual culture and to continue participating in that culture as a peer (123).

Ironic nods toward one's biological sex occur backstage among performers, as well. However, in these situations, it seems to serve a different function. One Louisville, KY informant offered the phrase, "beat ur mug," which is used by performers as a phrasal synonym for applying makeup while suiting up in drag before a show (Appx. D). Here, the performer's "mug," a very connotatively male expression for face, is being beaten into a more female visage. There seems to be a threshold being established in this example between masculinity and femininity right before a stage performance. The phrase's imperative form, then, implies a command for the performer to cross this threshold and surrender himself to the female persona he is becoming.

This template, however, has also generated the phrase "paint your mug," used by two of my respondents, one from Terre Haute, IN and another from Louisville, KY (appxs. D, G). Here, again, we have the phrasal suggestion of a masculine veneer being replaced by a feminine one. The term "fish" as a complimentary adjective also enjoys some circulation within the Midwestern community. For instance, "girl you look fish" is a way to commend a drag queen on her feminine appearance, said a Louisville informant (Appx. C). Variation in the term is attested to by an Indianapolis drag queen who uses the term "fish" as well as "fishy" (Appx. F). The connotation of female genitalia behind this word in its reference to the feminine appearance suggests something unmistakably bawdy that, when used as a compliment, both praises the drag queen's skill and expresses a playful in-group jab at the subjects they are portraying.

Rules concerning use of third person pronouns or emphatics, such as "girl," in reference to a female impersonator vary within the folk group. According to many of those surveyed, when performers are not wearing drag or are not in character, referring to them by their drag name, as "she," or with feminine emphatics is inappropriate (Appx. E, G). Another group has stated that it is only appropriate to refer to those who perform in drag as "she," regardless of outward appearance (Appx. D, F). Referring to a drag queen as "he" or by her birth name while she is donning a feminine persona, however, does not seem to be appropriate usage to anyone in my sample. The existence of common rules to govern how a performer is addressed or referred to creates a clear threshold that separates the performer's male and female lives. Standardizing the community's use of "she" for performance purposes also makes the performer, herself, in charge of how she is perceived during her set. She might decide to upset the illusion by removing a wig, but ultimately, it's her performance and another person's use of the wrong pronoun might hijack the control she has over how she is perceived.

The masculine-feminine dyad, a central opposition within drag culture, reasserts itself when performers overreach in becoming their female persona. According to Newton, the use of hormone supplements and surgical procedures to achieve heightened femininity often carries stigma within the folkgroup, meriting the title, "hormone queen," for one who partakes in these practices. Newton writes that this resentment arises from a perceived violation of one of drag's fundamental values, namely that female impersonation depends on the underlying maleness of the impersonator. "'Hormone queens' are placing themselves out of the homosexual subculture, since, by definition, a homosexual man wants to sleep with other men," she writes (123). Many of my study's informants acknowledged the practice but voiced some disapproval. When one was asked how she would go about appearing more like a woman and whether it is important to appear as feminine as possible, this informant immediately responded with, "some girls have surgical procedures done to help with the illusion. I have not and will never have any part of that" (Appx. E).

According to McNeal, the relationship between female impersonators and gay male culture is not the only conflict that manifests itself in drag performances. Playfully insulting speech directed toward heterosexual female audience members is one of drag performance's regular features (345). Mc Neal's field work uncovered jabs used at a gay night club such as: "You don't think you're at Hooters do you?" and "eight miles of dick in here, and you won't get eight inches of it." She argues that doing this allows drag performers to direct their frustrations with a larger hetero-normative society into a form of humor founded on the "inverted moral order" that drag performances create – one in which the heterosexual attendees are the marginalized minority and non-heterosexuals reign supreme (357).

In my fieldwork, however, I discovered that teasing occurs toward not only female audience members, but also male ones and fellow performers. A Terre Haute informant reports that during a show's downtime, while an upcoming performer is changing, she enjoys picking on both audience members and drag queens as a means of stalling and warming up the crowd, showing a much more practical motive behind the practice than that of social inversion (appx G). This is a fairly common type of communicative practice among the female impersonators I surveyed, and a lot of the insulting focuses on the heavy drinking that occurs at drag events either in the onstage banter between performers: "Queens like their booze and we talk about them being drunks etc. It's all in good fun and just being caddy, [sic]"—or between the performer and a heckling audience member who's had too much to drink: "I'll usually respond to whatever they're talking about, unless they are drunk, then I just say 'Drink your juice, Shelby'" (Appxs. F, E). A Kansas City respondent described taking a narrative approach to insulting: "We're basically insult comics. ... I like to tell just enough of a story [about a performer] to get the crowd's imagination going, and then leave it there" (Appx. A). There is an element of invitation for the viewers to access the performers' offstage lives in all of this repartee and onstage intra-group narrative, strengthening the bond between the folk group and spectators. Within the folk group, insulting seems to function similarly to banter between married couples, with the same operating principle as that of a celebrity roast: if it's done out of humor and respect for the recipient, then it actually maintains cohesion and fondness between performers.

The web offers a wide assortment of resources for aspiring drag performers. One site, for instance, sells video and audio tutorials on developing more feminine communication skills, offering lessons in mimicking a more feminine pitch, resonance, dynamic range, enunciation, vocabulary, grammar and body language (heartcorps.com). There are hundreds of video tutorials pertaining to drag makeup, hair and wig styling and body modification. Online stores, such as Drag-Queen.com, sell breastforms, heels in men's and women's sizes, corsets, wigs, hair removal creams and even feminine hormone supplements. Many of these items are reportedly used by Midwestern drag queens, with the exception of hormone supplements. There especially seems to exist a great deal of stability across my study's informants in creating the illusion of breasts. Five informants referred to one or both of two practices: duct-taping the chest to create cleavage and/or shading the area to give the impression of contour (Appxs. A, B, D, E, G). Two of my Missouri correspondents also reported wearing hip-pads under the costume to create more feminine lower-body curves (Appxs. A, E). The use of multiple pairs of panty hose was also reported by a Terre Haute, In. source who typically uses 7-8 pairs, and by a Springfield, Mo. informant who reported using 12-15 (Appxs. E, G).

It's very likely that this regularity in technique came from the practice of circulating tips within the community, which I encountered in my research. Objects such as costumes and wigs are even exchanged among performers, according to an Indianapolis source (Appx. F). This transmission of tips, attitudes toward style, and the clothes, themselves, might give rise to many of the current costuming trends within the drag community. In reviewing my informants' individual profiles and photos on the Drag Queen Registry's website, I've noticed that costumes very often seem to hearken back to the glamour stereotypes of a previous age. For instance, boas, fur stoles, waterfall necklaces, and heavily sculpted wigs are common among several of my sources, each nodding to 1940s and 50s high-end fashion. One of my Louisville informants even impersonates Marilyn Monroe, with a costume featuring the iconic white dress and curly blond wig. Adhering to the opposite gender's exaggerated, bygone standards of beauty can be seen as a humorous, shared transgression of traditionally imposed masculine roles.

Shared transgression seems to be a major theme of both previous research and my own findings on drag culture. In performers' dress, in the dynamic between themselves and a heterosexual audience, and in their naming practices, we find a public act of rejecting values imposed by society's gender roles and heteronormativity. This common outward reaction undoubtedly strengthens unity within the group, but there do appear to be other internal folk practices that also foster that sense of community. For instance, the transaction of costumes and make-up tips and the highly observed process of "drag mother" tutelage within the Midwest community are evidence of a performance endeavor that requires a high amount of communication and training within the group. Phrasal ways of expressing ideas that are specific to this genre, and the use of good-humored insult, are further evidence of a tight-knit community and an oral lore. The Midwest folk group of female impersonators is teeming with evidence of common customary and oral lore, and further study would need to be done to in order to uncover all of it.

Works Cited

Halberstam, Judith. *Female Masculinity*. Durham, NC: Duke University Press, 1998. Print.

Hilbert, Jeffrey. "The Politics of Drag." In *Out in Culture: Gay, Lesbian, and Queer Essays on Popular Culture*. Ed. Corey K. Creekmur and Alexander Doty. Durham: Duke University Press, 1995. 463-469. Print

McNeal, Keith E. "Behind the Make-Up: Gender Ambivalence and the Double-Bind of Gay Selfhood in Drag Performance." *Ethos*. 27.3. (1999): 344-378. Print.

Moore, Fiona. "One of the Gals Who's One of the Guys: Men, Masculinity and Drag Performance in North America." In *Changing Sex and Bending Gender*. Ed. Allison Shaw and Shirley Ardener. New York: Berghahn Books, 2005. 103-118. Print.

Newall, Venetia. "Folklore and Male Homosexuality." *Folklore*. 97.2 (1986): 123-147. Web. 19 Oct 2010.

Newton, Esther. "The Drag Queen." In *Transgender Studies Reader*. Ed. Susan Stryker and Stephen Whittle. CRC Press, 2006. 121-130. Web. 19 Oct 2010.

Appendices A-G:
Responses from Email Interviews

Ed. note: stage-names only are used; potentially identifying information has been altered or deleted.

Appendix A: E-mail survey from Ginger Kay Belmont (Kansas City, MO.)

1. What factored into your decision to do public drag performance?

This was a way for me to develop a permanent character...it wouldn't be for just a few weeks of a production or one weekend...this was for long term.

2. How did you come up with your stage name?

Ginger–something spicy and a bit flirty...Kaye–my drag mama is Sandy Kaye and I wanted her name....Belmont–old money–richest woman in the south during the Civil War (did I mention I was a History Teacher) so she's a bit spicy and flirty with some old fashioned southern charm and strong family values...a cross between Blanche Devereaux and Julia Sugarbaker with just a hint of the other characters from those shows to make things interesting.

3. How do you usually respond to heckling from an audience?

Join in...I do this for fun...Ginger doesn't get her feelings hurt easily

4. Do you or any of the performers you know have any drag-themed names for the items or people that you work with? Could you name a few?

Not sure I get this question but I will say that we have fun making up drag names such as Pat McCooter, Twila Twatlicker, Clamydia Jane, Tara Panties, and the list goes on...these names have been taken don't get any bright ideas be original when choosing a name

5. Did you have any mentors within the drag community? If so, describe your relationship with them.

Sandy Kaye...has been performing for many years...She got me started...I love and respect her though I don't see her much any more....Belle Starr...I work with Belle She is one of my dearest friends and I have learned MUCH from her...she has been my mentor for many years and will always be my friend

6. Did you have to undergo any type of initiation to become part of the drag community in the area where you perform? Could you describe this process?

You have to put in your time...prove yourself worthy of a cast spot...some take longer than others to get to that point but you still have to do your time as a newby...

7. How do you tailor a performance to suit a particular audience?

Some audiences like different genres...i can perform most any genre a music...some crowds like surprises...I have removable parts of costumes and sometimes do a "suicide" number (the crowd gets to choose the song)

8. What are some of jokes or phrases you notice getting a lot of circulation in drag performances?

OMG! now that's a list....we always talk about boobies, pussy, cock, and muscles. Cornfed tits...bald/nasty/big or whatever pussy. We are basically insult comics and it works best if you can insult yourself and fellow entertainers (never use things hurtful...if you have to you can make them up) I like to tell just enough of a story to get the crowds imagination going and then leave it there. They get to have fun with it.

9. What are some of the ways in which you or other performers try to modify appearance in order to portray a different gender?

Is it important for you to be as realistic as possible? jesus...girdles or waist cinchers; hip pads worn under tights to make a "feminin" figure....obviously boobs....make up and wigs...we also use duct tape to make clevage and to "girdle" the stomach....every girl has her own "secrets" and every performance or costume could use different methods of modification

Appendix B: E-mail survey from Sassy Sassafras (Kansas City, MO.)

1. What factored into your decision to do public drag performance?

I guess my whole drag franchise started when I was about 8 years old believe it or not! I remember I would ask my papaw to make me "costumes" for my favorite characters on TV or in movies. They all happened to be, surprise surprise, female characters, so he was making me a lot of dresses and other feminine garments complete with accessories! So it started pretty young with me parading around my living room in lipstick and a gown!

I was very open with my young love for drag until adolescence when I started to see the negative stigma around female impersonation and being gay in general. I went into the closet after that and only did drag in the privacy of my own room. Usually consisting of just me wearing a Halloween wig styling it in front of my mirror. I grew up in a VERY conservative household in a VERY conservative town, so I'm sure that had something to do with it too. It wasn't until I turned 22 (I'm 24 now) that I finally came out to everyone, including my family, thus freeing me from my hidden drag life and hidden life in general! I remember my first "coming out" experience in drag was when I went as Cruella De Ville to a Halloween party. I remember loving the reaction I got from the people there (most didn't even recognize me!) and I felt pretty because of it! This is obviously a great feeling! Since then I have tried to make drag a part of my everyday life! I'm not a live performer per say but I still love making videos and keeping up my websites! I do hope to get to actually perform and make it a second career one day but it's not in the cards for me at the moment! My parents do know I do it and they don't really mind anymore. Do they love it....no, but at least I didn't get kicked out, right?! My mom actually thinks I'm very pretty as Sassy! Haha!!

2. How did you come up with your stage name?

Sassy Sassafras....actually my friend and I got into a conversation one day about drag and doing it and, just kind of jokingly, I said "I wouldn't mind doing drag." She immediately was like "OMG! You have to!! Let's make you a name!" I remember us going around and around knowing it would need to have something to do with having sass because I'm a very sassy person in my male life! So it basically came out of my own personality trait and thus Sassy Sassafras was born! I guess she helped to birth Sassy!

3. How do you usually respond to heckling from an audience?

Since I'm not a "performing" drag queen but rather an "internet" drag queen, at the moment at least, I don't really have to deal with heckling or anything like that. Being a younger drag queen, I haven't yet experienced a lot of what maybe the more experienced ones have. I can tell you at the party I mentioned above, I overheard someone saying to another person there, "Well the fag has come out tonight." I just remember thinking how ignorant and stupid that person sounds.

I don't think I would give it a second thought though if someone was to really heckle me. Sassy isn't a confrontational queen by any means. She is too classy and glamorous for that! She has thick skin and she rises above adversity in any form and comes out stronger! Will she sass the hell out of you....YES! But nothing too extreme or downright mean! All in good fun....until I cutchu! :)

4. Do you or any of the performers you know have any drag-themed names for the items or people that you work with? Could you name a few?

Most of the Queens I know have names that either they just made up on their own or their Drag Mother gave them. I guess in a way my name goes along with how my drag personality is. Sassy character named Sassy Sassafras.

5. Did you have any mentors within the drag community? If so, describe your relationship with them.

No, I did everything all on my own. My biggest supporter is the same friend that helped come up with my name but she doesn't do any type of drag at all! There ARE some people that help younger performing drag stars in developing their talents and personality. They're called Drag Mothers and they are usually older, more experienced Queens who take them under their wig, per say.

6. Did you have to undergo any type of initiation to become part of the drag community in the area where you perform? Could you describe this process?

Since I'm still not doing any live performances in my area I haven't had to do anything to that effect. I will say doing internet drag is a little harder and more intimidating in my opinion because you don't have that immediate response from your viewers so you never know if anyone likes you or not haha!! I would love to start performing and getting out and about but at the moment I'm very content uploading my silly vids and pics to my websites! So far I've been pretty successful doing it.....I'm doing an interview now, aren't I! Haha! ;)

7. How do you tailor a performance to suit a particular audience?

What I usually do when I make a video for my page is think of some important topic that I feel I could bring Sassy's sass out in the best. I'm always trying to do something that is near and dear to my heart too. One thing that people might not know is that my videos are ALL improvised on the spot so what I'm saying is literally what I just thought of at that moment. I love organic work and I feel that it comes across more real and earnest than if I had rehearsed something beforehand. I think that's important when you're doing anything to always have some form of sincerity and realness in what you say and do no matter how crazy or off the wall it really is!

8. What are some of jokes or phrases you notice getting a lot of circulation in drag performances?

Dirty jokes! Hah! I don't think I've ever seen a performance of a famous Queen that didn't include some form of dirty or innuendo-laden jokes or stories. Important events and political commentary have taken a leap onto the drag stages as well it seems.

9. What are some of the ways in which you or other performers try to modify appearance in order to portray a different gender? Is it important for you to be as realistic as possible?

In my look, I tend to go along the lines of realism as much as I possibly can. I buy the best wigs I can find and the best make-up too. It all adds up to making you look the best you can. I've tried to make Sassy as real as can be complete with real opinions and thoughts as though she was a real woman. I basically tell people that Sassy is me as a woman hah!

I think it helps that I'm really in tune with my feminine side as much as my masculine side. It's really easy for me to come off convincingly as a girl because I understand femininity very well.

In trying to hide the annoying traits that make us look like men ;), we do all sorts of tricks. We usually have to use a generous amount of make-up, mainly foundation, to cover up any stray beard hair and to make us seem more feminine. I don't even have to get into "tucking", do I?? Let's just say nothing takes the drag fantasy away quicker than when you have an extra pair of breasts hanging out your short skirt! Some Queens I know even shade their chest to make the cleavage have a more realistic depth to it.

Appendix C: E-mail Survey from Satine St. Claire (Louisville, KY.)

1. What factored into your decision to do public drag performance?

A lil pre info,

I was 15 when this happen. I came out when I was 13 as a gay boy. And was very fourtunate to have accepting parents.

Well it started with a Halloween party in which I was helping with lights and dj'in. I dress up as Marilyn Monroe or try to. And I really enjoyed the attention and how I notice people wanted to see more of me in drag. I never felt like i was going to do drag, it first scared me, but I started to play with makeup in my room. I very much enjoyed painting my face and dressing up. So that lead me 3 years later to start performing at a after hours coffee house. Which lead to more ventures in drag

2. How did you come up with your stage name?

Satine came for the word satin. And st. Claire came from a horror flic in which people were in a crazy house and nurse st.Claire was the only sane one and it was a funny c flic thus came my last name.

3. How do you usually respond to heckling from an audience?

I let it not detract me from why I'm there and my vision for the piece. I may throw a slight glar of disapprovial. I'm here for ur enjoyment and if ur laughing in a non postive way I choses not to react.

4. Do you or any of the performers you know have any drag-themed names for the items or people that you work with? Could you name a few?

Well yes

Paint is makeup

Beating a face is applying makeup

"girl you look fish" means you look very femmen and female

Shalack means hairspray

Mary can be said in any context to say hi or heeeeyyyy

Squrill means girl.

Other than that a poppy pin is such wigs are wigs dresses and gowns are such jewelry can be called sparkle.

5. Did you have any mentors within the drag community? If so, describe your relationship with them.

I really never had a drag mother so to say I did have a performer that I know hurrican summers take me backstage and show me how she applys makeup, this happen when I first started to play with drag.

6. Did you have to undergo any type of initiation to become part of the drag community in the area where you perform? Could you describe this process?

Not at all lol I just started and they noticed and ask me to perform.

7. How do you tailor a performance to suit a particular audience?

I always try to think what I would enjoy and what I like about other drag shows. I do some mairlyn impersonation and also other classic Hollywood idols but I do like to play with current fads and also love to create a story for the spectors to connect with

8. What are some of jokes or phrases you notice getting a lot of circulation in drag performances?
Are you a virgin??
Looks liked I scared them.
Sweating like a whore in church.

9. What are some of the ways in which you or other performers try to modify appearance in order to portray a different gender? Is it important for you to be as realistic as possible?
Some performer get plumped which is silicon enjextions in the cheeks chin lips and even fore head, hips and butt and chest. I myself have had rhinoplasty and septoplasty for both health and stage reasons but mainley for myself. I don't advicoate plumping bc of the health risk envolved and also I am a drag queen a man in a dress. There are performers who are transgender who go through lots of surgery to look more female but me I love the illusion of what makeup can do and how much of an art form it is to go from man to woman. I do have naturaley boyish looks which makes it eaiser to tranform with makeup which is just a plus for what I enjoy doing.

Appendix D: E-mail survey from Felicia D. Knightt (Louisville, KY.)

1. What factored into your decision to do public drag performance?
I wanted to be a star in theatrics,and it looked like fun

2. How did you come up with your stage name?
Felicia comes from the movie "Pricilla Queen of the Dessert' D=diva and Knightt Comes from one of the drag parents i have

3. How do you usually respond to heckling from an audience?
i'm a emcee so i can handle myself quite well...and professionally

4. Do you or any of the performers you know have any drag-themed names for the items or people that you work with? Could you name a few?

"beat ur mug"- painting/makeup ..like when you beat your mug..ur getting up in drag

5. Did you have any mentors within the drag community? If so, describe your relationship with them.

My mentor and friend......The Mistress of Mayhem...Hurricane Summers..known all over the united states in gay bars galore

6. Did you have to undergo any type of initiation to become part of the drag community in the area where you perform?

No....its like star search.....if you have talent,you be discovered...

Could you describe this process?

amatuer nights to start.....you then go on to performing more and more as you get better and better

7. How do you tailor a performance to suit a particular audience?

depends on my mood and the time of year..holidays of course and bar type

8. What are some of jokes or phrases you notice getting a lot of circulation in drag performances?

ok one of the ones i use toward hecklers........."oh its ok i knew his mom and dad when they were brother and sister"......or...."10,000 sperm and your the one that made it thru

9. What are some of the ways in which you or other performers try to modify appearance in order to portray a different gender?

shading and contouring on face/plus lashes make a difference..plus some queens duct tape their chest together to form cleaveage....

Is it important for you to be as realistic as possible?

the better the illusion, the better the show

10. Why do you do it?

i do it for fun, its fun being a star on stage, it gives me a sense of excitement emotionally and psychology...love attention, fun, and for me..i promote "being real with yourself no matter what u do"

11. Could you describe any hierarchies or divisions of power within your area's drag culture (if there are any)? How do performers make their way up the ranks?

non e i know of..and we make our way of ranks..with crowns and with years of experience..with getting better with performances.

12. What are the rules for using gender pronouns?

i refer to most drags, and twinks as "shes"

Appendix E: E-mail survey from Desire' Declyne (Springfield, MO.)

1. I'm a Musical Theatre major in College (or was) and I started doing drag because I wanted to be able to play the characters I would normally not get to play because of the fact that I am a man.

2. My stage name is Desire' Declyne... Originally I had come up with the name Celine Carnae, but one day, my friends and I at work were playing a joke on one of the gals in the office, and filled out an application with the name Visa Declyne, I liked the last name so I came up with Desire' Declyne... I spell my first name Desire' so it reads like desire, so the full name could be read Desire Declyne which is kinda the premise of my whole childhood. :)

3. I've never really had heckling so to say, when I'm talking to a crowd if they have something to say, I'll usually respond to whatever they are talking about, unless they are drunk, then I just say "Drink your juice Shelby"

4. The one I use the most is the word "tea" meaning gossip, I'll usually either walk into the dressing room and say "Avon calling!" or WHATS THE TEA?

5. I don't have a drag mother per say, but I have had some of the most amazing mentors with the art of female impersonation. One being Alexandra Hart, who was Miss Gay Springfield America in 2005. She taught me how to do the makeup. Robyn Hunter, current reigning Miss Missouri

USofA At Large helped me with my hip pads and my pangentry work... Those two have been the most important in my starting out....

6. The only real "initiation" I had to undergo was shaving my goatee... :)

7. Usually I am very femanine when I'm performing, unless I'm doing a certain number that I could pull off any masculine type acts...

8. Not really except for when we do shots... which some places we will do anywhere from 5 to 10 shots and some places we do none... it just depends.

9. We play around alot with each other... calling each other whore, slut, bitch, or "love your hair, hope you win"... Back in Springfield, one of my dearest friends and I would be downstairs in the dressing room getting ready, and we would just be tearing into each other... but none of us ever take it personally because we know that the other is joking. Trust, you would know if a drag queen was saying serious things... lol

10. Some girls have surgical procedures done to help with the illusion. I have not and will never have any part of that. With the help of duct tape, I am able to create a hourglass figure, and cleavage. With my hip pads I am able to give my legs that more femanine curve. 12-15 pairs of pantyhose. and of course the makeup, lashes, nails, and wigs.

11. I do public drag performances because I like to entertain, it's a way for me to get that rush that I normally get from doing a musical or play when I'm not working on a musical or play... Entertaining is the biggest bone in my body, (well... not the biggest. lol) but I just really love to entertain and to see everyone dancing and singing along with me!

12. Sometimes we choose songs based on our emotions, other times we choose for entertainment value. Friday I did a gospel song and the audience went NUTS! (video at http://www.youtube.com/watch?v=Bb-r51j-h2k) It really depends, but I do believe that everyone should see a drag show at least once because it is just as important as art... it actually is an art.

13. It's all about making a name for yourself, you get a following, you become more popular, you define your style, perfect your painting, then just make that audience roar and you'll be set. Some queens are big on families, and some rely on their family ties to boost them up to the top but it really doesn't work that way. You have to work for it. It's just not an overnight kinda thing.

14. Well, for me, I tell people, when I am a boy I am [*deleted*], and when I'm in face, I'm Desire'. Some people call each other girl 24/7 that just don't fly with me lol

Appendix F: E-mail survey from Sequoia Pentecost (Indianapolis, IN.)

1. Why do you do public drag performance? (what do you feel you gain from it psychologically/emotionally?)
I do drag for the entertainment value. It brings a lot of joy to others causing laughter and excitement. Psychologically, it allows you to become a different person—allowing your alter ego take full control. Emotionally, it creates happiness because you see the joy it brings to so many others. I, unlike other drag performers, have no desire to be a woman or want to live my life as a female. It doesn't do anything for me sexually. It's like halloween on a more regular basis.

2. What do you feel your audience gains from experiencing a drag show? (is it just entertainment or are there any messages you want them to walk away with?)
See above

3. Are there any pre or post show rituals that you, yourself, or any of the other performers engage in? (warm-ups, good luck rituals, etc.)
Not really. Most of the time you are so preoccupied with trying to get yourself ready in time to perform.

4. Do you or any of the performers you know have any names for the items or people that you work with that are unique to the drag community? Could you name a few? (For instance of my informants told me about "drag mothers" and the phrase, "beat your mug")
Yes, there are drag mothers–these are typically more tenured or more experience drag queens that help our younger or more inexperienced drag queens who are trying to hone their drag skills. Drag mothers teach younger queens the tricks of the drag trade. Another term that is used is "fish." As in you are really looking "fishy." This means that you are really looking

like a women. "Fish" refers to women. I'm sure you can draw your own conclusions as to why.

5. Did you have any mentors within the drag community? If so, describe your relationship with them.

No...I had no mentors. I just came in full force and learned/studied on my own. I didn't have a drag mother.

6. Could you describe any hierarchies or divisions of power within your area's drag culture (if there are any)? How do performers make their way up the ranks?

Performers make their way up the ranks through honing their skills—getting really good with makeup, having fabulous costumes, and perfecting their drag act. This really comes from experience and exposure to the community.

7. Do you engage in any playful insulting with the other performers or audience members? If so, why? And could you give an example or two?

Yes. We "read" each other a lot for the way we look, how we act, or what we do. For example, there is a queen that we call Cadillac Barbie—she is older and we tease her about being the oldest indoor living attraction. Other queens like their booze and we talk about them being drunks etc. It's all in good fun and just being caddy.

8. How tight-knit is the drag culture in your area? For instance, do you like to trade/compare performance, body modification, costuming, or makeup techniques with other members of the community, or is it more competitive?

It is both. There are some clicks in drag like in any other groups. Within the clicks it is very common for queens to trade costumes, makeup tips, wigs, etc.

9. What are some of the ways in which you or other performers try to modify appearance in order to portray a different gender? Is it important for you to be as realistic as possible?

I think we all want to try to look pretty and do our best to portray "fish," however, to me I don't go as far to modify my body thorugh surgery etc. like some do. All of my modifications are thorugh padding, tape, and make up. I think this is the most traditional and more creative. It takes a lot of work to look feminine when you don't have the right equipment.

10. What are the rules for gender pronouns? When do you feel it's appropriate to refer to a drag queen as "she" and when is it appropriate to refer to one as "he"?

Drag queens are always referred to as "she." Even when a drag queen is dressed in boy form, it is common to call him by his drag name.

Appendix G: E-mail survey from Anita Shav Beaver (Terre Haute, IN)

1. Why do you do public drag performance? (what do you feel you gain from it psychologically/emotionally?)

I perform for the simple reason of being able to reinvent myself. I'm a Southern Baptist minister's son, and all my life I've been expected to act a certain way and be a certain kind of person. When I'm on stage, nobody knows a thing about me that they don't see in a 5 to 7 minute number. I can be anything and anybody I want to be. I can be sassy, slutty, simple, sophisticated, or just plain stupid and at the end of the night walk out and nobody know who I am. It's a type of release from the ordinary for me.

2. What do you feel your audience gains from experiencing a drag show? (is it just entertainment or are there any messages you want them to walk away with?)

Honestly I think the audience is both entertained by the show and they get messages from it. I mostly do it for the entertainment value (let's face it, I'm a 220 pound crazy bitch who likes to wear attention-grabbing outfits and make people laugh until they wet themselves), but I know some queens that really like nothing more than to speak to people with their performances. I just try to make people have a good time and laugh a little, which I believe is a medicine all in itself.

3. Are there any pre or post show rituals that you, yourself, or any of the other performers engage in? (warm-ups, good luck rituals, etc.)

Personally, I don't engage in any type of rituals other than just plain getting ready (doing makeup, putting on outfits, etc). Most of the queens I work with down a few shots to loosen themselves up, but I'm not a drinker.

4. Do you or any of the performers you know have any names for the items or people that you work with that are unique to the drag community? Could you name a few?

Oh honey child YES. Drag mother – the person who helped you get your start in drag. Drag sister – anybody that has the same drag mother as you. We call each other sisters or "girls". The term "beating your mug" or "painting your mug" refers to putting on your makeup. We use the term "getting my body on" to describe putting on our layers to give ourselves a more feminine figure.

5. Did you have any mentors within the drag community? If so, describe your relationship with them.

When I first encountered the drag community at 16 years old, I was fascinated by it. I have several mentors in the community, and thank God every time I perform for their strength, dedication to the art of female impersonation, and their willingness to help. The include Asia LaBouche and Vicki St. James from Talbott Street in Indianapolis, IN; Jeana Jones, Brittany Sebastian, Annastacia DeMoore, Ruby Lockheart, Staci Stevens, Traci Dalton all from Terre Haute, IN; and the late Briana Baxter also from Terre Haute. Each of these girls hold a special place in my heart for all of the advice, care, and love they have given to me over the years. Each in turn has acted as a drag mother to help me along the way. Their support has been a very firm foundation during my 6 years of entertaining.

6. Could you describe any hierarchies or divisions of power within your area's drag culture (if there are any)? How do performers make their way up the ranks?

There really aren't any hierarchies around my area, but I've heard of them in larger towns. Basically it's just survival of the fittest. Those with the determination and skill work their way up the ranks quickly, and those without it flounder and die out.

7. Do you engage in any playful insulting with the other performers or audience members? If so, why? And could you give an example or two?

Heavens yes. I'm a comedy queen. I love nothing more than to pick on my audience during downtime, and pick on my fellow performers backstage. It helps to lighten the mood, but also teaches that nobody is safe from the deadly and vicious tongue of a queen that has to stall (insert evil laugh here).

8. How tight-knit is the drag culture in your area? For instance, do you like to trade/compare performance, body modification, costuming, or makeup techniques with other members of the community, or is it more competitive?

In my neck of the woods, the drag culture is a vicious, cut-throat, no-nonsense, no holds barred, battle to be the ultimate diva. Queens will say and do anything to belittle others and make themselves look better, all with the hopes of winning a title or going someplace other than here with their careers. Thankfully, I'm the only comedy queen for miles around. I don't have to be cut-throat. I can just be me and be happy and nice to the others.

9. What are some of the ways in which you or other performers try to modify appearance in order to portray a different gender? Is it important for you to be as realistic as possible?

To me it is an Art. The ART of Female Impersonation. No, I don't want to be a woman, but I want to portray one as best I can when I'm on stage. There is a glitz and glamour to it. I love it when a woman comes up to me and says "I've never seen a man look this much better than a woman before. You're amazing. You pull off a womanly look better than me!". I'm not going to lie. It's tough. Some queens use duct tape, others use special clothing. For me, to give my lower half a feminine look, it requires 4 corsets (start with XL and go down to M or S), 2 body cinchers (L and M), 2 panty girdles (L and M), 7 or 8 pairs of pantyhose, and hip pads (couch cushions contoured down to roughly resemble T-bone steaks). To improve my bustline, I again go with different sizes. 4 bras (start with 38B, then 40C, then 42D, then finally 44DD) and padding (3 socks rolled up inside each other per "breast"). By the time I'm done, you could touch me anywhere on my body and not be able to tell I'm male.

10. What are the rules for gender pronouns? When do you feel it's appropriate to refer to a drag queen as "she" and when is it appropriate to refer to one as "he"?

Believe it or not, this is the easiest question to answer lol. When a performer is in drag, it is a She. When the performer is out of drag, it is a He. At least this is what rules I live by. But I'm not going to knock you out if you flub up and call me the wrong thing. It simply comes with the territory.

Carnie Lore and the People who Bring Life to the American Carnival
Ruby Jenkins

This 2010 paper is a classic of fieldwork in a classic genre (occupational lore), covering the classic categories (e.g., lingo), with a classic presentation handout which has been used as a model for a decade of folklore classes.

Over the past century and a half the idea of the carnival has manifested itself in many different ways—whether it be to audiences watching the train-traveling circus of Barnum and Bailey make its way across the country as early as 1872, or to the *Ripley's Believe It or Not* crowd watching the fabulous Mr. Ripley display and explain his findings from across the globe, or to those who now are watching Cirque du Soleil in Las Vegas.

People flock to the idea of a festival, a chance to win a prize, spend a day with their family, a chance to tug the bearded woman's beard, or to ditch your family and catch the strip show happening in tent four.

When I began this project, I recalled the large street celebrations of my past, thinking that it would be fun to examine the ways that people remember carnivals. However, the

more I researched and did my field work, the more I learned about the complex and intricate lives of the people who worked at these carnivals. My project focuses first on a history and explanation of who Carneys are, where they work, and how they have changed over the past 50 years. I focus specifically on American carnivals, and my research was conducted with people from ages 20 – 60. The topic of my research is the lore surrounding carnivals. One of the scholars I modeled my research after is Donald J. Ward, past director of Comparative Folklore and Mythologies studies at UCLA from 1978 to 2004.

Who Are Carneys?

Carneys (also spelled *carnie* and *carny*) are not the easiest group of people to define. Carneys are typically defined as a group as the "men" who work at carnivals.[1] Kevin Morra has been a carney for the past

twenty years of his life and writes a blog entitled *Diary of a Carny* under the name "Who Cares?" Morra's blog has provided the invaluable first-hand insight into the world of carnies that my paper conveys. In one early entry (April 2006) Morra states his feelings about the term 'carney.' He writes, "I don't like being called carny, and neither do most that have been out here for awhile; we prefer being called 'Show People.' The public will always call us Carnies though, so that's how I will address us here."[2] The term 'carney' may not be the most appropriate to use based on this comment. However, the term is so embedded in their culture, and used so perfectly in combination with Morra's complex relationship with his work (which will be explored further later in this paper), that

---

[1]Donald J. Ward, "The Carny in the Winter," *Western Folklore* 21 no. 3 (July 1962):190.
[2]Morra, "Carnies or Show People" *Diary of a Carny*. Blogspot. 1 April, 2006.

I will use it in this paper. However, carnies work at all the manifestations of a carnival, whether it is a fair, freak show, sideshow, at-show or circus. A fair is typically an economic institution, with the primary goal of boosting the economy of a certain area and promoting and selling goods from that particular area. The freak shows and "at-shows" were generally a part of a larger sideshow at an even larger carnival or circus, but are in and of themselves different from each other. The side show "describes a particular kind of show or exhibit that developed in the mid-1800s under the guidance of P. T. Barnum and others; it featured dancing girls, magic acts, and especially human oddities (known as 'freaks' in the business)."[3] Freak shows are usually traveling displays of human deformities that are a result of a medical condition, genetics, or fakery (for example bearded ladies, giants, dwarfs, Siamese twins, etc). The "at-shows" display "feats of strength and athletic prowess such as weightlifting, boxing, and wrestling."[4] The "at-shows" have recently developed into the world of professional wrestling. Carneys also include the people who own and maintain the rides at carnivals as well as the people who sell the food there.

The history of the carney goes back centuries. However, my examination of their folk group spans roughly the last hundred years. Carnies have a wide range of places where they can work. Traveling shows still exist, as well as the opportunity to appear at fairs such as state fairs. Cirque du Soleil, Barnum and Bailey's, and numerous other circuses are not only profitable institutions but also legal and well paying. On August 18th 2010 an article was published on Statesman.com interviewing a husband and wife human cannonball duo. According to the article there are only ten human cannonballs in the entire world.[5] These big circuses have become very institutionalized, yet the traveling carnies that my blog fieldwork

---

[3]Carol L. Russell and Thomas E. Murray, "Life and Death of Carnie," *American Speech* 79 (Winter 2004): 402.

[4]Ibid. 403.

[5]Helen Anders, "Joining the circus? Here's How That Works!" *Statesman* //www.statesman.com.

focuses on show similar discontent within the smaller carnie arenas. As stated earlier, Kevin Morra writes a blog on blogspot.com called "Diary of a Carny." This blog began in April 2006 and seems to have been abandoned in 2008. One of the entries dated December of 2006 begins,

> I find it ironic that my Carny life should end just as the curtain lowers on the Carny Culture of today, it's last dying exhale. The hard living, road happy people of yesterday are few and far between now, replaced with clean cut, drug free, South Africans or others the shows can import for cheap. Most of the big shows are owned by corporations now, not families anymore.[6]

Interestingly enough, the previous quote suggests that Morra is about to leave the carnie world; however his blog continues for another two years. The last entry he writes in 2008 does not express the same lament that this one does. Instead his last entry laments a carnie romance that ended with a girl named Sarah, whom he dated for two years despite their significant age difference. However, he expresses contempt at the outside hires later throughout his blog:

> Gone are the days when you worked your way up, season after season, sweating in the sun, setting up, tearing down, learning every inch of the ride until you got to the point you could "feel" when something was wrong. When you had "proved" yourself, you became the foreman.[7]

Beyond the importation of labor, he likens the change in carnie culture from the past fifty years to the change at the turn of the century.

> I suppose it was the same at the turn of the century, when the industrial age came along and mechanical rides replaced the

---

[6] Kevin Morra, "The Reason I Started this Blog." *Diary of a Carny* Blogspot, 24 Dec. 2006.
[7] Ibid.

sideshow tents and girlie shows, fortune tellers, tattoo artists, and soon dominated the Midway. I'm sure the Carnies of that era felt much the same way.[8]

I attempted to contact Kevin Morra to ask further questions, however, he has yet to respond to my email. This community of outliers seems to bond and feel a sense of comfort in their travel-based lives by knowing that the carnie life is not for everyone and that being a carnie means being a part of something greater. In one particularly reflective entry, dated October 2, 2006, Morra writes that although he doesn't have the white picket fence that his brothers have, "if you truly want to be unhappy, try doing what other people think you should be doing." He also writes that a

Carnival is a good place to hide, no one really gives a shit who you "really" are. You can give a fake name, fake SSN, I know all the tricks. No one will find you if you don't want to be found, and no one in Carny land will ask too many questions.[9]

However, in a blog dated April 2007 he records a problem in the changing economy of the carnie.

Here's the problem, a major one for the new guys that have bought the Carnival world. They require background checks on new employee's, drug testing, and valid government ID ... The new "Rules" the corporation has put in place lock Carnies out in the cold, most of them can't pass a drug test, or a background check, sad but true. Locking them out was the intention. The corporation wants to really "Clean" things up they say, like they're so much fucking better, spare me.[10]

As stated earlier, Morra's relationship with his job, as many carnies, is a complicated one. Morra seems to transverse the philosophical territory between hating the injustice of pay and social exclusion and taking pride in this aspect of his work. In one entry dated April 2006, he criticizes the book *Memoirs of a Sword Swallower*, in which he writes,

His book is a quaint romanticized version of what Carny life was like in the forties and it's bullshit. I'll tell you why. Most of the people were treated and payed like dogs, even worse

---

[8]Ibid.
[9]Morra, "Where I Fit In," *op. cit.*, 2 Oct. 2006.
[10]Morra, "My Prediction," *op. cit.*, 24 April 2007.

than they are nowadays, so I highly fucking doubt that the characters he describes in his book felt all that romantic about it. They were just barely surviving, and I'm willing to bet that they would rather have been doing something else, but they were misfits, and couldn't last at anything else in the normal world. I'm not just talking about the freaks in his book, I'm also talking about the other Carnies too.[11]

The discontent with pay and lodging is repeated throughout his entries. He also writes about the rough life of carnies. He writes about drug use (specifically marijuana when he directly refers to 'shake' at one point, which is the tail-end, stems of a bag of marijuana)[12] and alcohol, as well as about fights he has been in.

In addition to this, he also writes about the experience of sex on the carnival lot. His blog frequently laments all of the one-night-stands he had and all the children that he could have that he will never know. Like all of his blog, he writes about his sex life with a distant, removed, and remorseful tone. About one one-night-stand he writes, "we finally ended up at a motel fucking the night away. In the wee hours of the morning I told her I needed to go get cigarettes, and I never went back.... I didn't give a shit about her. That's the way I was in those days. A fucking prick."[13] The same callous, yet, remorseful language and attitude is used when describing "lot lizards." "Lot lizards" are women who have had the worst end of the carney experience possible. Women who "are runaway girls...working on a ride, getting paid shit, and trying to survive off shake...[and] four dollars a day in change."[14]He writes about one specific woman he remembers who had "fucked and sucked her way across the country on the Carnival, that's how she survived, that and shake."[15] This sad picture of a woman destroyed by a life of poverty is not the first thing that non-carnies tend to think of when picturing carneys. As desperate a picture as lot lizards create, Morra does not condemn just the carny world for these conditions. In the entry "So You Wanna Be A Carny," he records a story of one summer when he left the carnival to hitchhike on his own. He wrote,

I met every kind of weirdo you can fucking imagine that summer. I found it interesting how some seemingly "Normal People" act when they think they will never see you again and that

---

[11]Morra, "Memories of a Sword Swallower," *op. cit.*, April 2006.

[12]Morra, "Lot Lizards," *op. cit.*, 21 April 2006.

[13]Morra, "The Things that Haunt Me," *op.cit.* 26 April, 2006.

[14]Morra, "Lot Lizards," *loc. cit.*

[15]Ibid.

no one gives a shit about you. I had "seemingly nice" old guys wanting to suck my cock, wanting me to suck their cock, all the while showing me pictures of their wife and kids, talking about what a good life they had. I spent a lot of hours riding in vehicles with "normal looking" fucking weirdoes. I returned to the Carnival after that summer. It's a lot safer, and it's home."[16]

Diary of a Carny seems to be a fairly well read blog in the carnie community. Kevin Morra was interviewed by Wayne Keyser on the Ballycast.com website in 2008. *Ballycast* is a blog which promotes itself as *Ballycast! Blog and Podcast of the Carnival, Sideshow, and Burlesque.*[17] The blog posts interviews with current entertainers as well as living past entertainers. This blog represents an interesting insight into the relatively current world of carnies. One interview dated February 4, 2008 is an interview with Lady Aye of the Pyrate Sister's Bump 'n Grind House. The interview introduced Lady Aye as a woman

> … who's cooked up a unique combination of burlesque and side show arts. She does the glass walking and straight jacket strip tease, block head, and more. Her associates do the stripping, and sometimes a narrator ties it all together framed as a 1950s b-movie horror flick in a magical combination called the Bump 'n Grind House.[18]

The same "Episode #10–Lady Aye" page contains a link to an interview with The Amazing Vanteen, a promotion of the website about the exploits of Vanteen, the magician of 40 years who died in 2006.[19] Later on the page there is a "carny food recipe" for a Long Island iced tea, which calls for a "scant jigger" of several of the ingredients. The entire *Ballycast* website contains over forty interviews with various carnies who have been working in the business for decades. This archive of interviews shows the continuation of the carnie folk tradition despite the vast changes it has undergone over the past

---

[16]Morra, "So You Wanna Be a Carney?" *op. cit.* 26 April, 2006.

[17]Wayne Keyser, "Episode #11–Kevin Morra of 'Diary of a Carny," *Ballycast: The Blog and Podcast of the Carnival, Side Show, and Burlesque*, 15 Feb., 2008.

[18]Keyser, "Episode #10–Lady Aye," *op. cit.*, 4 Feb., 2008.

[19]*The Amazing Vanteen*. Website. n.d. http://vanteen.tripod.com/.

century. *Ballycast* (as well as Wikipedia) also has a glossary of "carny terms," or terms used only by carnies. This cant is an important part of the construct of the carnie identity and will be explored later in this paper.

As stated earlier, carnies are a group who turn profit off their status as outliers from society. They do this not only by being physiologically different from the majority of society (such as "freaks"), but also by having a different lifestyle. Circuses and carnivals traditionally travel through part of the year, but tend to have a home base when they settle for part of the year. Carnivals and fairs abide by seasons, traveling in the summer and dissipating in the winter. In his article, "The Carny in the Winter," Donald J. Ward analyzed the Los Angeles carnie folk group during the off (or winter) season. His main informant's name was Ronald Burke, a carney (as is his father). Ward's article reports that the carneys he studied are male, can vary in age from young to elderly, but are mostly middle aged. His article says that their backgrounds in education and social standing vary, and that all the carnies he interviewed enjoy their way of life.[20] Ward also reports that the carneys are able to sell anything, and that they have a unique language in which to communicate with other carnies so that non-carnies do not understand. This language, called "carnie" has frequently been referred to as "Z-Latin" or "carney Pig Latin."[21] The cause of this titling is that the base construct of this language is as follows:

> Carnie adds [iəz] (which he represents orthographically as eeiz) to only the first syllable of words beginning with a consonant, an option that we mentioned earlier occurs only rarely, he makes no provision for words beginning with a vowel.[22]

The article goes on to say that some carnie languages have an "'utterly meaningless phrase' a *suissant a leeizali* at the ends of sentences 'to confuse the hearer.'"[23] Carnie is generally spoken either to exclude and haze beginning level carnies or used so carnies can communicate a scam to each other without their target (or 'mark' as they call them) understanding their plans. However based on the article "The Life and Death of Carnie", the most prominent use of carnie died out after the 1960s, when knowledge and understanding of carnie became widespread knowledge. My fieldwork supports this; the oldest person I interviewed could not recall any language that carneys used that was unique. The language Carnie takes

---

[20]Donald J. Ward, "The Carny in the Winter" *Western Folklore* 21. 3 (July 1962): 190.
[21]Carol L. Russell and Thomas E. Murray, "Life and Death of Carnie," *American Speech* 79 (Winter 2004): 406.
[22]Ibid. 404.
[23]Ibid.

two forms. The first is the use of Carnie as a language, and the second is the carnie vocabulary, as explored by Louise M. Ackerman in her article "Carnival Talk." Some words carnies use include,

> PIG IRON—The metal construction parts of the rides which are reassembled at each new location, GRIFT or FLAT JOINT—a dishonest concession, PATCH—an advance man who squares things with local authorities so that trouble does not develop after the carnival is on location.[24]

The invention of their own language, as well as the fact that they profit off of confusing non-carnie 'marks' shows not only their decided exclusion from society, but also their profit from it.

The separation from society was no secret, in fact it constructs part of the magical illusion that carnivals have. If carnivals did not have the strange allure of the fantastic, the otherworldly, and perhaps even of the sleazy, they would not be carnivals. One of my informants recalled that "it seemed to be the place to go if you were a freak, sort of out of the ordinary."[25] Carnies took what excluded them from society and used it to form their own society. Through the course of my research, I was not able to find much academic research about lore surrounding carnies. However, based on my fieldwork, there seems to be a distinct idea that non-carnies have of carnies. In the process of my fieldwork in order to protect the dignity and privacy of my informants I offered the option to remain anonymous. Also, I structured my questions so that they do not elicit mention of either sexually deviant or illegal material. I included in my interview release form a section where the interviewee could write in their own "restriction description."

When interviewing non-carnies about their experiences at the carnivals, carneys seemed the most distant part of their memories. The goal carneys have of distancing themselves from society works. When asked about what my interviewees liked most or remembered best about the carnivals in their past the most common responses were fried foods (such as fried Oreos, cheesecake, pickles, and funnel cake), beer, rickety rides (most come with a name having something to do with twisting, for example "The Scrambler" or "The Octopus" or "The Mixer"), and winning shoddy prizes from seemingly rigged games for three times face value. One particularly memorable story involved a three day carnival in Effingham, Illinois from VL (name redacted). As a child she went to the

---

[24]In *American Speech* 35.4 (December 1960): 309.
[25]J.C. interview, 11 Nov. 2010.

fair all three days, and every day tried to win a goldfish. On the final day of the fair one year, after she had won only one goldfish, the carney ended up giving her all of the leftover goldfish. She took all 20 goldfish home with her and put them in a bowl, only to find all of them dead the next morning. VL mentioned in her story that she remembered thinking it seemed desperate of the carneys to give away all the fish, and wondered why they did not take them to the next town. That was, until she saw them dead in the morning.

Carneys tended not to come up unless the interviewee was prompted with a direct question. In all of the interviews I asked my interviewees to describe the physical appearance of a carney. All of the responses I received stated that carneys were creepy, smoking, tattooed, dirty, poor, men who weren't to be trusted. The only term I could think to categorize such stereotyping of this category of people was racism, yet carneys adhere to no one specific ethnicity, and are only bonded by their lifestyle choice, employment, and perhaps social class. Several interviewees prefaced their descriptions with disclaimer-statements such as, "This is kind of a harsh description." One interviewer, D.H., stated that carnies:

> seemed very insular. You know, it's...this sounds mean... but it's a skill-less [job] for people who didn't manage to do something else. So in that sense they're very much replaceable. However, it's kind of like the migrant workers who pick the fruit. Anybody can do it, but who the fuck wants to go work in a carnival or go pick fruit?[26]

Clearly the distance between the carney and non-carney societies exists based on very real tensions. However, the interviewee responsible for that statement was also the only interviewee who had ever had any contact with someone who did actually run off and join the carnival. He told me the story of a friend of his named Judge, whose girlfriend left him one summer to join the carnival that annually passed through their hometown of Birch, Missouri. Judge was lamenting the loss of his girlfriend to my interviewee, and when he tried to comfort him, Judge offered the simple

---

[26]Interview with D.H.

lament, "It happens." Kevin Morra addresses the carney/non-carney social view with the following quote.

> We hate society as much as they hate us, we call them lo-
> cals, they call us Carnies, scammers, losers...and a lot of other
> names I suppose. Some give us a hard time, they're always
> watching, on the lookout for us to rip them off. We all drank,
> too much, did too many drugs, and fucked too much at one
> time or another; what's left is what you see when we come to
> your town.[27]

After a relatively long inter-view, I asked one of my intervie-wees (a 22 year old male) if he had ever had a personal interac-tion with a carney. To which he replied, "You know ... I don't think I've ever actually had a conversa-tion with one. Which is regret-table."[28] The trend amongst non-carneys seems to set carneys in the fuzzy backdrops of their rosy mem-ories of their days at the carnival. I theorize that the reason for this resides in the second-order nostal-gia that people feel for the magic of carnivals from the turn of the cen-tury. Even carneys themselves feel nostalgia (in some ways) for the days when the magic seemed more real and the illusion was better maintained. Society's—both carney's and not—vague memory of magic seems to be supported by the will to suspend re-ality in the face of brightly colored lights. The fieldwork I have collected exhibits that whether or not carnivals have changed over the past fifty years, both carneys and non-carneys believe in a semi-romanticized idea of the carnivals in the past. The reality of the contemporary carney life explored in this paper is so separate from the shows that they put on—the carnivals they construct—that non-carney lore about them, while some-what accurate, just barely scratches the surface of what their culture is.

As the twinkling lights of the carnival *that was* dull like the slowing turn of a dying carousal, a new, brighter, light takes on the past magic

---

[27] Kevin Morra, *Diary of a Carny*. Blogspot. n.d.
[28] Interview with G.P., 9 Nov. 2010.

of the carnival. This new bright light is television. Today it is politically unacceptable to host "freak shows" as they did one-hundred years ago. However, since our desire for 'at-shows' and freak shows are not being satisfied by carnivals they have manifested themselves in television; a setting twice removed from the actual situation. When asked what they thought the modern freak show was, one of my interviewees brought up *The Jerry Springer Show* and reality television as her idea of the modern freak show. Jerryspringertv.com (the official *Jerry Springer Show* website) advertises the episodes "Trannys Throwdown" and "You Slept With a Porn Star," which sell elements of sexual promiscuity and strangeness to their audience, much like a carnival. Reality T.V shows people in situations different from, and generally more desperate than, their own—and makes a show out of their lives. I would not, however, argue that the folk-group carney has shifted to include television personnel. Carney is a profession and lifestyle choice that is inextricably linked to the job of working at a carnival, fair, festival, or circus. However, television provides an outlet for observing our fellow humans at their strangest without the stigma of 'freak' attached to them.

My intent in collecting this research is to set it against the true accounts and history of the carnies that I have already compiled. One photo database that I have found extremely useful is called *Black and WTF*.[29] This is a photo archive of old black and white photos that have either been found in thrift/antique stores, that people had in their homes, or that are from other online archives. All of the photos display strange out-of-the-norm behaviors, and many of them depict carnivals. All of the photos in this essay, except for the first one, are pulled from this website. The first one is from the *Amazing Vanteen* website, http://vanteen.tripod.com/.

After my extensive fieldwork, I find myself revisiting my own memories of carnivals. The newly researched information does not change the memories that I have. Instead it puts the memories into a new context. The carnival has throughout history been a means of escape, both for carneys and non-carneys. However, the carnival is just that—an idea. Non-carneys remember carnivals with carneys in the background because their escape doesn't include knowing how the carnival was assembled or who did it; and the carneys hide in the background assembling the carnivals for precisely the same reason—to hide from the outside world. The carnival as a means of escape has created a symbiotic relationship between carneys and non-carneys, which is exemplified by the way both carneys and non-carneys remember and talk about carnivals.

---

[29] See blackandwtf.tumbler.com.

Bibliography

Ackerman, Louise M. "Carnival Talk." *American Speech* 35 (December 1960) 308-309.

American Carny: True Tales from the Circus Sideshow. Dir. Nick Basile, Perf. Jillette, Penn, Todd Robbins, Ses Carny, The Great Nippulini, Simon Lovell, Chris McDaniel, Jennifer Miller, Harley Newman, David Oliver, James Taylor. Cinema Epoch, 2007. Film.

"Amazing Vanteen." *The Amazing Vanteen-Magician*, vanteen.tripod.com/. Web.

Anders, Helen. "Joining the Circus? Here's How That Works!" *The Statesman.* 18 August 2010. Web.

Black and WTF. blackandwft.tumblr.com/. Web.

"Carnytown News & Business Network." carnytown.com/main/. Web.

Chemers, Michael M. *Staging Stigma: A Critical Examination of the American Freak Show*. New York: Palgrave Macmillian, 2008.

"Discover More!" *Ringling Bros. And Barnum and Baliey; The Greatest Show on Earth!* www.ringling.com/. Web.

"The Fabulous Mr. Ripley." *Ripley's Believe It or Not!* www.ripleys.com/mr-ripley/. Web.

Keyser, Wayne. "Episode #11—Kevin Morra of *Diary of a Carny*." *Ballycast: The Podcast of the Carnival, Sideshow, and Burlesque.* 15 Feb. 2008. Web.

Morra, Kevin. *Diary of a Carny.* diary-of-a-carny.blogspot.com/ Web.

Prosterman, Leslie. "Food and Alliance at the County Fair." *Western Folklore* 40 (January 1981) 81-90.

Russel, Carol L, and Thomas E. Murray. "The Life and Death of Carnie." *American Speech* 79 (Winter 2004) 400-416.

Thurston, John. "Origins: Carnie Talk." *Writers Block*. www.writersblock.-ca/fall 2001/origins.htm. Web.

Ward, Donald J. "The 'Carny' in the Winter." *Western Folklore* 21 (July 1962) 190-192.

Interviews

Non-formal interviews: 9/19 interview, 5 minutes, 44 seconds

- Cuba, Missouri, the juggaloes, cult following.
- Carnivals scare me because the carnies assemble the rides.
- when he got older saw rednecks groping their girlfriends inappropriately
- 'feelin' each other up'

Non-formal interview: 12/19 interview, 7 minutes

- "Creepy"
- "Carnies scary, poor, and have no teeth…spinney rides…hometown in Illinois….I definitely feel like they have a culture because they hang out all the time."

Interview with JC, age 57, November 9, 2010

R: "Ruby Jenkins recording for her folklore paper about the life of the carnival

J, "I'm (name deleted), 57 years old, not 58, I grew up in a rural town, pop. about 5,000, mostly an agricultural based town not that I lived on a farm, but it was a rural community. Grew up in the 50s or 60, you know. And just when the circus or carnival came to town it was THE thing to do. And I remember that you could even go watch them set up. You could watch them unload the elephants and people would put up these amazing tents, in like an hour's time, and it was unbelievable how they could do that. And they did it probably done it hundreds of times a year and everyone knew their part. And up it went and you could watch the elephants. And once the tent was up, someone would give elephant rides.

R. Like immediately afterward?

J. Yep. Once their job was done. Then someone would. And you would walk up this ladder, and two or three people could ride at one time, and yeah. It was neat. That was the thing to do.

R. And did you grow up around here?

J. Southern Illinois

R. And how were carnivals received in your community? Like, you said when the carnival came to town you're saying the thing to do was exciting…

J. Well the carnival coming to town was diff than the county fair. The county fair had carnival rides and amusement parts,... it had amusement, but when it was just the carnival coming to town... that was just awesome. You could go and buy tickets, and I'm sure my mom and dad gave us a dollar which would buy tons of ticket, and you would just ride and ride and ride. Then you'd puke and it was time to go home. The county fair was different because you had you four age groups.

R. Four age groups? What are those?

J. Four age groups are, future farmers and they ran different projects that they worked on like livestock, cooking, canning... you know. . . .

R. Yeah, you're fine...

[Blank space and ruffling sounds]

[Continued interview with JC, 14/19 20 minutes 27seconds]

R. Continuation with JC's interview. I have a couple questions, easy straight forward, I think you've already answered some of them. How often would you go to these carnivals? And how often would they come to town

J. I don't know, it seemed like once a year.... I don't know but I'm sure they had a schedule.

R. Right. Did the carnival have a name?

J. You know, I don't know it. I'm sure there was.... it wasn't like Ringley's Barnum and Bailey's type thing, it was some cheaper version that would travel.

R. It's interesting... the carnival, I'm sure they do.... When they come to town would you go there once a day or... how often would you go?

J. Oh yeah they might be there three or four days, but yeah it was the build-up; you had to be really good.

R. What did your parents think of you going to the carnivals?

J. Well, you know they would hold that over our heads, like "okay!..." We probably got a dollar to go. We were old enough to go on our own, we were 10,11, or 12, but our parents never worried about it, you know it was a different time. You know now I would never dream of letting my kids' 10, 11, 12 year old girl go. But you know.... It was always implied that you should never talk to, never um, never be involved working with the carnival. That ... I can't remember her saying that they were ever bad. It was just ...

R. Implied. Do you remember any specific ways it was implied? Or how this implication affected your view of the workers at the carnival?

J. Hm... I just, no. Course they never would have talked to us the way you
   would talk to a child nowadays.

R. How was it different?

J. Well, sex was never discussed; it was hard enough for parents in the
   fifties and sixties to talk about menstruation, you know. My parents
   just gave me a box with all the information in it, you know... nor
   would they have discussed child abduction or child abuse or the
   child being molested or anything like that. I may be extremely
   naive; I know it was happening in the fifties and sixties ... but they
   would never discuss it with us. They just simply said do not ever
   talk to or...

R. Did you ... you said that your parents would never discuss sex with you,
   and was that when you were older? 3:22

Interview with GP, Age 22, November 9, 2010

Lisbon, Iowa – Sauerkraut Days

0.00 Every day visit, young with friends and old with "the creepy carney...
   that weird guy at the balloon throwing stand" talk of "rigged game."
   G and his friends theorized that the guy who ran the coin pushing
   stand fixed it so they wouldn't know. G's view of carneys "more
   or less ... these are kinda harsh descriptions ... dirty people, not
   well kept, rude, smokers, lots of time missing teeth, slightly creepy.
   Those were, like, my perceptions. And typically any type of carney
   story was along those lines." Says that describes who works at the
   carnival

5.30 G says "creepy" generally tends to apply to men with a tendency
   towards sexual pushiness (rape); "quiet" is a part of the creepy atmosphere. "They're quiet they're never really paying attention to
   you ... that's why they're creepy I guess. I never really witnessed
   any gesture or comment or anything that really gave me like a solid
   reason to be like 'wow, that guy is creepy.'"

7.00 The creepy people didn't affect his wish to be at the carnival, but it
   did give it a different stigma. Associates with circuses, interesting
   but with a weird atmosphere with weird people who can do weird
   skin-stretching tricks. Weird unexplained air of mystery ...

8.31 Circus was more artistic and with more talent and skill obviously.
   Like a show rather than a service.... I guess that's the main difference. Both diff, they're both a traveling type thing.

9.20 R. Were women carneys/creepy? G. Well, I could be wrong, but
   I think I remember predominantly males being employees.... Fe-

males ran the games and not so much the rides. I can't really think of any times that I thought "wow that woman is creepy."

10.15 R. what was your fave ride? G. Oh yeah, the mixer. The whole thing went around in circles and each arm went around in circles; then you could make you individual car go around in circles... R. Fave game? G. Oh yeah, throw a balloon and win 5x5 glossy images in cheap clear glass frames with images in them like Michael Jackson and Space Jam or *Sports Illustrated* models.... And you could win if you waited for the carney 'guy' to start the games again and refill the board and it was easy to hit them.

14 Description of the fair, beer tent and community based stuff on one side of the main street, then the other side of the main street would be the traveling stuff like the games, rides, and some of the food stands.

17.3 Mm... personal interaction... only to the extent of being handed a prize. I don't think I ever had a conversation with any of the.... Yeah. Which is kinda regrettable. Yeah.

Interview with VL, age 21, Lake St. Louis Missouri

0.17 Three night carnival. First night noticed that there was a game where you could win these goldfish. 1st night, one gold fish, second night no gold fish. Last night they were giving them away and so we took them home and put them in a mason bowl thinking that tomorrow we'd get them an aquarium of sorts. And in the morning, all 20 of them were dead. There were a lot of them. I haven't really trusted carnival games since. (3.33) Why don't the goldfish go with them instead of with us to die?

1.27 I was between the ages of 6 and 8, um. I remember I thought it was desperate of the carnies to give all these fish away because I knew they were going away. I thought they could just give them away to the next county, but....

2.1 I remember people saying that the carnival rides were dangerous because they're not as established or safe ... people like her parents.... The carnival was like a yearly thing, Effingham Carnival. The carnival didn't have a name. It was the same fair because I remember the same "scrambler" ride

4.3 V. 'By virtue of calling someone a carney it has a negative connotation, but I don't know where I heard that. I remember feeling like I knew how the carnival was supposed to be ... but I don't know where I first encountered that. I don't have any specific encounter with a carney....

5.28 My boyfriend at fine arts academy in high school, he met this guy Jed or something who had to leave his hometown or else; he'd go away with the carnies. He was from 'Go all the way down to the boot heel and then turn around, and that's his town.'

6.55 Terminology? I probably wouldn't call someone a carney. Like 'the way you don't call someone a queer, you don't call someone a carny.'

9.3 I'm sure there is some drug use and some violence in the culture... but it seems more old time-y. Now it seems more like fun entertainment instead of mystery and intrigue

10.33 There are not freak shows at carnivals, like, you're not supposed to notice that anymore. It's not politically correct to notice someone being a freak but... someone being put on display... I think maybe television has taken on that role. Like you can watch Jerry Springer say, 'My 500-lb wife loves me but is cheating on me with a woman'

11.31 I guess in that respect would you think that it still remains in a certain social class? V. In a freak show what would be considered a freak, like super tall women, I don't immediately associate with a certain class. Bearded women, I don't think of super rich women being bearded because they have the financial ability to remove disability.

12.3 The lady at JC Penny with a beard. Not lore about her, just comments about her. Don't assume social class.... She's a lady with a beard. More than one inch.

13.4 What about Discovery Channel shows like 'Siamese Twins!'? But it makes it okay because you're learning about it.

14.54 R. Are you alright with me using this in my paper? VL. Oh, yes.

Interview with DH, age 23, Lake St. Louis Missouri

0.00 Fried food, fried Oreos, fried cheesecake, fried pickles, beer, anything on a stick that smells like cholesterol

2.3 JB (name redacted), from Birch, Missouri in the bootheel of Missouri. STORY. DH knew JB from fine arts academy over the summer a few years ago. While missing and talking about their significant others, JB got kinda bummed out. He got very sad one day about halfway through, and he explained that every year a little circus or whatever it was comes through his town and inevitably several people leave with them. Go on the road with the carneys. It's a thing that happens every year.

3.44 I don't know why, I can't imagine that they travel anywhere other than shitty little towns like Birch Missouri, I mean there's not a great call for them in Madison Square Garden, BUT his girlfriend had left town with the carnival and had, like, left him a note that his mom, like, read to him over the phone or something. Or like written him a letter, years ago ... but he was just really depressed and I remember that quite vividly because I tried to pin the story down from him because his girlfriend effectively ran away with the circus ... and I remember his face because it was so sad but just accepting; he just kinda goes, 'it happens.' And that's amazing to me!

5.00 R. Is there some sort of romantic allure of the carnival? DH. I don't think it's fair to say that there is a romantic allure anymore. I think the allure in this particular situation is the desperation of someone wanting to leave the situation they were in. The lure of the carnival that we all go to is very much a lure of the past. I mean, you never go to a carnival and play the latest laser tag game or the latest in virtual reality. You go there to win rigged games for crappy little stuffed animals and eat down-home deep-fried foods and ride rickety old rides that haven't been approved since the '50s. It's very much something yearning for the middle of America in the past or perhaps the boardwalks of the coasts ... in you know, 50s, 40s, 60s.

6.05 Definitely [more of a romantic allure in the past (in response to R. question)]. Well, I mean, the carnivals of the old days were like the state fairs. They used to be something that people would travel hundreds and hundreds to do that, and that was a big thing state wide. Nowadays the people that live around there, the places being held that go to it, and the people who go to it regardless of being held. It used to be like the World's Fairs. Think of Coney Island then versus today. When it was shiny and new and exciting and a hot dog was a nickel and now it's.... You find puke everywhere you go and it's broken down... burned out. Disneyworld they do a really good job. [Interjection from VL.] On the first day of Disney world the concrete was so hot that people's shoes went through it...

7.40 R. In relation to hyperreality and amusement parks in America today, how do you think that relates to carnivals today? Would you still call someone who works at Disney world a carney? Even though they're a part of this fantastical super reality? Or are they something that belongs in a different category? D. Different category because it falls into the category of Six Flags where one time I had a birthday party and we rode the train and every person there waved and I remember quite vividly asking one 'do they make you do this?' and he just nodded. And I think the difference there is the static, very corporate, feel where as you know, it's a brand. Where a carnival is a nameless red and white stripped tent that periodically comes and goes.

8.40 I mean, I would say the romance of it is gone 'cause especially when you think of how many horror scenes have been set there, like *Something Wicked This Way Comes*. Um... and I mean ... who isn't terrified of carnival fun houses or carnival clowns? It seems to me that there is an unknowable aspect of it and that's what I think contributes to the allure and dangerous aspect of it.

9.03 I went to a carnival when I was between 5-8, years ago, Missouri State Fair? My parents thought that ... my parents were big into baseball cards ... and I really wasn't. My grandpa used to give us good valuable cards. And I went to the carnival and played this shooting game and won the big prize, and I remember that I wanted this big stuffed animal, but my parents didn't want to carry it around so instead they got this sealed box of baseball cards and like, it was huge. I mean, BIG box of baseball cards. All kinds of different designs and stuff.... . I don't know what's valuable in baseball cards ... but it was special. A big collection. And to this day this box of baseball cards, I wasn't allowed to open it ... and to this day it sits in one of my cabinets in my room, unopened.

10.39 Crushed under stuff over the years. And I remember that one very vividly. Now if there were any recurring ones I went to ... I doubt it.

11.00 R. What do you think it adds to the atmosphere of the carnival—the idea of the carney as a gift giver? D. Well, he's not a gift giver. You didn't even earn it. You pay three times face value to overcome some rigged challenge and they give it to you out of sympathy. As a child I think all the glittering light and all the strange, just, foreign-ness of going to buildings made out of plastic, and people, you know, instead of giving people money, you give them tickets... . You know, it distances you from the fact that you're spending money by making it a third unusable currency.

11.56 You interject this third, middle currency that is beyond worthless that they can't even use.

12.07 I did go to one recurring carnival, my St. Patrick's carnival. It's in the basement of the church that I went to.

12.30 R. It sounds like the act of receiving relatively useless things is a big part of carnivals for you. How would you associate carneys as a part of this memory? Attitudes you had towards them? Were they more of a backdrop for...? D. They seemed very insular. You know, it's, this sounds mean... but it's a skill-less [job] for people who didn't manage to do something else. So in that sense they're very much replaceable. However, it's kind of like the migrant workers who pick the fruit. Anybody can do it, but who the fuck wants to go work in a carnival or go pick fruit?

13.11 R. And from that you have the saying, 'Run off and join the carnival'? Where do you think that comes from? D. JB's girlfriend. I think it comes from this desire that comes from the 40s, 50s, 60s, where, you know, people didn't travel very much.... People who lived in Missouri didn't end up living in California. And the carnival was a way to travel, if not great distances, [at least] out of the situations that they're in. So I mean, in that sense I think the lure of the carnival has faded except in these shitty little towns, because people do.... The world is smaller than it used to be.

14.00 I don't remember how the carnivals were received in my town. My parents were always really pissed at the amount of money I spent on the unwinnable games. The amount of crap food covered in sugar I would ingest in the course of the day. And on the rare occasion that I would come home with something I won, it was something huge and unwieldy and like impossible to get into the car–like 100 glasses or 32 goldfish or a huge stuffed animal.... You know it was always something impossible to transport. I never won 32 goldfish. The one goldfish I did win my parents poured it out in the parking lot and said it would be better that way. My parents were not good people.

15.00 No idea how often I went to carnivals. Difference between a renaissance fair and a carnival—they're both cultures gone by... but there are less wife-beaters at a "Ren Fair."

16.00 I feel like carnivals are a celebration of everything tacky, and you know, cheap fun, regardless of how much they cost.

16.21 I think you could dispense with carnivals tomorrow and roughly an 8th of the population would give a shit.... I'm saying not a lot of people would care if we didn't have carnivals anymore, but we would probably lose something. What that is, I'd be hard pressed to say. Even if it is just the opportunity to eat, you know, fried dough slathered in sugar.

17.02 R. Do you feel carneys have their own culture? D. I don't know. The fact that they're relocating their township from place to place, and the fact that they would spend so much time together, they're a closeknit group. I mean ... what takes a group from, you know, friendships and habits and traditions, into a cultural aspect? Is it time? ... Is it validation from an outside source?

18.00 In that sense if it's a family carnival, people who have been doing it for generations, then it's very much a culture. As it is, I think we have a culture in America of things that are really replaceable and trash-able and the culture of the carnival very much fits into that. We have a culture of instant gratification. I think carnival culture epitomizes the extremes of American culture. You have the capitalistic function... but also cheap and tawdry, with easy access, that Americans love. There is very little highbrow carnivals.

20.45 When normal people in the early years and today look back on sideshow freaks and think, 'Oh, these poor exploited people,' [they forget] these were the only jobs people could get and they made a lot of money in relative comfort and were among people who understood, treated, and cared for them. Um ... I think nowadays it's any teenager who doesn't feel like going past or even graduating high school can... I mean... there're jobs. They're not great jobs. And nowadays it's cheap labor, high profit. The commoditization of carnies, yeah it's definitely happening.

22.00 R. Do you think the freak show still exists in modern America? What form has it taken? D. Well, there's daytime talk shows. There's reality TV; there's awkwardfamilyphotos.com. ... Human nature, and especially in America where we either desire to be so famous and beautiful that we are in the top 1% or mundane enough to be in the middle 50—we don't want to be in that lower quadrant. And we seek out ways to make ourselves feel better. Whether it be by watching *The Biggest Loser* to say 'Haha, I'm more in shape than those fuckers,' or .... Then, by the end of it you feel awful and maybe motivated to get off your ass.... I mean today we watch morons and assholes on tv.... I mean, we watch it in different ways.

23.00 We don't go to a tent but we don't have to. It's piped directly into our tvs and living rooms. R. Do you think TV has changed the idea of the carnival since we don't have to leave our homes? D. Television, no. Technology yes.

24.00 DH, 23, English major Truman State U, grew up in Lake St. Louis, is comfortable with me using this in a paper. "I'm okay with that."

24.45 Bearded lady with disease who works at JC Penney.

This does not cover all of my interviews. But these are the interviews in which I found the most relevant information. RJ

Handout

The handout reproduced on the next two pages was designed for a Folklore Colloquium presentation in December 2010. RJ

December 4, 2010   Ruby Jenkins

The Life of the Carnival: Carney Lore and the People Who Bring Life to the American Carnival

Who Are the Carneys?
- Three different spellings: Carney, Carnie, Carny
- Work at all manifestations of the carnival:
- Circus (for example Barnum and Bailey), "at-shows" (feats of strength/physical contortion shows), freak shows and side shows ("particular kind of show or exhibit that developed in mid 1800s under P. T Barnum featuring dancing girls magic acts and human oddities" ("Life and Death of a Carnie").
- Many carnivals have become institutionalized, yet the traveling carneys that my blog field-work focuses on show similar discontent within the smaller carney arena.
- People who assemble, own, and maintain rides and serve food.
- Donald J. Ward (past director of Comparative Folklore and Mythology studies at UCLA) defines carneys as typically "men" who work at carnivals, (however, there are female carneys, at least today).
- Kevin Morra, current carny and blog author of "Diary of a Carny"
- My research focuses on carneys from the last century.

Kevin Morra "Who Cares?"
- Contemporary Carney
- "Diary of a Carney" 2006-2008
- Complex relationship with employment
- States, "Gone are the days when you worked your way up, season after season, sweating in the sun, setting up tearing down, learning every inch of the ride until you got to the point you could "feel" when something was wrong. When you had 'proved' yourself, you became the foreman."
- Social exclusion, bad pay, drugs ("shake"), alcohol, casual yet remorseful attitude about sex.
- "Lot Lizards" - "runaway girls…working on a ride, getting paid shit, and trying to survive off shake …[and] four dollars a day in change."

- "Normal People" Morra left the carnival one summer and instead hitchhiked across the country…
- "I found it interesting how 'normal people' act when they think they will never see you again and that no one gives a shit about you. I have 'seemingly nice' old guys wanting to suck my cock or wanting me to suck theirs all while showing me pictures of the wife and kids, talking about what a good life they have…I returned to the carnival after that summer. It's a lot safer, and it's home."

Ballycast, Ringling Brothers, Lady Eye
Carney the language:
- Donald Ward and Los Angeles carnies off season, "The Carny in the Winter"
- "Z-Latin" also called "Carnie" or "Carney Pig Latin."
- Adds [iəz] to only the first syllable of words beginning with a consonant
- "Suissant A leeizali"
- "Marks" the word carnies use for non-carnies they are attempting to sells something to.

Non Carneys:
- Carnivals = Fried Foods + Beer
- Rickety rides, usually about twisting "The Scrambler" or "The Mixer"
- Prizes - The thrill of winning something useless. Goldfish
- Carneys not mentioned by non-carney interviewees until prompted.
- Carneys are "creepy, smoking, tattooed, dirty, poor, men" who weren't to be trusted.

The distance between us and them…

"We hate society as much as they hate us, we call them locals, they call us Carnies, scammers, losers… and a lot of other names I suppose. Some give us a hard time, they're always watching, on the lookout for us to rip them off. We all drank, too much, did too many drugs, and fucked too much at one time or another, what's left is what you see when we come to your town."

December 4, 2010   Ruby Jenkins

Television, the new Carnival; Jerry Springer and
beyond.

Bibliography:

Ackerman, Louise M. "Carnival Talk." American
    Speech 35 (December 1960) 308-309.
Boylan, Robert. *Black and WTF*. Driven by
    tumbler.com. http://blackandwtf.tumblr.com/.
    "Carnytown News & Business Network."
    http://carnytown.com/main.
Chemers, Michael M. Staging Stigma: A Critical
    Examination of the American Freak Show. New
    York: Palgrave Macmillian, 2008.
"Discover More!" *Ringling Bros. And Barnum and
    Bailey; The Greatest Show on Earth!*
    http://www.ringling.com/.
Jillette, Penn, Todd Robbins, Ses Carny, The Great
    Nippulini, Simon Lovell, Chris McDaniel,
    Jennifer Miller, Harley Newman, David Oliver,
    James Taylor. *American Carny: True Tales from
    the Circus Sideshow*. Directed by Nick Basile,
    2007.
Keyser, Wayne. "Ballycast; The Podcast of the
    Carnival, Sideshow, and Burlesque."
    http://ballycast.com/?p=30"
Morra, Kevin. "Diary of a Carny." http://diary-of-a-
    carny.blogspot.com/?zx=64b65412 c72b02d2.
Prosterman, Leslie. "Food and Alliance at the
    County Fair." Western Folklore 40 (January 1981)
    81-90.
Russel, Carol L, and Thomas E. Murray. "The Life
    and Death of Carnie." *American Speech* 79
    (Winter 2004) 400-416.
"The Fabulous Mr. Ripley." *Ripley's Believe It or
    Not!* http://www.ripleys.com/mr-ripley/.
Thurston, John. "Origins: Carnie Talk." Writers
    Block. http://www.writersblock.ca/fall
    2001/origins.htm
Ward, Donald J. "The "Carny" in the Winter."
    Western Folklore 21 (July 1962) 190-192.

Ruby Jenkins
email@truman.edu

Facial Cosmetics: Practices of Truman State University Students
Morgan Jones

In this 2015 study, the investigator was drawn to applying folklore to behaviors and artifacts so common as to be of no analytical interest. She tested cosmetics use and users for their susceptibility to analysis according to the rubrics applied by contemporary folklorists: conservation, variation, structural and functional analysis, emic and etic perspectives. The investigator took special interest in issues relating to investigator/informant status, which to her presented ambiguities. Of most interest to her were the categories that seemed to emerge spontaneously from the data. Broader social implications become prominent.

As a young woman who somehow managed to miss the makeup experience except for yearly or biannual dance recitals, I am quite interested in why women wear makeup, both the emic reasons—the reasons they themselves offer—and the underlying functional reasons which anthropologists have posited. I approached this project with several questions: where had I missed the transmission of knowledge about makeup? How do women apply makeup? Why do they do it? In order to complete this project, I had to set aside my preconceived notions about the "girly-girls" who wear makeup in order to learn about the behavior. I had a very low number of responses to my survey – unsurprising, given that not all women wear makeup and that men, most of whom do not utilize cosmetics, make up a certain percentage of Truman students who might otherwise have responded. I conducted eight interviews with girls I know who wear makeup.

Despite the small sample size, my informants contributed more data than I can completely discuss for this project, so I have chosen to mostly focus on the two broadest areas of interest to me: what girls do to make themselves up, and why they do it. My findings show that there is a spectrum of makeup practices which ranges from elaborate to basic and that there are three main focuses of the makeup routine: skin, eyes, and lips. The skin receives the most attention, followed by the eyes, and then the lips. I focused on each woman's daily makeup routine for an average day, and have defined this as the order in which they apply products and what kinds of products they apply (such as mascara, lipstick, etc.).

Methods

To conduct my survey, I used an online survey through Google Forms, a free format which allowed me to share the survey repeatedly on Facebook. When it was time to reap my responses, the program also gave me an easy option to put all of the responses into a Google spreadsheet. Additionally, I conducted interviews with any girls I thought might discuss makeup with me (convenience sampling) and whom I felt comfortable approaching (unfortunately, I am shy person, and found setting up interviews to be terrifying, though the interviews themselves were more enjoyable than I had anticipated).

I began by typing up as best as I could an informant's responses to my questions. Many of my informants were so enthusiastic that I was unable to keep up. After the first or second interview I began using a voice recording app on my phone to record the interviews. I kept the records for this project, but did not go back and transcribe the interviews word for word, because many of my informants expressed discomfort with the idea that they would be directly quoted (their responses would occasionally be populated with "um"s and "like"s, and they felt that direct quoting might make them sound shallow or unintelligent). I assured them I had no intention of utilizing direct quotes, as at the time I was having all I could do to get the gist of their answers down, and even then I often had to ask them to repeat themselves. To write my paper, I compiled handwritten drafts of my four interviews. I used color-coding and highlighting to find patterns and to indicate to myself the categories that seemed to be emerging. [*The transcripts were excluded from the final project published here. –Ed.*]

Analysis

Transmission

One way of thinking of folklore is as some knowledge or behavior passed from individuals to individuals. Taking this approach, it makes sense to begin with a brief overview of the sources from whom the informants learned the skills of makeup application. Of my fourteen informants, seven list mothers as a teacher or as one factor in their knowledge about makeup, and more discussed the mother in their responses about how they learned makeup. It was not uncommon for them to explain why they did not learn from her if that was the case.

It seems fairly common for girls to have turned to other sources of information if their mothers did not wear much makeup. Seven listed the internet, either blogs or online articles or YouTube—with YouTube being more common. Only two of those who reported the internet as an influence on their knowledge of makeup also listed their mother as a teacher. Internet influence was more likely to coincide with identifying as self-taught, learning through experimentation with friends, or being instructed by a friend. Three listed friends as sources of knowledge. Three listed themselves as self-taught. Only five listed a single source of knowledge about cosmetics. For the most part this knowledge seems to have been imparted through more than one source, and it seems likely that even the young women who responded with only one source have learned through other means, but that those means did not spring to mind at the time of their response.

A number of informants said they had only hazy recollections of being taught to use makeup or when they first began to wear it. This is an indication that wearing makeup is not a clearly demarcated rite of passage. However, makeup use on a regular basis begins in a defined window. Although informants may have earlier experience with it if they were dancers or involved with theater (further studies might explore the practice of stage makeup and its transmission), every informant gave their age when they first began to wear makeup regularly as being between twelve and fourteen years, although it was more common for informants to identify their age by grade or level of school at the time. The majority of informants began wearing makeup regularly in seventh or eighth grade. Only one informant stated that she did not wear makeup regularly until high school. There does not appear to be a correlation between starting age and what source transmitted the knowledge to them. The most relevant study I found suggests that using makeup is one way in which girls begin to create their individual selves as separate from their mothers, and the informants' ages at the time they began wearing makeup regularly seems to fit with that use (Gentina 117, 119). The means of transmission does not appear to impact the behavior which makes up a woman's daily cosmetics routine in terms of how many steps there are, what features they emphasize, and which kinds of products they use.

Routines

Conservation & Variation

There is a lot of variation in the everyday cosmetics routines of college students. However, there are patterns of conservation. Most informants use some sort of base to give themselves an even skin tone, even if they then highlight and darken it to recreate the contours and shadows/highlights of their face. Six report using foundation and concealer, four use some form of foundation, and two use a multipurpose product known as BB cream, something between a foundation and a moisturizer. There also seem to be three main areas of focus for makeup application: the skin of the overall face, the eye area, and the lips. The everyday makeup routines fall along a spectrum from basic to elaborate. Each end seems to have its own concerns, possibly indicating different, very slightly separated folk groups. It is possible that these slight variations are expressions of folk groups which are not based on or around makeup usage, but are based on having different customs regarding makeup, or different expectations regarding appearance. My data did not expand beyond an individual's use of makeup to the social groups they identify with, so I cannot be certain about this point.

The Spectrum

I developed the spectrum from Basic to Elaborate makeup practices based on patterns I perceived in the data and in everyday life. Some women do intense, dramatic makeup with unusual or vibrant colors and others do very light, subtle makeup so it can be difficult to tell if they are wearing any at all. My data supported this observation. Some informants use only two, three, or four makeup products with equal numbers of steps in their routines. These I categorized as Basic, at one polar end of the spectrum (the natural spectrum might in fact start even before Basic, including women like myself who wear no makeup on an ordinary day). In the middle I placed informants who use more products/steps than the Basic group, and informants who do more aesthetic shaping with their cosmetics, such as filling in eyebrows or applying blush to certain parts of the cheeks or face, which is more than the Basic group tends to do. On the opposite end of the spectrum from Basic, I placed the routines which I termed Elaborate. There were only three of these in my informant pool. They each have at least fourteen steps to their everyday routine, pay far more attention to aesthetic shaping than the group in the middle, and use more products. This was the most defined and obvious category I observed.

The Basics

There were seven women in the basic group, making it the largest. On this end of the spectrum, the routine focuses on two or three main areas. The first and most important is the overall face, as marked by the application of foundation or similar products. The women in this group are more likely to forgo concealer and do not use BB cream in their everyday routine. However, two of them do use concealer. One uses only foundation, concealer, and powder. The other will wash her face, apply lotion, and then concealer, but forgo foundation. For one of the women in this group, Woman 4, the routine begins and ends with foundation, specifically CoverGirl Ultimate Finish Liquid Powder, which claims to be liquid, powder, and concealer all in one. Another informant will only use moisturizer. This is the very reserved end of the spectrum.

In addition to foundation and the attention to the face, most of the women in this group go on to concern themselves with the eyes. Eyeliner or mascara is used to define and draw attention to the eyes. One of the informants uses both, one uses eyeliner but will occasionally add mascara if she feels like it, and two use only mascara on a regular basis. The same informant who only uses moisturizer does not use either eyeliner or eyeshadow, but will use eyebrow pencil to fill in her eyebrows and an eyelash curler to curl her eyelashes. This indicates a variation of the focus on the eyes. Two of the members of this group also show a faint attention to the lips, not as strong as the focus on the eyes. One uses tinted lip balm, the other Chapstick. This group's attention to the lips seems to indicate a utilitarian approach and possibly a toning down of attention to the lips.

Elaborates

On the other end of the spectrum, some informants have elaborate daily routines. There are three informants in this group, making it the smallest. In this group, the attention to the skin of the face is more intense. Two of them follow a very similar pattern with regards to their face. They begin by priming their face with primer. Then one uses the multipurpose BB cream and the other foundation and concealer. They both use a powder next. One specifies that the primer is to set the layers under it, the other does not say. After bronzing, blushing, and highlighting their faces, they specifically prime their eyelids, and then use natural shades of eyeshadow. The third person follows a similar pattern, but shows slightly more variation; she begins with a lotion, not a primer, and then applies liquid foundation before using three different concealers for various parts of her face and applying a setting powder before she bronzes, contours (using a grey-toned bronzer), blushes, and highlights. Interestingly, it is described in painter's terms: using a primer. One of the informants in this group said she thinks of makeup as an art form, and that seems to be reflected in the behavior here. The face is treated like canvas, primed and gone over in layers upon layers to create beauty.

The eyes are given more attention and rendering in this group as well. Two of them fill in their eyebrows before turning their attention to the area closer to the eyes. One of them brushes her eyebrows later in her routine. Two of the girls, the ones who prime their faces, prime the eyes—which I take to mean the skin of the eyelid and under the eyebrow—specifically. They all apply eyeshadow. The women who use primers prefer to use natural shades: one uses browns or lighter colors, the other a neutral shade on the lid and a darker shade to indicate the crease. All three women use eyeliner to further accentuate the eyes and mascara for the lashes.

The third area of attention on the face, the lips, shows the most variation here, and though it is given more attention than in the basic group, it still does not get as much as one might expect. One of these women uses lipstick, another lip gloss, and the third only Chapstick.

The Mid-Spectrum Routines

The third group, the middle of the spectrum, contains four girls. These are the routines which fall between elaborate and absolutely basic. Looking at the three main areas, again starting with the face, three of the women use foundation and concealer. One of these begins with a moisturizer before her foundation. The fourth young woman uses BB cream and follows it with a powder to reduce the shine and set the cream. She is the only one in this group to use setting powder at this stage. Two of these girls use blush, and one ends her routine, after doing her eyes, with a light powder.

Turning to the eyes, this group comes closer to the elaborate end of the scale, as two fill in their eyebrows. All four use mascara. Two use eyeshadow and eyeliner most days, one uses them occasionally. In this group, attention to the lips is medium. One person uses lipstick, one Chapstick, and the other two nothing.

Interpretation

Functionality

Now that we have examined the similarities and variation in the daily cosmetics routines of Truman students, let us turn our attention to the functions of these routines. These practices boost young women's confidence, offer a chance to express creativity, and help them establish their

social roles. They also provide status indicators and demonstrate characteristics of ritual consumption. Makeup allows young women to adhere
to societal notions of femininity, the beautiful, and the good. Boundary
patrolling by older women helps to teach younger women what is and is
not appropriate for certain life periods—as seen in the use of lipstick.

Emic Explanations

Let us begin with the informants' responses about why they use makeup.
A number of informants gave more than one reason for wearing makeup.
Two say they use makeup partly because it is their routine. One of the
two notes that the morning routine involving makeup is relaxing. Four say
they enjoy doing makeup or find it fun. Two report doing it to enhance
their beauty. Five want to cover acne, blemishes, or other facial flaws or
imperfections. Three say that they wear it or feel other girls wear it for
themselves and not for others. Eight responses involved something along
the lines of they like how they look while wearing makeup/don't like how
they look without it, feel more confident or pretty while wearing it, or uncomfortable when not wearing it. These findings demonstrate variations—
such as the emphasis that it is a routine—and conservation—the interest
in covering perceived flaws and creating a more perfect appearance. None
of these results seemed unlikely or unduly surprising. These results are in
accordance with Gentina's discussion and study of adolescent French girls'
makeup usage as a consumption ritual:

> "… teenage girls' self-image (Fabricant and Gould, 1993; Bloch
> and Richins, 1992), identity (Marion, 2003), concern about
> physical appearance (Chang et al., 2008), and social role (Sol-
> omon, 1983) have all been found to motivate the use of makeup.
> This is consistent with previous research in social psychology
> which has shown that makeup enhances physical attractive-
> ness, self-esteem, feelings of social confidence, and social in-
> teractions (Cash et al., 1989; Cash et al., 1985; Miller and Cox,
> 1982; Theberge and Kernaleguen, 1979)." (Gentina 117)

Self-image and concern about appearance seem to dominate in my findings, but one informant noted that cosmetics can be a "useful tool," and
the other reasons are likely there, although not necessarily consciously.
Makeup helps informants feel more secure and more beautiful. Gentina
argues that makeup is useful because it helps girls to feel more beautiful,
and my data agrees with that. Makeup allows girls to cover up perceived
flaws and to enhance their appearance. Gentina's statement that girls use
makeup to develop their identity relates to girls' use of makeup to begin to shape a persona distinct from the parent, especially the mother,

though this self-creation continues past the point in life where that may be necessary (119). College students, for example, have reached the point of physical separation from the family household, especially if they have come to Truman and away from their hometowns, and are not generally perceived by other students or professors in the context of their parents. If a college student spends most weekends at school, she is spending approximately seven months out of a year away from home. College students are in a transitional phase between adolescence and adulthood, so that the principles of makeup use to create identity are probably still in play, but they are different, as Gentina's study focused on girls fourteen to eighteen years of age, while most of my informants were eighteen or older. As for social role, that is similar to identity, but Truman students' social roles, while sometimes requiring good looks, revolve around being students at a rigorous university.

Mass Culture's Influence

Cosmetics can come to increase self-esteem on the one hand, as the skills and knowledge enable the woman to make something beautiful from her face, but also decrease a sense of natural beauty. The decrease in the belief in one's natural beauty occurs because the implication is that the woman's face is not normally beautiful or has flaws which must be covered or hidden. The makeup itself is referred to in ways which reinforce this message. Note that seven of my fourteen informants report using the product referred to as "concealer" or "coverup"; two others use BB cream— a product which works as a concealer among other things—and one more uses another product which is also a concealer combined with other products. Concealer is used to cover particularly problematic spots such as pimples or uneven coloring so that the face looks more even overall. The implicit message is that every day when a woman is putting on a public face, she is concealing her skin. So ten of my informants use concealer (though some of them said they use makeup to cover facial flaws).

The message that a woman's face is naturally imperfect is perpetuated by mass culture cosmetics companies. These companies profit from the folk behavior of makeup use and its continuation. This makes the individually passed-on behaviors involving cosmetics difficult to separate from the individual's adherence to mass cultural aesthetics. There have recently been movements to call out the commercial nature of the beauty industry, such as attempts to show model photographs before and after Photoshop; but given the structure of American society, that is unlikely to effectively combat what Bartky terms the "fashion-beauty complex" (39). Bartky compares this complex to a religion in the ways it "cultivates in its adherents very profound anxieties about the body.... It then presents itself as the only instrument able, though expiation, to take away the very guilt and shame it has itself produced" (41). Although not a folkloric analysis, Bartky's work is relevant here because contemporary facial cosmetics—the products and industry—are mass cultural products used in ways which I classify as folk behavior. Makeup use is an everyday behavior for many women, and was usually learned face-to-face or in direct communication with someone, even if that someone was a creator of a YouTube video talking into a web cam. This behavior is affected by the way mass culture teaches girls to look at themselves.

Not surprisingly, given the changing social norms and mores of gender, most informants seemed to feel that "Why do you wear makeup?" was a question to answer carefully. Several brought up the fact that they were aware girls can be pressured into wearing makeup, but then asserted that they do not feel pressured to do so. Most phrased their answers in ways which emphasized personal choice in the matter: "I just do it for me," or "I like the way I look with makeup on." It seems likely to me that all of my informants are in some way pressured to use facial cosmetics through mass culture, if not in direct communication with others. Although these particular informants may not feel pressured, if they did, they might not want to admit it, or might not even admit it to themselves. Bartky suggests that one reason women resist feminist rhetoric is that women rely on certain feminine rituals to give themselves confidence and improve their self-image (41). While ideally American society would be moving to a place where women no longer feel imperfect, attempts in the meantime to tell them they do not have to feel that way may not be welcome, because they are seen as attempts to destroy the behaviors which enhance self-image (Bartky 41).

Current Truman students are part of a generation caught up in changing gender norms and ethical mores regarding social expectations of women. After several waves of feminism, there is recognition that society should not demand that women wear makeup, but it is clearly a tradition that has not disappeared, although it seems more optional now and among our age group here at college. As our generation matures and further generations emerge, we may witness a trend changing from what was once compulsory becoming optional, and even eventually being frowned upon. My informants' responses indicated their awareness of the social implications of the question "Why do you wear facial cosmetics?" They attempted to answer in a way which did not make them seem reliant on makeup for these reasons, but which still affirmed their decision to continue the practice.

I believe they use makeup because they have chosen to do so, but I also believe Bartky still applies, even though her book is twenty-five years old.

On the comparison of makeup to artistic expression, such as we saw with the elaborate makeup practices of three informants, she writes: "since a properly made-up face is, if not a card of entrée, at least a badge of acceptability in most social and professional contexts, the woman who chooses not to wear cosmetics at all faces sanctions of a sort which will never be applied to someone who chooses not to paint a watercolor" (71). Women are still, for the most part, expected to wear makeup to interviews and jobs. It is part of looking like an adult and behaving appropriately.

The conflicting messages girls receive about makeup from feminist standpoints and commercial culture may explain why many informants placed emphasis on girls wearing makeup to please themselves and on their being happy with the resulting look. My informants were definitely conscious that superficial expectations are placed on girls. One informant said that she has seen lots of ways girls have been shamed, that girls do wear makeup to get others to like them, and that she has seen images showing the difference makeup can make. So she will wear it to make a guy think she is pretty if she's going on a date, but mostly she does it for herself. Another informant reported an Instagram game in which a person would post a photo taken without cosmetics and tag three people, who would then have to post a similar photo; and even though she does not feel she wears makeup (she wears only foundation and mascara), she found the game on Instagram frightening. This game takes on the structure of a dare, which suggests testing social behavior by breaking the approved standards, and implies that makeup is still seen as a proper thing to wear in public, and that it is still a standard of female behavior by which women will be judged.

While it is unfortunate, this stigma attached to not wearing cosmetics may indicate a strong societal idea that women are still supposed to be ornamental or aesthetically pleasing in some way. This most likely explains a particularly striking survey response. Asked, "Why do you use facial cosmetics?" she wrote, "I don't like my face without them, and also people always comment when you don't, and it hurts. In the end it's just easier to wear makeup and fit in than deal with people telling you you look sick." This response is perhaps an outlier, but indicates societal reinforcement of the choice to wear makeup. At least in some circles, makeup is still considered a good thing for women to use. Among my interviewees, makeup did seem to be a personal choice made because they enjoyed it. Since they are people wearing makeup regularly or semi-regularly, that was the answer that made sense to them. If I had also interviewed informants who do not wear makeup on a regular basis, the answers would probably have been very different. The assertion of personal gratification and agency works mythically to establish a story of psychological agency beyond influences of the beauty industry and social codes. I would need a much larger sample and more in-depth study to determine how factually true it is that today's college students are not or do not feel pressured to wear makeup, but the responses indicate that there is "truthiness" to the assertion of individual choice, even if it is like our assertion that we all share individual choice in clothing selection.

Elaborations and Correlations with Emic Explanations

Among informant data, I noticed a correlation between two of the young women who fall toward the elaborate end of the spectrum and their reasons for using makeup. Two informants responded that they use makeup because it allows them to express their creativity. Another, on the basic end of the scale said something similar about special occasions making them "feel pretty in a more artsy way."

Etic Analysis

Most social behaviors are polydetermined and emic responses are not always the entire story. Cosmetics require time and effort to apply, as well as knowledge of how to apply them, and—not insignificantly —cash. This suggests that beauty is important or meaningful, if we are societally willing to spend or encourage women to spend large amounts of money, time, and effort making themselves appear a certain way. There is some-thing significant about the extravagance of the consumption. Buying and wearing large amounts of makeup, including a great variety of colors, sig-nals that the woman can afford to do so and that she has the time in the morning to apply many fine layers to her face. A woman who makes such choice is either demonstrating her wealth or is making an effort to appear wealthy. She also appears elegant, in that she is proclaiming that she does not have to rush in the morning and her mornings are not hectic, but or-derly. For such a woman, makeup and the routine which she uses to create her face, are assertions of order. This can subconsciously indicate that she has an orderly household, and because of traditional stereotyping, that she runs an orderly house, the domestic front traditionally being the woman's sphere.

Like wearing a white shirt, such ornamentation is also unlikely to last long if the woman has a physically strenuous job. Makeup, like other tra-ditionally female modes of outward signaling, such as dresses, long hair, and heels, announces that women have fewer practical needs than men. A woman is also unlikely to have the time to wear fine makeup if she must be at work early in the morning. Thus not only purchasing large quantities of cosmetics, but also wearing them, indicates an upper-class or middle-class lifestyle. This can be understood by other members of society, even if not consciously stated. This phenomenon is similar to the way authors may characterize someone as fussy and detail-oriented by noting that all of their pencils are sharpened to the same length and are lined up evenly on a desk. The reader will not necessarily think, "what a perfectionist!" but they will not be surprised later when the character is irritated by another character's scuffed shoes or crooked tie. When another person sees a woman wearing lots of carefully applied makeup, they subconsciously realize that the woman in question is either putting on a display or wealthy, or both. This can make the woman a more attractive partner in more than the visual sense. Men are not usually accused of being gold-diggers, but can there be any harm in marrying an heiress?

Women recognize this aspect too. Many girls have a more elaborate routine for special occasions—dances or dates, for instance. This not only makes them more physically attractive, but communicates their own resources and social standing. Performing a more elaborate routine can be their way of telling others that the event in question is important to them; thus they wear makeup to work or a job interview. If the event were not important, they would not have sacrificed the time and money to prepare for it in terms of cosmetics. By doing elegant makeup, they also demonstrate that they are mature and skilled in feminine things. Not everyone can apply makeup well.

Three Focuses

In America, women are considered beautiful and adult if they have even, flawless skin, accentuated eyes, and sensuous red lips. My data indicated that those are the three main areas to which women pay attention cosmetically: facial skin, eyes, and lips, in that order. Almost all informants use some product for the skin, and most then pay some attention to the eyes, with lips being the least attended area.

It seems likely that the reason most attention in cosmetics is paid to the skin is because smooth skin is seen as youthful and therefore innocent but at the same time desirable and mature, since adolescence is associated with blemishes, while adulthood is not. Also, given the common dyads children are exposed to in mass culture, there is a strong tendency to link physical imperfections with moral failings. For example, in many children's movies, the antagonist is recognizable because of his or her ugliness, potentially scars or wrinkles, and associations with dark colors, while the protagonist is rarely homely, but instead is often handsome or pretty. A group's standards of beauty are often connected to its concepts of what is good and what is true. I think it likely that the belief takes the beautiful skin and eyes which reflect the standard of childlike innocence and demureness previously desirable in a woman and connects them with the smoothness that announces adult availability. I would like to think we are transitioning away from the societal belief that childlike submissiveness in a woman is "good."

In the past, women were expected to behave passively. Given that expectation, it is possible that the accentuation of the eyes emphasized women's roles as observers. Perhaps among college students the emphasis is on their roles as observant learners. The inverse of the attention to the eyes is the comparative lack of attention to the lips among college students. The students I interviewed spend a lot of time on their face and some effort on their eyes, but they don't spend much time on their lips. There is the most variation in lip cosmetics—in whether they use them at all. Eyes and skin are almost always attended to in some way. But with lips, nothing is often an option. Although a brief question I put at lunch to a group of girls was dismissed with the explanation that lipstick is expensive and requires multiple applications per day, something else is going on with the lips. As Foltz-Gray wrote in 1996, discussing herself, as a child, watching her mother don lipstick, "My mother's lips were ... the source of her kiss and the stem of her wrath." This is not a scholarly source, but it illustrates that lips are often active. Highlighting them can indicate a woman's capacity to act, to speak or kiss. Deemphasizing the lips, through which women speak and take action, on some level deemphasizes the role of doer. So why do the girls I interviewed visibly downplay their lips?

Context of Truman

I think this may be because of the context of Truman students. Truman is a college, and college students are often occupied with schoolwork, but Truman students especially pride themselves on being nerds, hardworking and academically stressed. Sometimes evening conversations sound less like chat and more like masochistic boasts about who has the most homework in the upcoming days or week or who has spent the least amount of time on sleep. Truman students are not alone in their belief that they are special and especially put-upon academically, and since this was my subject-pool, I wanted to illustrate the social atmosphere of the university in order to discuss its possible effects on students' makeup use.

Truman students pride themselves on being accomplished, and with such a large proportion of female students, it is not surprising that so many of our student body display even more personal accomplishment with their cosmetics. Cosmetics are arguably a more difficult medium for indicating sophistication than clothes or shoes; most clothes do come pre-made after all, and styling an outfit is only the ability to match the pieces well;

but cosmetics need to be applied at least once a day—requiring levels of consistency—and they must also alter according to each new day's needs, showing a breadth of knowledge, and requiring personal commitments of time and money beyond simply dressing in the morning.

Makeup Habits Change

As discussed earlier, not everyone has clear recollections of their age or the time they began, suggesting that this is not a clearly-defined rite of passage; but it does seem to mark something. At least one informant noted that when she was learning makeup her mother's routine was not satisfying because it was appropriate for a mother-age-and-status working figure, but not for a young girl.

Some informants reported changes in their makeup habits early, during middle school, and again during high school, and a third time with the move to Truman. Not every interview covered this topic, but two which did suggest that girls become less focused on their appearance and more confident as they get older, reducing the amount of makeup they use and how often they use it, especially now that they are busy. One informant who does more elaborate makeup, had a period of ten months some time before college, during which she was very busy and didn't do much makeup, and when that period of her life was over, she rediscovered makeup through YouTube tutorials and saw it more as an art form than a necessity. Gentina offers an explanation for this trend:

> "Successful incorporation leads a person out of the liminoid [transitional] state with a revised self-concept and an increased self-esteem (Schouten, 1991b). Thus, for some informants, using makeup is no longer necessary to feel comfortable in public. This is consistent with Noble and Walker (1997), who found that the reliance on symbolic possessions so critical in liminal states significantly decreases once the transition has been completed." (Gentina 120)

Essentially, during times of transition and change, in this case the transition into late adolescence, girls use makeup to help them redefine their roles; and once they feel more comfortable in the role which makeup has helped them establish, they experience a reduced need to wear it as a display.

Makeup usage changes with age and context. Middle and high school, with regularly recurring interactions can definitely be a place where physical display is more important, while Truman, with more random and infrequent social interactions, tends to be less so (although several informants mentioned that they use makeup to hide the dark circles under their eyes and look as though they are sleeping in a healthy manner). They do this despite Truman's—and other colleges'—culture of bragging about lack of sleep, demonstrating a pressure to be pretty or healthy in addition to being successful and the sort of person who sacrifices health for grades.

Boundary Patrolling

The questions I put to my informants did not elicit much evidence of boundary patrolling habits in this folk group, the deployment of badges and shibboleths to determine who is a member of the group, and who is not. If I were to do this project again, I would want to inquire more intensely in this area. However, one informant did discuss boundary patrolling as done by an older woman.

She reported that when she began experimenting with makeup at age thirteen, her mother, described as very conservative and as someone who does not believe in wearing makeup, took her daughter's makeup away because she said the girl was too young to wear it. I remember that growing up, it was not uncommon to hear someone saying that X, whoever she was, was too young to be wearing and worrying about makeup, and the undertones seemed to be that makeup was for signaling availability for courtship and an interest in boys. These statements are examples of boundary patrolling by the older generations, not just by women.

Maternal disapproval was more marked in Gentina's study, where the girls used makeup in defiance of their mothers in what Gentina calls "a ritual of initiation." She writes, "As a ritual of initiation, the consumption of makeup products distances the child from her parents, in particular the mother, while amplifying the teenage girl's belongingness to a larger system of peers" (Gentina 119). The girls chose to wear makeup despite their mothers' unhappiness with the situation, because, as I have said earlier, it allowed them to assert their independence from the mother.

Final Thoughts on Lipstick

Although the girls wore makeup and made their mothers unhappy, the mothers' boundary patrolling had an effect. My informants, as I have said before, describe routines that attend to the eyes and the face to make them more beautiful and desirable, but often do not bother with that symbol of female sophistication and mature authority: lipstick. Highlighting the mouth sends a powerful signal. If only two of the fourteen informants use lipstick on a regular basis, it indicates some sort of symbolic use. It is possible that not using it daily allows for its use to be noticed as a declaration of specific, special events; but I think wearing lipstick indicates that someone either feels very competent and is near the beginning of true adulthood or is paying more attention to sexual or social norms. Gentina's informants were also uncomfortable with lipstick:

> Teenage girls were reluctant to use lipstick, regardless of the color, because they associated lips with sexuality and femininity. Because they had not assumed adult sexual roles yet, some of the informants considered lipstick use as inappropriate for them. For these informants, even though using makeup demonstrated their desire to separate from their childhood role, they also seemed to have difficulty fully separating. They were not quite ready to totally reject their childhood. (Gentina 119)

Thus Gentina's informants had reasons for downplaying the lips. If I could do this project again, I would include a question about lipstick specifically to see if I would get similar answers. Even though I did not raise explicit discussions about lipstick, my findings with regards to the lips seem to be consistent with Gentina's. As discussed earlier, lipstick demonstrates adulthood and adult roles, which, judging by the conversations I overhear around campus, many Truman students are not so eager to embrace. Wearing lipstick also signals sexual confidence and maturity, as Gentina states. The sexual implications of lipstick may be deemed inappropriate in a setting which prides itself on rigorous attention to the scholarly.

However, the reluctance to emphasize one's lips may be transitory. Gentina's informants, younger girls, were uncomfortable with black eyeliner and lipstick (119). Their discomfort with eye makeup is inconsistent with my findings. Twelve of my informants report some form of attention to the eyes as part of their daily routine, in the forms of eyeshadow, mascara, eyeliner, or accentuating the eyebrows. This exhibits variation in the approach, but conservation in the area accentuated. Most of my informants seemed fairly comfortable with eyeliner and eye makeup, although one did report not knowing how to use mascara. I hypothesize that the use of eye makeup is affected by age. Younger girls feel that drawing attention to the eyes is—like drawing attention to the lips, although to a lesser degree—more adult behavior. Young women of college age deem eyeshadow, eyeliner, and mascara appropriate behavior for themselves, but do not yet feel mature enough for the ultimate feminine makeup: lipstick.

Conclusion

I had fourteen informants for this project, a small sample of the folk group of all of the girls at Truman State University who wear makeup, but I collected a good deal of interesting information. From the fourteen, I determined that there is a spectrum from basic to elaborate in terms of how much makeup a young woman does. Six were basic. There were three strong examples of elaborate makeup practices, and the remainder fell towards the middle of the spectrum.

Each makeup routine focused attention foremost on making up the skin of the face, concealing acne and perceived faults, smoothing the tone, and then drawing highlights and shadows back out on the even tone of the foundation. This preoccupation with the fineness of the skin has symbolic associations with virtue and is implicitly linked with indoor work and middle or upper-class status. The obsession with perfect skin and beauty is perpetuated by mass culture advertising, which markets the desirability of the unattainable for profit. The next most significant details were those around the eyes, the metaphorical windows to the soul, be it through eyebrows, eyeliner, eyeshadow, or the eyelashes. The attention given to the eyes may develop with age, as women begin to feel more mature and confident with their increased sexuality and feminine social roles. Finally, there is a dismissal of the lips which seems to indicate that Truman students are not ready at this stage of their life to claim complete adulthood and the sophistication, responsibility, and sexual maturity it implies.

Truman students—and students from other colleges—are hardworking, accomplished, and driven by the narrative that they are the cream of the crop. This narrative makes it unsurprising that female Truman students devote time to crafting put-together appearances. These appearances serve a number of functions. They serve as indications that the woman wearing cosmetics manages to keep her life somewhat orderly and has the money, time, and skill to use makeup. Makeup usage can also indicate that a woman is of a certain social class. A well-made-up face is aesthetically pleasing and gives the woman a boost in confidence. The conspicuous consumption of makeup can be used to indicate that the woman takes an event or person seriously, and can be used to encourage courtship. Most college age women say they do not feel pressured to wear makeup and assert that it is a conscious choice, though one reports negative social feedback if she does not. The use of facial cosmetics is a polydeterminate and useful folk behavior which is heavily influenced and, at this point, reliant on mass culture and mass production.

Works Cited

Bartky, Sandra Lee. *Femininity and Domination: Studies in the Phenomenology of Oppression*. New York: Routledge, 1990. Print.

Foltz-Gray, Dorothy. "Lipstick: A Love Story." *Health (Time Inc. Health)* 10.5 (1996): 38. *Academic Search Complete.* Web. 1 Nov. 2015.

Gentina, Elodie, Kay M. Palan, and Marie-Hélène Fosse-Gomez. "The Practice of Using Makeup: A Consumption Ritual of Adolescent Girls." *Journal of Consumer Behaviour* 11.2 (Mar/Apr 2012): 115-123. Web. 28 September 2015.

Role Play Groups as Folk Groups
Chelsea Muzar

In this 2013 paper, the investigator reports factually on the lore, verbal and behavioral, of a virtual folkgroup, and reflects on the dynamics which take it beyond a discrete, shared activity, a game plain and simple: "To be involved in a community requires a commitment to caring about the other members of the group and offering help when it is needed."

Role Play Definition

Role play games, as defined by Jerzy Kociatkiewicz at the Institute of Philosophy and Sociology for the Polish Academy of Sciences, "are an activity in which a group of people (called players) creates and role play characters in a world devised by the...Game Master" (71). Though this definition is true for the traditional tabletop RPGs (role play games), it does not quite apply to the online spectrum of gaming. RPGs online can be conducted between two people or an entire group. Common places where people participate in these games are online forums, social media sites, chat rooms and, of course, in the massive multiplayer online role play games (MMORPGs) such as World of War Craft and League of Legends. While MMORPGs are one of the most common forms of online gaming, this paper will not be focusing on them. Instead, this paper will be looking at the table RPGs described by Kociatkiewicz and focusing on the RPGs that are created on the social network of Tumblr. While role play in its basic form can be considered simply a game, the groups that build themselves around RPGs seem to develop structured communities that have certain expectations of their players. There is a need-to-know the language of the games, the rules, the qualifications of a "quality player," and in some cases the ability to take characters from popular books, movies and television series and portray them uniquely, yet accurately. The combination of slang, rules, beliefs and community barriers support the idea that role play groups, especially those online, have formed their own folk communities.

Unlike the traditional tabletop game, the role plays conducted on Tumblr are forced to function a little differently. Since they are hosted online there is no face-to-face communication and the games are written down instead of verbally crafted, much like a collaboration on a story. The first player writes the opening scene, which leaves a chance for the second player to respond. The interactions go back and forth until the game is finished or the players grow tired of it and the game is dropped. These games are also not limited solely to pre-planned three hour periods meeting in a location like those of the tabletop games. Since they are online, the players can log into their accounts whenever convenient and post a reply or just check and see the progress of their story.

During a tabletop game, the Game Master (GM), who is in charge of enforcing the rules, controls the fictional world. As Kociatkiewicz noted during his involvement with the games, "My role as Game Master in this session clearly put me in a privileged position of power" (75). The game can be solely created by the GM, meaning they've come up with the entire idea, but the more common approach is that the GM springboards off ideas from a book or online file of a specific game. These books come with their own rules, character sheets, and structured expectations. One tabletop RPG player who was interviewed explained that after the world is created, "the players...usually take on the role of the stories' protagonists [and] they work together to tell their story." And the players do *tell* their stories, though certain things must be written down, like specific pre-plotted ideas or game scores; still, most of the interaction and the storytelling is verbal. Despite the fact that the game may come with a book and instructions, the players themselves work together to weave a compelling, unique tale. Of course, it's unique in the sense that no two players are alike: no two people will have the exact same reaction to an event that happens in the game, and the roll of the dice is fair but the outcome is always random.

Within Tumblr there are two different groups of players. There are the Group Players, who will be referred to as GPs and operate much as in the tabletop games. They are often, though not always, restricted to playing only with other members of the group and must follow the plot and rules of the administrators or GMs ("game masters"). The Independent Players, referred to as IPs, on the other hand, have the freedom to create and drop games with as many people as they choose. In an interview, two players spoke about the topic. RT, a well seasoned Tumblr role player, wrote that "group role players are generally, as the name suggests, a group of people who come together in order to fulfill a select plot and at times will refuse to role play outside of their group of people." (RT). GPs may be more biased and selective in their gaming but there are reasons behind it. Another interviewee, J, wrote:

> When you're an independent blog, you aren't part of any group, so you don't have any connections and are stuck looking for your own crowd. It's the opposite with group role plays. When you're a group role player, you're already tied in with others that are a part of that group, so you aren't alone...since you automatically have people to interact with (J).

Both categories of role play have different applications and functions for their players. GP offers immediate connection, while the other offers personal freedoms. In Group, the player has to apply to be accepted. She is hand-picked by the administrators who have the assumption that she will further the game. These administrators are usually role play partners that have decided to create a larger game and include more people. Sometimes, if the group is too large, more administrators are recruited within the game. These people are usually veterans or those gamers who have been involved in the game the longest.

Tumblr Group RPGs oftentimes offer preplanned connections with people. The administrators can pair two characters up and label them as a couple, as siblings or as enemies. The basic plot and game ideas have already been chosen for each character in order to create a complex and structured gaming experience. GPs must often deal with a schedule, a specified number of posts they must provide each week. If they do not meet the quota then they are removed from the game or they are replaced. Group Play can be very strict as compared to Independent Games since GPs are held responsible for their game time.

It's up to the IP to find the niche that he belongs in. Here the groups that are established are organic and those who are drawn to each other are usually people with similar interests and writing styles. Most often specific fans of TV series, movies, games and books branch off into their own smaller groups within the IP spectrum of the community. The IPs are freer to pick and choose those people whom they want to start a game with, making their experiences more organic.

Telling a Story

Kociatkiewicz writes that RPGs are "an activity, or perhaps an art of moderately regulated joint telling of stories" (73). Writers tell stories and create worlds that people believe in, if only for the moment. In RPG the players are collaborating on a story. For example, the world could be the world of fairy tales and fables, the characters could be Little Red, the Wolf, and Grandmother. The players could roll dice or take turns for the order of who gets to tell the narration. They each tell different snippets of the story or, to complicate things, they could use the dice to mark up points and attack, hinder or aid other characters. The story will never turn out exactly the same each time it's played. However, the system of tabletop RPGs seems to be more structured than what would happen in an online setting. Their games come with books, PDF files, online dictionaries, rules and regulations that are set up by the people who create and sell the game. Below is an example of a "Character Sheet" from the game Grimm.

Grimm character sheet from Fantasy Flight Publishing Inc.

This would make it nothing more than a very complicated board game; however, the individual groups can stray from the original rules and create their own. This is similar to "sandlotting," which happens when the rules of a game are changed to benefit the group. The term "sandlot" was usually applied to baseball but, according to the folklorist and etymologist Peter Tamony, it eventually "came to denominate unorganized sports" in general (Tamony 268). Though tabletop role play is not a sport, the concept of sandlotting can still be applied to the games. One of the rules used in the Truman RPG group, as gathered from tabletop role player MO, states, "Don't say no; go with it," which means don't protest what happens in the game just because you don't like the outcome; accept it and move forward. MO is the GM (Game Master) for several of the Truman RPG's. She conducts her games based on sheets like the one seen above; however players can edit the world which the books provide for them in order to fulfill the needs of the group. They create their own terms, such as "Ghosts are persons who have graduated from Truman but still use the online forum" (MO). They still value the importance of telling the story, of creating a world and controlling the outcomes of its inhabitants, basically of playing God.

Still, as serious as that sounds, according to Kociatkiewicz, "RPGs are actually more akin to the childhood play of make-believe" (Kociatkiewicz 73). That quote was echoed by MO when she wrote, "RPG is structured make-believe." But when children play make-believe, they indulge in games like house, wedding, doctor, teacher and so forth and the suggestion is that, "Children may indeed imitate the reality of adult custom" based on what they've seen older children and adults do in daily life (Sutton-Smith 34). Essentially they want to be a part of the older world, so they create their own version of it. But what do role players achieve by playing make-believe?

On Tumblr the players are writing a thread, or as MK, a Tumblr role player wrote, a "chronological list of interactions between characters, a series of one reply after another." A thread is a post on the Tumblr blog that is used to write the story of two or more characters. Many of these stories are written about interactions between the supernatural and the natural world, gods and mortals and the uncanny. It seems that many players online prefer to write with a character who has some sort of supernatural gift or who has come from the heavens. Austin E. Fife believes that "an author is inevitably involved in the process of myth formation" (229). Fife, however, is talking about how writers take a pre-existing myth and create something more from it, a sort of retelling. This still applies to RPGs since it is normal to see players using gods and goddesses from many pantheons, angels, demons, mythological creatures–and if it is not a real character taken from a myth, then it's a hybrid. Many players use pre-established characters from television shows, movies and books. There seem to be very few true "mortal" or "non-magical" characters used in the game–and if the character is mortal, they are usually some sort of super-hero or secret agent. Or if they are both mortal and non-magical, they are usually still aware of or involved in the magical world.

The most common plot of these threads, according to all who were interviewed, is the formation of a relationship, usually with romantic intent, between two characters. These plots seem to function as a way for the player to become closer to another person through the game. The observation was made by one player, NT, that "many people are actually afraid [or] too shy to 'follow' the people they like or talk to them about wanting to RP." It seems that many of the players have some form of self doubt or anxiety, with a high amount of posts being written about fearing a lack of "quality" in their abilities to write and portray their characters in a way that everyone will find enjoyable. These fears may be because the player is not only looking for a connection between two or more characters but is also looking for a connection between other players or partners as well.

The players claim that they participate in the games and threads in order to relieve stress and to enhance their writing ability. "[I role play] to practice my writing and create stories out of the ideas stored up in my head" (J). It is an exchange of ideas, "a creative outlet, but beyond that, for me, it's a chance to explore...the different views others have of the characters" (MK). It is also a chance to escape the pressures of real life:

> To me, role playing is an escape. I use it as a means to get away from real life. I like to step away from the real world and enter the world of whatever character I'm playing at the moment. It's a way to remind myself that not everything is bad, that I have friends online and off [who] can help me out of my own head by getting into our character's heads (RT).

When asked about the communication between players—that is, the use of OCC (out of character) conversations with partners—most of the interviewees stated that they spent the same amount of time role playing as they did simply talking with their role play partners about normal mundane things. As Fife points out, there are many "hours spent discussing materials, methods, organization" and so forth when two writers collaborate (237). Still, regardless of whether or not they speak out of character with their partner, some sort of bond is formed through the creation of plot and the collaboration of storytelling. A relationship is created and a sense of community is provided for those whose needs aren't completely met in the world outside of the internet.

When observing some of the posts made by members of the RPG community on Tumblr, a common thread ran through their complaints about "the real world." They didn't fit in with what was expected of them in social situations and they felt more comfortable making friends online than in common face-to-face interactions. When asked if she felt she was part of a group, RT said that role players are "definitely a community and I would even go so far as to say family. We're there for one another. I feel like there are people I can go to and talk to when I need to and that, to me, is a community and a family." (RT).

To add to the aspect of community, almost every player who was spoken with claimed that they were drawn to the role play community because of a friend. A friend taught them how to create the games and function properly within the group. They walked the new player through the beginning processes of becoming involved in a game. Though most of the games did not start on Tumblr, the horizontal learning of how to play the games led them to the social media site or the tabletop RPG clubs.

Burt Feintuch wrote an article about community and what it means, and he states that, "in community there is responsibility, integration, and obligation" (150). It is not simply a place where people go and hang out and leave all cares at the front door. To be involved in a community requires a commitment to caring about the other members of the group and offering help when it is needed. Feintuch makes an observation about a local neighborhood: "[A community] stood for neighbors who would lend a hand when you needed to raise your barn, who would be there when you needed help, who would monitor your children and shared your religion" (150). The sense of community is much like that in RT's comment. The games are not just structured time to play pretend but a chance to have that sense of community and support.

Barriers in Online Games

Getting started in the Tumblr RPG community can be difficult and oftentimes is overwhelming for a new gamer. First there are the mechanics of the site itself, which are constantly changing and causing massive uproars amongst the bloggers. Then there's the actual communication between the players and, even though someone might be new, if they can't follow the established rules then they will be shunned and perhaps even shamed from the group. In her study of groups, Noyes labels these barriers as "boundary mechanisms," which are used to mark the boundary lines between someone who is an insider and someone who is an outsider (Noyes

465). Just like many other groups, RPG bloggers don't want outsiders in the community.

The easiest way to find out who is a member of the group is through the use of slang because "competence in and use of such varieties of speech mark one's initiation into the shared knowledge of a specific group and are continuing signs of one's participation" (Brenneis 239).

Below is a list of common terms used by those in the Tumblr role play community gathered from observations and from my various interviewees.

Canon Character— A character that belongs to books, television or movies

Drabble— A short-short story about a verse or situation including one or more characters that is usually written by one of the players

FC — Face Canon. An Actor or Actress that represents the "face" of the character or who the player believes that character would look like in the real world

Headcanon — A fact about a character that is created by the player

IC — In Character.

M!A— Magic Anonymous. Someone who contacts the player anonymously to give them a "magical command" such as: "you are now trapped in a cat's body for 24 hours"

Mary-Sue — An original character that is without flaws (the term "Mary-Sue" came from Paula Smith's story *A Trekkie's Tale*. In Verba, Joan M. *Boldly Writing: A Trekker Fan & Zine History: 1967-1987.* Second ed. Minnetonka: FTL Publications, 1996. Bwebook.pdf. 2003. Web. 19 Dec. 2013. Wesley Crusher was said to be a male version of Mary Sue in episodes of *Star Trek the Next Generation.*

Multi Para — Multiple Paragraph. A type of role play that involves more than one paragraph

Multi-verse — More than one verse in available for the role player to use. This is usually for the purposes of interacting with more characters and having more relationships develop between characters.

Mun — The person who controls or writes for the character

Muse — The character who is used in the games

OC — Original character. A character created by the player

One-Liner — A type of role play where the interactions are usually just one or two lines of dialogue

OOC — Out of Character. It's used to let everyone know that the player, not the character, is speaking

Para — Paragraph. A type of role play that consists of having a paragraph that mixes dialogue with action

Reply — One player's written response to another's writing

RP — Role play

`Self Insert` —A character that is basically the player or the writer

`Ship` — Who the player believes the character should be in a relationship with, usually romantically

`Starter` — The opening of a game, usually consisting of a sentence or a paragraph written by one of the players

`Thread` — The story between characters that can take the form of a One-Liner, Para, or Multi-para game

`Verse` — A "universe" in which the character resides

Certainly there are more terms, but these are just examples of the basic slang that is used amongst the players that can be picked up within the first few games sessions. There are also other ways that the players patrol the boundaries of their group. They hold certain expectations of those who play canon and original characters. If someone is playing a canon character then it is expected that they do not stray too far from the source's characterization without reason. Original characters cannot be too perfect, too kind or too angst-driven lest they be labeled a Mary-Sue or Self-insert character. (Usually these prejudices are pointed at original female characters.) If these expectations are not met, then the player may have their blog and their character, but other gamers will often refuse to participate in games with them.

There is also a certain set of rules that everyone must follow in order to be accepted in a community. These rules may appear on sites or blogs that explain how to role play but they are not linked to one single person. In the interviews that I conducted, the Tumblr players gave examples of some of the basic rules. MR, an off and on again role player on Tumblr, wrote that "there are a number of rules every role player should follow. I'm not entirely sure who made them, as until fairly recently (in my case anyway) they were largely unspoken and just KNOWN amongst anyone in the community" MR. continued by explaining an important rule:

> Some of the more important ones are basic understanding and patience. To understand that it is just a game. To understand that you can only control your [own] character(s)...never do anything you or your partner don't consent to or don't feel totally comfortable with. Be patient with your partner(s) as they're only human and have real lives outside the computer.

This is summed up perfectly by another Tumblr role player, MK, who says, "First and foremost, the greatest rule is respect your fellow role players."

Respect is an established rule, but there are other rules that stem from that base. RT wrote a list of more rules that players are expected to follow, whether they are aware of them or not.

> *Do not power play [which means the controlling or injuring of another character without the character's role player's permission].*

> *Do not god-mod [make your character all powerful or unable to be hit in a battle].*

> *Do not metagame [where one character knows everything about another character].*

There are some others, such as not to start OOC [out of character] fights, not to send hate on Tumblr to people, to keep fighting private and not make it public, etc. Following these rules keeps the peace in the role play community.

It's been observed that when someone breaks a rule they are sometimes put down or shunned from the community. Written blog posts or PSA (public service announcements) are circulated essentially labeling this person as an undesirable. They are sometimes attacked by extremist members of the group, called names, sent hateful messages—even though this goes against one of the basic rules that was pre-established in the community, suggesting that it is all right to attack outsiders or those who are now seen as outsiders while it is not all right to attack those within the community—and so forth in order to get them to take down their blog and leave Tumblr. Sometimes the person who has broken the rule is simply ignored. They may or may not lose their current partners or opportunities for potential partners.

There are a few people who seem to purposefully act against the rules. These people are more likely to have several PSAs posted about them with listed warnings to avoid them completely. They are more likely to lash out at the group. They attack the players who refuse to participate in a game as well as their partners. One notorious Tumblr user, who will be called D, was observed sending mass messages of "anon-hate" to certain players who refused to play the game the way D wanted. D has well over 20 PSAs posted about them and has been rejected by most in the community and reported to the Tumblr Staff in an attempt to have their account removed.

Along with the basic rules that role players have, each person usually comes up with their own individual rules that they ask everyone to respect. They may stem from the rules mentioned earlier but they're usually influenced by the way the player role plays. For example, KT, another Tumblr role player, writes that her rules include, "third-person past tense" as the form of writing she prefers her partners to use. Not every player uses third person, some use first. These rules may be created in order to shrink the IP (Independent Player) community down into smaller groups.

Following the basic rules also leads to the discussion of what makes a person a good role player. There are many instances on Tumblr where people are praised for their abilities in the community. They are referred to as *"senpai,"* which is Japanese for "senior at work or school" (*EUdict.com*) and according to MK, "in the role playing community, I imagine [*senpai*] refers to a more senior member (in terms of time role playing or quality) of the community that one admires" (MK).

There are collective beliefs about what makes someone a good role playing partner. All those interviewed had almost the same response to the topic. The traits that are looked for in a good role player consist of: someone who knows how to write well, respects the characters they play with, respects the other players, who has a good understanding of their own character and has developed them beyond the static state. A good or "quality" role player appears to be someone who is established in the community and is usually well respected or admired by their peers. They follow the rules established in the community and conduct themselves in the proper manner. Someone who is opposite of this vision is described as "selfish,...doesn't take rp seriously" (MR), as "someone who refuses to hear out the other mun and cannot take criticism" (RT), and someone with poor writing skills. While there seem to be specific terms for someone who is a good player, the poor players are only labeled as bad players or sometimes as bad people.

Role players have slang, certain rules they must follow in their community, and certain beliefs about what makes someone a good or poor player. These things are set into place to create a dividing line between players and non-role players (no-rpers). For the purposes of this study, non-role players are people who are not involved in role play in the Tumblr and online forum communities or in tabletop play. Interviewee NT said, "I personally have nothing against no-rpers as long as they keep their noses out of our business.... Most probably think us role players to be weird, I think." Another player wrote, "Role playing is writing and is common nowadays. I don't care for non-role players. They probably think of role playing as a sexual activity" (J). The barrier built up between the groups is not only for the players to feel comfortable in their own community but also to help them protect themselves from persons they believe would mock something they enjoy participating in.

This fear may come from the belief that role play is strange, that it goes against the norm and will be seen as wrong. While most players seem to be comfortable talking about their time spent role playing, they do not openly label themselves as role players. NT wrote, "I don't see people walking on the streets announcing that they role play." RT's response echoes J's idea that non-role players believe that the activity is sexually based. "I think the idea of it as it exists in the public thought is taboo. People, as I've found, generally think that role playing is some obscene act that people in costume do" (RT). Role play in the online Tumblr community, however, does not seem to be normally used to reach a sort of sexual gratification; rather it is used to build relationships that the player lacks or wishes to expand upon in interactions outside of the internet.

Something notable happening more and more in role play is the use of mythological and folk tale characters in the games. This rise could be linked with commodified movies, graphic novels and books like Marvel's *Thor*, Rick Roidan's *Percy Jackson* series, and *Supernatural*'s use of folk tales and urban legends. The Canon Characters or "a character that was created for a plot in mind set in a specific universe, for example, Thor Odinson from the Marvel Cinematic Universe or the Comic-verse" (Anonymous player) are appearing more frequently within the community; they come from those commodified genres. There are hundreds of Loki blogs, hundreds of Thor blogs, and many Athena or Aphrodite blogs. There are blogs that contain werewolves, vampires, mermaids, ghosts, demigods, gods and so forth. Role players are taking the characters and stories that have been sold to them by corporations and making them their own again. No two Loki blogs are alike; each one is crafted by a different person who has a different view of the character. They are creating something that is uniquely their own.

This uniqueness expands into the activity of role play itself. Role players have established their own communities with their own rules, beliefs, slang, and barriers. They have created a system that separates their group from others, keeping out those who would be considered harmful to their community. Players who understand the slang and meet the requirements of group expectations are praised, while those who fail to do so are shunned. Popular characters are taken and adapted to fit the needs to the player and the game. Lasting relationships with game partners are created in online friendships, and communication outside of the games between players is considered just as important as the games themselves. People within the RP world have created their own communities that are, essentially, folk groups.

Bibliography

(Note: This paper is based on a series of interviews with ten persons; additional information came from gamers who voluntarily published their names in non-password-protected forums; however, identities have been obscured in keeping with current standards for protecting the privacy of informants. Ed)

Anonymous. Personal interview. 25 Oct. 2013.

BD. Personal interview. 7 Oct. 2013.

Bayard, Samuel P. "The Materials of Folklore." *The Journal of American Folklore*, Vol. 66, No. 259 (Jan. - Mar., 1953): 1-17. JSTOR. Web. 12 Sept. 2013.

Brenneis, Donald. "'Turkey,' 'Wienie,' 'Animal,' 'Stud': Intragroup Variation in Folk Speech." *Western Folklore*, Vol. 36, No. 3 (Jul. 1977): 238-246. JSTOR. Web. 7 Oct. 2013.

Burns, Thomas A. "Fifty Seconds of Play: Expressive Interaction in Context." *Western Folklore*, Vol. 37, No. 1 (Jan., 1978):1-29. JSTOR. Web. 14 Sept. 2013.

Feintuch, Burt. "Longing for Community." *Western Folklore*, Vol. 60, No. 2/3, (Spring-Summer, 2001): 149-161. JSTOR. Web. 7 Oct. 2013.

Fife, Austin E. "Myth Formation in the Creative Process." *Western Folklore*, Vol. 23, No. 4 (Oct., 1964): 229-239. JSTOR. Web. 14 Sept. 2013.

WG. Personal interview. 7 Oct. 2013.

Grimm Character Sheet. N.p.: Fantasy Flight Publishing Inc, n.d. PDF.

J. Personal interview. 4 Oct. 2013.

MK. Personal interview 30 Sept. 2013.

Kociatkiewicz, Jerzy. "Dreams Of Time, Times Of Dreams: Stories Of Creation From Roleplaying Game Sessions." In *Studies In Cultures, Organizations & Societies* Vol. 6, No.1 (2000): 71-86. Academic Search Complete. Web. 12 Sept. 2013.

Noyes, Dorothy. "Group." *The Journal of American Folklore*, Vol. 108, No. 430, (Autumn, 1995): 449-478. JSTOR. Web. 12 Sept. 2013.

MO. Personal interview. 7 Oct. 2013.

KP. Personal interview. 4 Oct. 2013.

MR. Personal interview. 2 Oct. 2013.

"Senpai." *Eudict.com.* n.p., 9 May 2005. Web. 3 Dec. 2013.

RT. Personal interview. 3 Oct. 2013.

Tamony, Peter. "Sandlot Baseball." *Western Folklore*, Vol. 27, No. 4, (October, 1968): 265-269. JSTOR. Web. 19 Dec. 2013.

NT. Personal interview. 6 Oct. 2013.

Red Flame Records and Early Independent Rock and Roll
Dylan Pyles

In this 2013 paper, the grandson of noted folklorist Lyda Pyles documents a little-known chapter in the history of rock-and-roll: one of the ephemeral independent rural and small-town music labels, and the local bands that recorded with them. What was playing on the big-market radio stations was very far from the whole story. It's folklore, oral history, local history and musicology, and engages subtleties of how folklore and mass- or pop-culture studies relate to one another.

Introduction

During the late 1950s and early 1960s, the landscape of pop music in America was dramatically altered by the arrival of rock and roll music as the sound of a new generation. Adolescents had more money than ever before and found themselves in a place where they could influence the world of popular media and its associated business of commodification – the conversion of common cultural property to bankable assets – and the monetization of youth itself. As Bruce Harrah-Conforth puts it: "…as the marketplace shifted its focus to the attention of youth and their parents' dollars, the focus of American life also shifted to youth" (307). Kids wanted to hear something loud, with a beat they could dance to – something just for them – and situated themselves as a commercial demographic that could demand it. Out of this demographic came a slew of junior-high and high-school aged kids who wanted to make music of their own, their own version of the music they worshipped, and who outfitted themselves with budget instruments to learn, copy, and appropriate the rhythm and blues based sounds of the artists they went wild for. Soon, a nationwide boom of underground music was taking place, with demand for live rock and roll as instigator.

It was during this time that small towns all across America cultivated their own "scenes," comprised of a handful of bands sharing the local dance and bar circuit. In Kirksville, MO and surrounding areas, a group called "The Red Blazers" rose to popularity by creating their own variations of popular rock and roll songs, while writing some of their own material based on those hits. Aspiring music mogul and Kirksville native Dick Lowrance, who had ideas for taking the insurgence of local groups a step further, managed the Red Blazers. As other artists – such as the Twilighters – sprouted in the area, Lowrance took them too under his wing, with hopes of uniting the scene into one core under the banner of his independent record label, Red Flame Records (Daniels).

Dick Lowrance, Red Flame and the Red Blazers

Between 1961 and 1967, Dick Lowrance produced and released records from artists local to Kirksville through Red Flame. A total of ten songs were recorded and distributed on five 45 rpm singles, eight of them featuring The Red Blazers with different vocalists; the first two being from Jonny Bragg & the Red Blazers, and three from Ike Haley & the Red Blazers. The Red Blazers also recorded three tracks sans vocalist. They were an instrumental group that took on various front men on vocal duties, with only one record that strictly features the core instrumental group. The only record released on Red Flame that didn't feature Lowrance's Red Blazers was by a group comprised of high school and college-aged musicians from Kirksville and surrounding areas dubbed "The Twlighters." The Twilighters released the label's final record in 1967.

Twilighters drummer Dave Daniels remembers the early days of the northeastern Missouri rock and roll scene, and how Dick Lowrance sought to unify all of the groups playing locally under one management flagship. Though Lowrance's intentions may have been entrepreneurial and profit-minded, he provided opportunity to young musicians through the connections he forged with smaller music industry figures, and he opened up options of recording for his groups in St. Louis, and of pressing the records through companies like Rite Records in Cincinnati, Ohio.

Beginnings: Dick Lowrance and Jonny Bragg

The Red Blazers were formed in Kirksville in the late 1950s, probably 1958 or '59. After playing many local gigs, friend and aspiring disc jockey

Lowrance, still a teenager, began to offer financial support and managerial services to the group with hopes of expanding their popularity around the region (Ellis). In 1961, at age twenty, he enacted his idea for an independently funded record label by pairing the group with vocalist Jonny Bragg and producing two songs, one co-written by Bragg and Lowrance ("Flame of Love") and the other solely penned by Bragg ("Storybook Love"). The songs, supposedly recorded at Technosonic Studios in St. Louis (where all of the Red Flame songs were tracked), would become the inaugural Red Flame release.

It was also around this time that Lowrance opened the small, short-lived Red Flame storefront near the town square in Kirksville; it only operated for a short period between 1961 and 1962 (Ellis). In addition, the Red Blazers hosted a Dick Lowrance-produced teen dance television program in Ottumwa, IA on KTVO, on Saturday evenings at five (Daniels). The program, like the storefront, was short lived; Donny Ellis estimates a run of only 6-8 weeks in 1961. Ellis remembers being invited by Dick to dance on the show, and Dave Daniels remembers The Twilighters being invited to play a set in the Blazers' place. Because the shows were shot entirely live, there are no surviving tapes archiving them.

Ike Haley

Soon, Bragg and the Blazers parted ways and Ike Haley took over vocal duties for the group; he recorded a string of songs with them over the next two years. Haley, an African American originally from Arkansas, had roots in classic rhythm and blues and added a new flair to The Blazers that contrasted the teen dance sound of the Jonny Bragg singles. His addition by Lowrance to the group further cemented music as a unifying philosophical entity within the cultural community of the Kirksville area, because Haley, in every sense, "added color" to a scene that was prepared to fully embrace black music and the related approach to rhythm and blues. The three songs he recorded with the Blazers are versions of Little Richard's "Lucille," "A Thousand Miles Away," originally a hit by doo-wop group The Heartbeats, and Big Jay McNeely's 1957 record, "There's Something on Your Mind" (Ellis).

All of these songs had a distinct rhythm and blues sound, aided heavily by Haley's extra soulful interpretations of what had become instant classics and dance hall favorites. It was his electric adoption of these well-known tunes that made his reputation as a performer, and by making them his own he participated in the common practice in underground music of appropriating mass culture into something rooted heavily in communal transmission.

Expansion: The Twilighters, Friar Tuck & the Merry Men

The Twilighters were founded in the early 1960s by upperclassmen from high schools in Kirksville and surrounding areas. They gigged rigorously on the local circuit, playing everywhere from bars (where their peers couldn't watch them perform), to school dances, to self-organized gigs at the National Guard Armory in Kirksville. Many member changes took place within the band, but the group eventually landed on what Daniels calls the "classic" lineup of the group–Randy Elmore, Gary Blurton, Everett Cassady, and himself. Daniels was much younger than the other guys, and admits he just tagged along.

It wasn't long before Lowrance recognized their youthful talent and invited them to record under Red Flame. This was in 1967, and Daniels remembers going to Technosonic Studios in St. Louis to cut two original songs—"Spellbound" and "My Little Angel." "Spellbound" was written specifically for that session; it has since gained attention in circles of 1960s garage rock scholarship, and its rollicking, simple structure and manic upbeat tempo are considered early examples of features that would later become punk rock.

Their sound wasn't the only feature of the group that can be rightfully considered as a predecessor to punk. Daniels remembers those self-organized gigs at the Armory the best, because it was "better to do it yourself." They would pay $50 to rent the place for an evening, pay the janitor $50 to clean up; and they would pack the place with kids at 75 cents per entry, clearing the profit margin by a landslide. This do-it-yourself ethic lends more evidence to the communal vitality of the early days of local, independent music scenes, which would come to full fruition in the punk rock movement of the 1970s and 80s. This was a music made by the locals for the locals, and organized entirely by the "kids" without outside help or influence.

Lowrance produced one other group, Friar Tuck and the Merry Men, out of Western Illinois (Blurton). Though the group wasn't released under the Red Flame banner, their sound is similar to that of the other groups, creating a fine continuity between the Midwestern local music sound that was being perpetuated by young musicians in the 1960s. They released one Lowrance-produced single on what could be an original Lowrance label, namely Sherwood Forest records. The songs on that single were "Peanut Butter" and "Try Me" (Ellis).

The Era of Smalltown Rock

The small town and urban boom of young rock and roll imitators of the late 1950s and early 1960s forged what could be considered a new folk community. Young musicians listened to rhythm and blues records to escape the pressures of school and parents; and their desire to learn instruments and imitate the new sounds stemmed from a communal and in some ways anti-academic approach to musicianship. If a young musician wanted to learn a song, they taught themselves and taught each other. In her book *The Musical Ear: Oral Tradition in the USA*, Anne Dhu McLucas talks extensively about the oral tradition involved in popular American music as it takes on a life of its own outside of the pop world: "The changes wrought by successive performers as they took on a piece and made it their own were seldom the result of notational changes; instead, they resulted from the individual stylistic characteristics of the genre" (49).

As ways to play different rock and roll or rhythm and blues songs were passed from musician to musician, stability and variation began to show up heavily in local interpretations of different hits or in the incorporation of those newly discovered practices into simple, original compositions. In other words, there was no book written on how to play the groovy new music taking the country by storm, so it was left to those who desired to learn it to create their own means of doing so. McLucas gives an exact description of the musical crevasse discussed here when she says that, "The bands generally start by covering the songs of the bands they want to emulate, but often branch out from there to do their own material" (67). This could be seen as an example of how something from mass culture can influence a folk group and lead to that group's appropriation of the culture into their own community.

An example of this is Ike Haley & The Red Blazer's recording of the song "Lucille," released about 1962. This song had been made famous in its original version recorded by Little Richard in 1957, during the beginning of the rock and roll takeover. Songs like "Lucille" enter the folk world when they are learned and passed on outside of–or better, underneath– the pop world and mainstream society. These musicians were creating a new mode of folk transmission in relation to the new form of culture, by learning these songs in the under-the-radar setting of small towns and urban areas. This form of cultural conductivity can be paralleled to the way Appalachian folk or southern blues music is passed on by means of one-to-one transmission in a rural community.

Folk Culture and Pop Culture

One major difference here is that the previously mentioned classic folk music settings date back many, many years in practice and don't show any signs of being derived from mass culture. Some would say this is what makes them distinctively folk, but an argument may be made that the evolving landscape of youth culture in America in the late 50s and early 60s allowed for a new type of folk ideology to emerge within centralized towns, in which young people are influenced more by mass culture than by traditional folk methods of cultural transmission, and therefore construct their own folklore influenced by–but not the same as–mass media.

Harrah-Conforth talks much about the folkloric qualities of rock and roll music and its community-binding effect. He mostly writes about the rite of passage involved in youths attending rock and roll concerts, paraphrasing Victor Turner when he says that "...due to the very chemical workings of our brains, human beings have no choice but to construct [folklore] to explain their world in what often appears to be a capricious universe" (308). This alone is prevalent in the notion of the necessity for American youth to construct their own folk communities in relation to the mass culture shift that rock and roll brought with it, at a time when consumerism became more focused on youth and their demands. Harrah-Conforth elaborates more convincingly: "...rock and roll, like all human products, has the capability of being used as a tool to both reorder and make sense out of that 'capricious universe'" (308). It's not as if young people of this time period were consciously trying to sift through and decide what was traditionally appropriate for them to base their community around, but instead, they actively recognized the need for their own ritualistic processes and created them as an abstraction from the mass media that heavily influenced their worldview and common practices.

Hannah-Conforth makes a great point—that "Those critics who have failed to see rock and roll as anything but a mass-market commodity have extracted the item from the process..." (310). This observation is borne out by the manner in which young musicians were learning the songs that they wanted to replicate, and creating their own spins on those popular hits as they adopted them from mass culture into their grassroots sphere. Just because something is commodified and mass produced doesn't mean that it didn't have roots in a folk community or couldn't inspire one.

During the early 1960s, the music itself was impacting the smaller cultural groups of young musicians through recordings, and the musicians were picking apart those songs and learning them, then rebuilding them in new versions that displayed stability and variation. This is exemplified in different stages within the singles that were recorded and released on Red Flame Records, from covers with slight variation such as Haley's rendition of "Lucille" to original tunes obviously based on the structures that were prominent within rock and roll trends at the time, structures based on approaches that the composers had learned and passed along within the group.

Wherever there is music–wherever there are musicians–there will be a folk community. There are certain traditional parameters of what can be considered folk music itself, but it is not entirely unfair to say that any type of music can be of a folk type once it enters the folk community and that community manipulates it and appropriates it in unique ways that are separate from the popular society which had propelled it or generated it. Soon, ways of playing a rock and roll song that was originally written for a consumer audience become so variable among independent musicians that the song takes on a folk essence of its own, due to its sacred and ritualistic significance to the non-pop community that embraces it and passes it along. This is evident in the story of Red Flame Records, an early independent music label that took on the job of uniting and perpetuating a small-town music scene with an inspired do-it-yourself ethic. It's this kind of grassroots planning and execution that proves ideas about music and art can be taken from the greater realm of society and be used on a folk level within a specified community.

Works Cited

Blurton, Gary. Personal Interview. 8 March. 2013.

Daniels, Dave. Personal Interview. 3 Oct. 2013.

Ellis, Donald. Personal Interview. 3 Oct. 2013

Harrah-Conforth, Bruce. "Rock and Roll, Process, and Tradition." *Western Folklore* 49.3 (1990): 306-13. JSTOR. Web. 11 Sep. 2013.

McLucas, Anne Dhu. *The Musical Ear: Oral Tradition in the USA*. Farnham: Ashgate, 2010. Print.

Appendix: Photographs

"Storybook Love" (Bragg) by Jonny Bragg and the Red Blazers,
Red Flame Records: Produced by Dick Lowrance.
Catalog # 101B. Pressed at Rite Music, Cincinnati, OH. 1961.
https://www.youtube.com/watch?v=aEruKkhIwNo

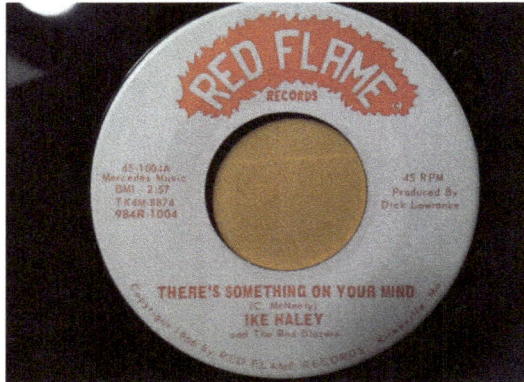

Ike Haley and the Red Blazers: There's Something on Your Mind
https://www.youtube.com/watch?v=RIerYt54qvw&feature=emb_title

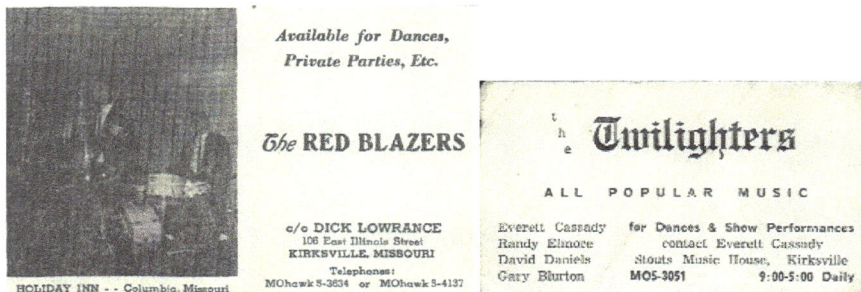

Available for Dances,
Private Parties, Etc.

𝕮𝖍𝖊 RED BLAZERS

c/o DICK LOWRANCE
106 East Illinois Street
KIRKSVILLE, MISSOURI
Telephones:
MOhawk 5-3634 or MOhawk 5-4137

HOLIDAY INN - - Columbia, Missouri

𝕿𝖜𝖎𝖑𝖎𝖌𝖍𝖙𝖊𝖗𝖘

ALL POPULAR MUSIC

Everett Cassady
Randy Elmore
David Daniels
Gary Blurton

for Dances & Show Performances
contact Everett Cassady
Stouts Music House, Kirksville
MO5-3051   9:00-5:00 Daily

Left: Red Blazers business card.(Ellis)

Right: Twilighters business card (Daniels)

Left: Twlighters Promo
        Gart Blurton & Dave Daniels (Standing)
        Everett Cassady & Randy Elmore (Kneeling) (Daniels)

Right: Twilighters live, mid-1960s (Daniels)

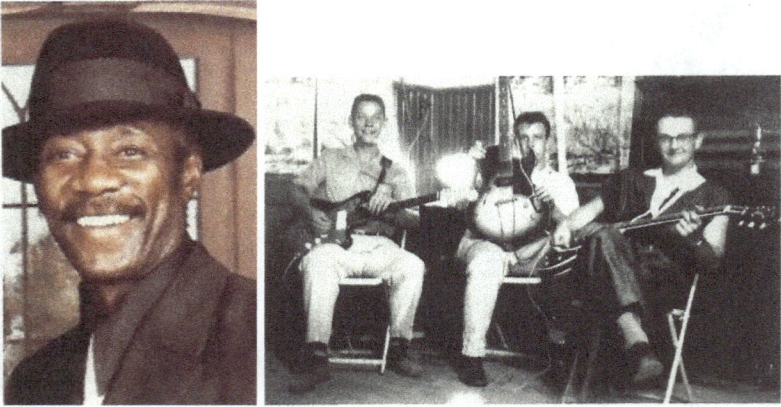

Left: Ike Haley (1935-2009) (Ellis)
Right: The Red Blazers: David Prather, Larry Smith, Bobby Rollins (Ellis)

The Red Blazers: Front Row – Bob Rollins, Dick Mohr, David Prather
Back row: Dick Lowrance, Nels Edwards, Jerry Hagmeyer (Ellis)

Southern Magnolias in the Neighborhood: Vernacular Architecture in Jefferson City's Moreau Drive Area
Rachel Spillars

In 2010, the investigator – one of the first Folklore minors in Truman's new program – chose as her capstone project to document her own neighborhood, which appeared to her in a new light after studying Howard Wight Marshall's work on folk forms in Missouri buildings. The project turned out to reach far beyond material folklore.

In 1911 the Missouri State Capitol burned down, sparking immense pressure from both St. Louis and Sedalia officials and lobbyists to move the Capitol location to their respective cities (Ohman 56). Governor Hadley settled the issue of location by a public decision in favor of Jefferson City. Before 1911, consistent efforts to move Missouri's seat of Government from Jefferson City since its transition from St. Charles had plagued the city's economic growth, effectively stalling any expansion (Grace 2). After the decision by Hadley in 1911, "Jefferson City entered a 'boom' period of economic growth.... The population of the town also increased dramatically, from 11,800 in 1910 to 25,000 in 1930. By the later date, most of the town's population lived outside of the original townsite in newer annexed suburbs east, west and south of downtown, while commercial and institutional buildings occupied the streets surrounding the Capitol" (Grace 2). During the expansion in 1910 to 1930, the majority of the houses in the Moreau Drive area were built.

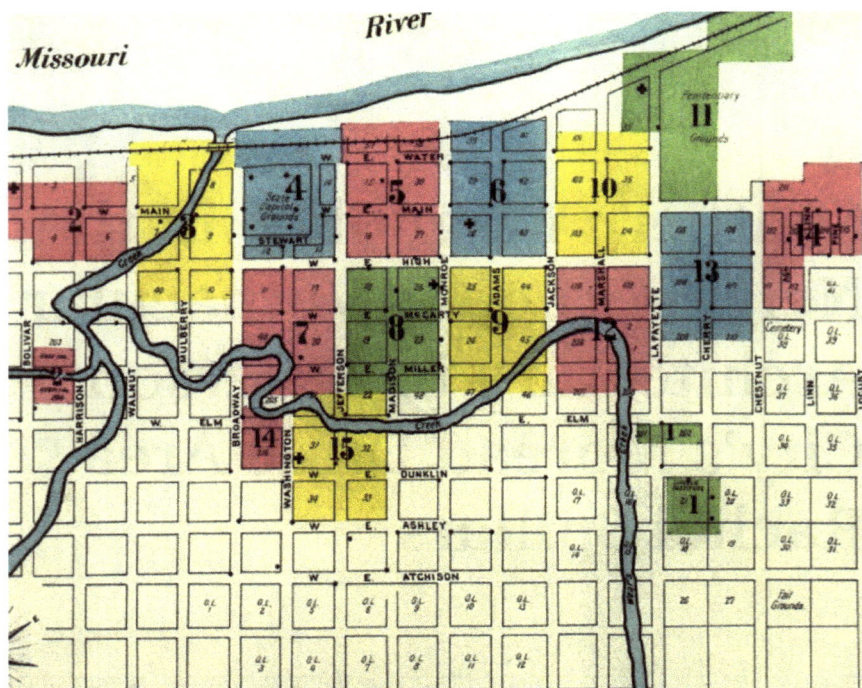

Figure 1 Sanborn Fire Insurance Map "Jefferson City, Missouri February 1908 #1." Capitol marked as #4. Fairgrounds located in lower right corner

Originally titled "Fairmont" as an allusion to the Cole County Fairgrounds which the street supplanted, Moreau Drive occupied farmland (See Figure 1). A few farm homes and a southern antebellum existed on the street, which, being two miles from downtown, had been considered on the outskirts of the city. Here, the expansion of Jefferson City produced a variety of houses and a strongly defined community. This paper aims to study the interconnectivity of the architecture of the Moreau Drive area's houses and stylistic development. In addition to the material folklore, the architecture itself, oral traditions regarding the development of the area and current customary cultural practices exist which help define the inhabitants as a community. The oral folklore intertwined with the development of the architectural types and styles, present and past, in the community. Therefore, the focus of the study deals with both the present and past incarnations of the homes and the folktales told about them. Growing up in the area, I heard firsthand many of the stories regarding prominent figures in the community, giving me many stories to draw on and a foothold in the community. The stories recounted here are from my experience. However, the area is large with many connecting streets, and a choice of location and houses had to be limited.

For the study, using the information from the MidMOGIS and direct observations on the houses, I chose an area of Moreau Drive that can be readily separated from the surrounding neighborhoods by geographic markers and the date of construction. The MidMOGIS allowed me to view the construction date of the houses, although some of the given times can only be approximated due to limited information. The houses span from where

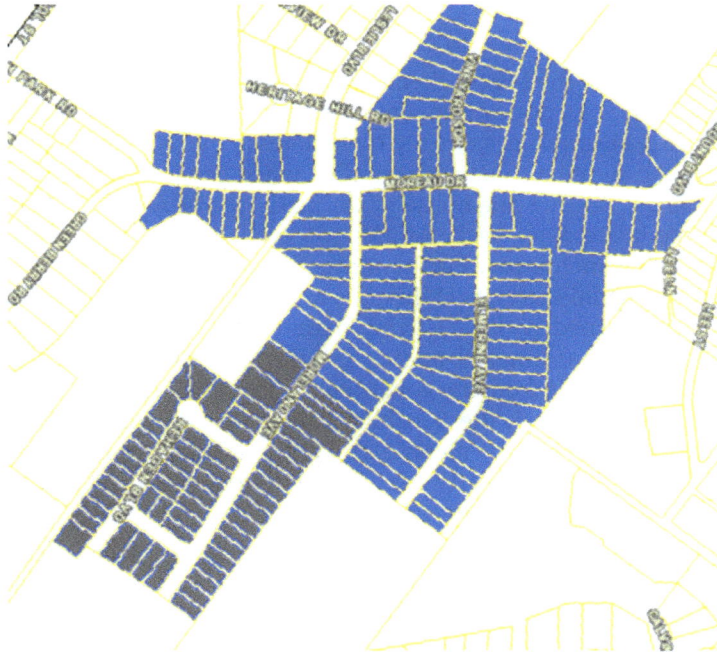

Figure 2 Map of Moreau Drive Area with land lots. Blue lots included in study. Grey and White lots not included due to national style trends, build date, or outside the scope of the area.

Moreau Drive branches off in Greenberry Road and Hough Park Road to where the Civil War marker stands between Moreau Drive and Fairmount Boulevard. Inside this area, four streets are connected to Moreau Drive: Moreland Avenue, which also branches into a few other streets, Elmerine Ave, Vineyard Square, and Leslie Boulevard. Excluding Leslie Boulevard and the branches of Moreland Avenue, all of the homes on these streets were documented in the study. Leslie Blvd. does not feature in the study because of a time difference in its creation and the national trend of its split level and ranch style homes (national trends in housing reflect non-folk architecture in that they are mass trends in type and style, with very little deviation over different demographics). Leslie Blvd.'s houses were built during the 1960's and 1970's, well after the construction of Moreau Drive and the houses therein. The style of the houses on Leslie Blvd. is consistent with mass market trends in housing styles during the 70's and 60's, namely, split-level houses and ranch style houses. A similar developmental scenario occurred in the streets branching off from Moreland Avenue. These homes were built too late to be included in the study, and have had very little change to their styles since their construction.

Information on the homes themselves is limited, and what information exists might be inaccurate or unavailable to the public. The MidMOGIS, as stated earlier, allowed access to the build dates of the homes, but even their information cannot be completely verified when house numbers and street names change, causing one house's information to be ascribed to another. Some of the home dates in the MidMOGIS are approximations because of inadequate documentation. Furthermore, there are few available photos of the houses' original exteriors. When the old Capitol burned in 1911, many state records burned with it, leaving many of the oldest houses without records prior to that time. In addition to the physical lack of documents, many are inaccessible from the government, according to various agencies' secretaries (even though the Sunshine Law in Missouri does not prevent anyone from looking at the materials). With a shortage of documentation from the government, the Historic City of Jefferson, the city's historical society, provided many photos and resources.

In examining the region's vernacular architecture, I mainly use the term and research concepts of vernacular architecture as detailed by Howard Wight Marshall in his *Vernacular Architecture in Rural and Small Town Missouri: An Introduction* and architectural terms as defined by the *Encyclopedia of 20th-Century Architecture*. The earliest folk, or vernacular, architecture of the area can be traced in the type of building, and the development of the community in the changing style of the building. Marshall defines the "type" of building as the structure of the home: the floor plan, the placement of rooms, height. Type is relatively stable over time, while style can change frequently, in ornamentation and personal taste. In other words, vernacular architecture type is functional, meeting the needs of the occupants, while style is the local decoration and an indication of the cultural and demographic identity to which a building ascribes.

Past ornamentation on the buildings is difficult to trace, especially in cases where the house has been renovated, to the point where the original structure is unrecognizable, impeding analysis of the vernacular types and changes in the community. How can changes be determined if the original structure is unknown? There are a few ways to tell if a house has stayed the same over the course of its life. The first and most definite way to determine any changes is to compare the home's floor plan with its original plan or to compare the home to pictures dating from its origin. However, pictures do not exist for all of the homes, nor are floor plans readily available. There were two ways of determining the extent of alterations in a home. The first is looking at the houses themselves. Vinyl siding, uneven roof lines, or windows that do not quite match up on the same line indicate a home that has undergone remodeling at least on the outside. For demonstration, three houses can exemplify these methods of determining change.

1302 Moreau Drive shows all the characteristics of extensive exterior remodeling: the back roof line is not entirely straight, the windows do not match up to the same height on the same level, and plastic siding is used on the back and upper levels, while the original brick is on the first level (see Figure 3).

Figure 3: 1302 Moreau Drive. Multiple additions, brick painted white, white siding. Type: original type unknown, possibly Georgian/American Foursquare

Figure 4: 1203 Moreau Drive. Multiple renovations. Type: Bungalow

Figure 5: 1106 Vineyard Square. Multiple renovations, painted stucco exterior. Spanish and Italian influences. Type: unknown/L-house.

The second, since I live in the neighborhood, is that I have seen which houses in the last ten years received remodeling and I have heard of renovations of homes from neighbors. An example of this is the house at 1203 Moreau Drive (see Figure 4). The house was "flipped" around 2003, when the property developer put on a beige-painted stucco exterior and replaced the front porch and window trimming. A similar makeover occurred for the home at 1106 Vineyard Square (see Figure 5). For 1302 Moreau Drive, 1203 Moreau Drive, and 1106 Vineyard Square, stylistic changes updated their appearance, and no documentation exists for their earliest appearances. It should be stressed that changes in appearance are not a bad thing and actually indicate what direction current stylistic choices are forming and changing in existing communities.

By comparing the type of home with the home's style and visible changes, the architectural history — the folk architectural history — of the community becomes clear. A home's type is relatively constant over time and tells of the original decorations and means of the family living therein. Style changes through time and indicates a change in community values and their desired outward perception. The types of houses in the Moreau Drive area are numerous: Tudor, American Foursquare, Georgian, Italian Renaissance, prairie, bungalow, French Eclectic. One of the most common home types in the Moreau Drive area is the American Foursquare.

Some debate exists as to exactly how "folk" the American Foursquare is. According to John Milbauer in the *Encyclopedia of Oklahoma History and Culture*, the American Foursquare is "substantially built," "conveys stark simplicity," and "is not a folk house, built from local tradition, but a popular style found across the country, especially the Midwest." He argues that the American Foursquare type is not a folk house type because of its move into popular style and use around the country and through mail order catalogs. William Young in the *Encyclopedia of 20th-Century Architecture* disagrees with Milbauer's assessment, giving the American Foursquare credit as a "vernacular design," an "efficient, self-contained box," whose basic shape, despite any additions, is always apparent (43-45).

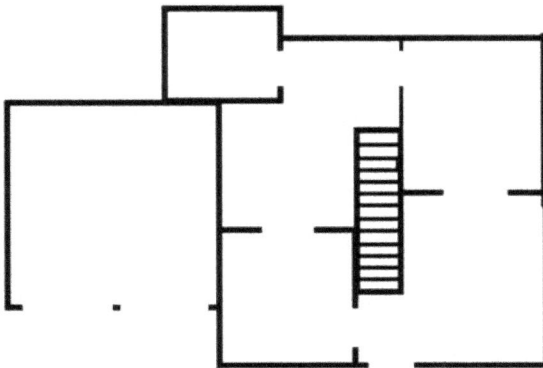

Figure 6: Typical floorplan of American Foursquare (garage often left off)

Figure 7: Example American Foursquare (this specimen from Colorado). This foursquare has the ubiquitous front porch, overhanging eaves, the dormer atop the hip roof, general square shape, and four sets of windows spaced over the first and second stories' front exterior.

But what, exactly, is an American Foursquare? All Foursquare houses have similar exterior aesthetics, mainly aimed at reducing cost. The houses almost always have a first story front porch, a large front dormer in the attic for light and fresh air, overhanging eaves for shade on the second story, irregularly spaced windows for more light and air, and sometimes windows without muntins to cut down on costs (Young, 43-44). The house type was "designed more for utility than for architectural or stylistic purity" (Young, 44). The American Foursquare saw its boom-period between 1910 and 1940 when the expansion into suburbs allowed Americans larger houses for the same amount of money. Essentially, the house is cheap, sturdy, and simple (see Figures 6 and 7). The American Foursquare also took to applied decoration, or, different styles, very well.

Although John Milbauer discounts the house type, mainly because of its association with prosperity and popularity, the American Foursquare is a folk house, for "vernacular architecture is traditional architecture. It gives a visible face and functional core to local patterns, ethnic and regional character" (Marshall). Alyson Greiner defines folk architecture as

> Architectural traditions [that] encompass not only the types of structures designed and built, but also the ways in which buildings are arranged upon the land, the methods and materials of construction, the functions that different structures serve, and the social, cultural, economic, and political milieu associated with particular architectural conventions. (*Encyclopedia of Oklahoma History and Culture*)

Vernacular home designs conform to economic situations, the owner's values and priorities, natural settings, and local access to resources. Additionally, as Howard Wight Marshall states, the "vernacular building is well represented in structures that may seem to be high-style, yet exhibit strong elements of local and ethnic cultural heritage, such as the Victorian town house, the community school building, the mail order catalog bungalow and the county courthouse" (Marshall). The Foursquares, and other house types in the Moreau Drive area, reflect these properties of vernacular architecture. For instance, the materials used for construction mainly consisted of brick or locally sourced rocks, to conform to resources available and the setting of Jefferson City. Jefferson City in general has a distinct lack of wood and plastic siding along houses. Some say this is due to a city ordinance requiring a certain percentage of a building's (home, office, school, etc.) exterior to be brick or stone, so as to support a local brick factory or to improve the town's aesthetics. The oral history suggests the social and political setting dictated a certain exterior, promoting the use of local resources for these homes (Figure 8).

Figure 8: 1203 Elmerine Ave. Hip roof with dormer. Front Porch design corresponds to traditional Foursquare archetype. Type: American Foursquare, brick exterior.

Figure 9: The Gingerbread House, 1212 Moreland Ave., also known as the Hobbit House. Timber framing wood on stucco exterior. Type: Tudor, stucco exterior, natural stone chimney.

Over time, as styles came and went, the exterior of the area's Foursquare houses changed to conform with the social and cultural atmosphere of the neighborhood. Specifically folk aspects for the basic type of the home became atavistic hold-overs for style, not function. For example, the Gingerbread House, also known as the Hobbit House and 1212 Moreland, and 1212 Elmerine both use atavistic timber framing. The lines crisscrossing the homes' front is timber framing, once used as part of a home's structural support (Figure 9). Now, home construction does not need the extra support the timber framing provided, but the look of framing stays on for atavistic decoration. Another example is the brackets under the roof eaves (Figure 10). Originally, these brackets helped support the roof's overhang, but now their main purpose is improving aesthetics. Brackets and timber-framing are relatively common in the neighborhood, lending an old-world style and feel to the homes.

Figure 10: 1212 Elmerine Avenue. Timber framing, brackets under eaves. Type: American Foursquare, brick exterior.

Some of the facades of the houses have changed drastically from their original forms. Changes do not mean that the folk aspect of the building is gone, rather, that a new folk social dynamic or group has introduced itself to the area. Stylistic ornament changes to the exterior are "characteristically applied as a sort of mask or Sunday clothes, put on the exterior of an otherwise humble building. The special architectural style that dresses up a vernacular building is a vital element in the building's social and cultural identity" (Marshall). Stylistic ornamentation in the neighborhood reflects cultural shifts, sometimes along national trends. By putting Greek columns on an otherwise plain building, a homeowner alters the perception of the property and neighborhood. Such is the case with Hyde House, 1204 Moreland Avenue (see Figure 11).

Figure 11: Hyde House, 1204 Moreland Ave. Ionic columns, ornamental second story door. Type: American Foursquare, brick exterior.

The house was built by the Gieseckes, the owners of a local shoe factory at the State Prison. Reportedly, Mr. Gieseckes used prison labor when building his house. Hyde House rests on a limestone foundation, common in the neighborhood and area, as limestone is in ready supply. Hyde House is named for Judge Hyde, a Missouri Supreme Court Judge. Before Judge Hyde, the home probably looked more like Figure 8. After moving in, the Hydes reportedly added the ionic columns and the second story door, which is for decoration only. Mrs. Hyde was known to serve sherry at the door to guests at her dinner parties. Hyde House prominently features a Northern Magnolia, a flowering tree very common to the area and used as more decoration. Hyde House's exterior changed to fit with the social and cultural identity of the Hydes and the community at large as peer pressure to conform to the neighborhood's elite ideal.

As with Hyde House, the oral folklore associated with the other large houses focuses on the families that built them or left an enduring legacy in the area. One home is the Vineyard Place, 1122 Moreau Drive. Vineyard Place is a Southern Antebellum house, with twelve-inch-thick limestone walls (see Figures 12 and 13)—as recorded by Smith and Bening for *The Historic City of Jefferson.* According to Nicholas Monaco, the current owner of Vineyard Place, the home was originally built in 1849 by Missouri Governor John Edwards, but it was never completed when his marriage plans collapsed.

Figure 12: Vineyard Place, circa 1964. Courtesy of Historic City of Jefferson.

Figure 13: Vineyard Place, present. Square columns, City of Jefferson. Note the "widow's walk." Type: Southern Antebellum.

Edwards then sold the house before the Civil War and headed west in search of gold. During the war, it is said that Union soldiers occupied the house, using it as an observation point. After the war and many changes of hands, Vineyard Place was sold to the Havilands, who had one child, Mayme Vineyard (Smith and Bening). Mayme Vineyard was an interesting person and is considered one of the founders of the neighborhood. She used $6,000 dollars of her own money to build a road when the city wouldn't, and then gave it to the city.

Figure 14: 1107 Vineyard Square. One of the homes built by Mayme Vineyard. Type: Prairie Influence, Eclectic.

The road is named Vineyard Square, after her. She built the residences on Vineyard Square, as well as twenty-three houses on Moreau Drive (see Figure 14). The homes, which used quality materials and had interesting styles, were sold very cheaply. She ended up broke, renting out rooms and selling chicken eggs, and the home fell into disrepair.

In addition to Mayme Vineyard's legacy, the home also has rumors of a secret tunnel in the basement, purportedly used as part of the Underground Railroad. This tunnel corresponds to other rumors of secret tunnels underneath the Capitol connecting it to other government buildings. Nicholas Monaco says he was pressured into buying the home and restoring it, redeeming the neighborhood with it (Smith and Bening, 5). Nicholas Monaco restored the home, much to the neighborhood's delight.

Louis Ott, known locally as the "Lumber Doctor," sold Monaco the Vineyard Place. Ott and his family made a lasting impact on the neighborhood in a variety of ways; and, along with Mayme Vineyard, he is considered one of the founders of the neighborhood. The Ott family is responsible for many houses in the Moreau Drive area, those they lived in, or those they built as rental properties. The lumber baron Ott built three homes in a row for himself and his two children. His children, Irene and Elmer, lend their names to Elmerine Avenue.

The homes built by the Otts for themselves reflect the transition from simple, affordable architecture to elite paradigm architecture. Louis Ott and his wife Pauline Ott built 1119 Moreau Drive in 1925 as an American Foursquare home resembling Figure 8. As the story goes, Pauline was traveling south and fell in love with the architecture (Brooks). When she returned to Missouri, she brought with her renovation ideas and two southern magnolia seeds. The result is the Ott Home with the southern magnolia from two intertwined seeds (See Figure 15). The two permanent homes Ott built for his children are not in the American Foursquare style. Rather, each has unique influences. These houses are larger and more opulent than the American Foursquare, and it should be noted that "people choose building styles and types for reasons. They may want a building with a popular style to make an impression on the neighborhood, to express well-being and success, or to reflect the fashion of the day" (Marshall). The first is the Castle House, 1117 Moreau Drive (see Figure 16).

Figure 15: The Ott Home, 1119 Moreau Drive. Ionic columns; note the Southern Magnolia trees (to left). Type: American Foursquare.

Figure 16: The Castle House, 1117 Moreau Drive. Atavistic timber framing, slate roof, and turret. Type: English Tudor, brick.

The Castle House is best known for its defining turret and Tudor style, making a grand impression on the neighborhood and elevating the area's status. The second home is 1201 Moreau Drive (see Figure 17). 1201 Moreau Drive's type of architecture has been described variously as Spanish Revival, Italian Renaissance, and Art Deco. Curiously, 1201 Moreau has a bell tower, usually reserved to churches, yet here used in a family home. In the area, these three homes, The Ott Home, the Castle House, and 1201 Moreau Drive, are noted as foundations of the community for their stately exteriors and historical significance to the development of the elite paradigm.

Figure 17: 1201 Moreau Drive. Bell Tower, tile roof, details in arch front doorway. Type: Spanish Revival, Italian Renaissance, or Art Deco.

More houses followed which the Otts either rented out or sold. The Otts rented 1322 Elmerine, a simple looking home with a unique patterned concrete floor (see Figure 18).

Figure 18: 1322 Elmerine Ave. Patterned concrete flooring, front door pilaster decoration. Type: Colonial/American Foursquare.

One home the Otts built, however, is not as widely regarded as their other homes. The home is 1303 Elmerine Avenue, known as the Honeymoon Cottage. Louis Ott built it for his daughter Irene Ott and her new husband, Percy Steppleman (see Figure 19). The relatively small Honeymoon Cottage is along the prairie house type, and styled a very bright pink. The residents of Elmerine, who refer to themselves as "Elmerinos," hate the house. While other homes along Elmerino fall into the American foursquare, bungalow, or Tudor-esque house type, none are pink. Elmerinos regard their street highly and formed a community around maintaining a rigorous standard of curb appeal. This gives landscaping and general home maintenance a high priority, which the Honeymoon Cottage currently bears. The Elmerinos will peer pressure homeowners to maintain their lawns and their homes to conform to the community standard.

Figure 19: The Honeymoon Cottage, 1303 Elmerine Avenue. Pink. Type: Prairie.

The enforcement of a community curb appeal, although not mandated, affects the entirety of the Moreau Drive area. Gardens flourish, and the Magnolia trees seen throughout the neighborhood stand as an emblem — and boundary, of sorts — for the community. Where the Magnolia trees are, the Moreau Drive community is.

Jefferson City's Moreau Drive neighborhood distinguishes itself by its architecture and myriad ornamentations. Although considered an elite neighborhood, the homes come from modest origins. Changes in the community appear in the changing architectural styles. The Hydes, Otts, and Mayme Vineyard transformed the area's architectural landscape, infusing their own histories with the homes.

Works Cited

Alyson L. Greiner. "Folk Architecture." *Encyclopedia of Oklahoma History and Culture*. Oklahoma Historical Society, 2007. Web. 1 August 2012.

Brooks, Michelle. "Family Adds Modern Touches, But keeps Character of Historic Ott Home." *Jefferson City News Tribune* 20 November 2011: n.p. Web.

Grace, Karen. "Jefferson City: An Architectural Biography." *Preservation Issues*. 5.5 (1995): 1-8. Web. 15 Apr. 2012.

"Jefferson City, Missouri February 1908 #1." Map. Sanborn Fire Insurance Maps of Missouri Collection. N.p.: Sanborn Map Company, 1908.

n.p. Special Collections and Rare Books. MU Libraries, University of Missouri. Web. 9 Mar. 2013.

John A. Milbauer, "Foursquare House," *Encyclopedia of Oklahoma History and Culture*, Oklahoma Historical Society, 2007. Web. 1 August 2012.

Marshall, Howard Wight. *Vernacular Architecture in Rural and Small Town Missouri: An Introduction.* Columbia: University of Missouri-Columbia, 1994. Online.

"MidMoGIS Area." Map. MidMoGIS. City of Jefferson, 2009. Web. 02 Apr. 2012. The MidMOGIS is a map which allows access to geographic data regarding homes and neighborhoods of Jefferson City. It is available online at www.midmogis.org.

Ohman, Marian M. *The History of Missouri Capitols.* Columbia, Missouri: University of Missouri-Columbia, 1982. Print.

Smith, Jenny and Carolyn Bening. "Vineyard Place: A Landmark Saved, a Neighborhood Revived." *Yesterday and Today* May 2012: 4-6. Print.

William, Young H. "American Foursquare." *The Encyclopedia of 20th-Century Architecture.* Ed. Stephen Sennott. Oxfordshire: Routlege, 2004. Print.

Girl Scouts vs. Boy Scouts: The Girl Power Paradox
Mary Stowers

This 2019 study integrates personal experience with interview and archive work, and further with sociohistorical inquiry, in a quest both personal and private, to make sense of the conflicts the investigator experienced in scouting.

Girl Scouts and Boy Scouts share a complicated past, intersecting and diverging at various points in history. While Boy Scouts began as a paramilitary movement in Britain and later moved to represent the clean-cut, All American Boy in the US, Girl Scouts began as a reaction to the existence of the Boy Scouts; from its outset, it attempted to represent a conflicted set of ideals, trying to both free girls from, and instruct them in, a cultural idea of femininity.

Each organization has had a complex relationship with shifting ideas of race, gender, and sexuality, which resulted in a stark divergence in their approaches and policies around 1970-1980. Boy Scouts redoubled their efforts to remain the old-fashioned, traditional scouting organization and affiliated itself with more conservative ideals. They tied themselves to a defense of traditional masculinity, sometimes to toxic ends: as recently as 2013/2014, policies around banning gay adults from the program were hotly debated. (Margolin). Meanwhile, Girl Scouts looked ahead, embraced issues of sexuality and feminist theory, and changed its public image accordingly, allying itself with left-leaning organizations such as Planned Parenthood.

GS, however, much more than its male counterpart, struggled with ideological dissonance between its origins and its current goals. Originally, the handbooks were filled with encouragement of what it means to be "womanly" and filled with activities suited to such a goal, while trying to balance this against feminine independence with badges like "aviation" and "adventurer" (Arneil 54-57). It's hard to pick a side when these coexist with badges like "homemaker," "childcare," and "hostess." ("Girl Scout Badges 1938-1962"). When approaching a study that examines both Girl and Boy Scouts, I wanted to take gendered differences into account and see how these differences still play a role, at least as recently as 2012. For the purposes of the project, I interviewed around 30 individuals ages 18-25 about their experiences with scouting from elementary to high school, focusing specifically on transgressive behaviors, visual signaling, and power structures within each of the groups.

Most of my research was derived through finding people on social media. Based on one facebook post, 32 people agreed to be spoken to, probably half of whom followed through with full responses (some of which in turn just contributed agreement/disagreement with issues or a personal anecdote). I conducted a mix of in-person interviews and questions over facebook messenger and over the phone. Though there were technical issues with the audio recording, I kept fairly meticulous notes and typed the interviews as close to verbatim as possible, reviewing my notes after each interview and asking any followup questions immediately after. My questions revolved around various questions of rule-breaking, self-regulation, personal anecdotes, and songs, stories or traditions that were used transgressively and passed from child to child.

Especially in Girl Scouts, the informants at least vaguely remembered crafting their own versions of songs, or using certain songs that might be considered inappropriate. One Boy Scout reported the mealtime "Father, Son, and Holy Ghost, who eats the fastest gets the most," was looked down on, and one Girl Scout said their troop favored violent versions of Christmas songs, specifically a variation on the Barnie rudie. "Joy to the world, that Barnie's dead! We all cut off his head!" Another girl mentioned that a specific rhyme passed around among the Girl Scouts was "R-A-P-E, get the hell away from me!", and specified that the girls would only ever share this with each other when the aids, leaders, and adults were not present. Three more confirmed they had heard this, if not in direct association with Girl Scout camp, from other elementary to middle school girls.

After a quick google search of "R-A-P-E, get your hands away from me" + "Girl Scouts", I found a deviantart post with many comments around variations of the chant, universally cited to have been heard around school age. I've included the post itself, but it's a post intended for a fandom community I didn't recognize; I focused mainly on the comment section.

(Deviantart)

Many of those commenting (circa 2010-2011) were surprised that others had experienced the chant as well. There were several threads that ended up being debates as to what the 'correct' version was. At least two mentioned they heard it at camp, one of them said they heard it at Girl Scout camp specifically. Many of the posts cited learning it from an older sibling or cousin; one said they taught it to their younger sister but changed R-A-P-E to N-O-P-E because their mother overheard and insisted that the sibling was too young for the more adult version, exhibiting some variation. There were a few exceptions, but the norm seemed to be female-to-female transmission of the rhyme at an elementary school age. The two comments specified to be from males remembered a bawdier version, demonstrating that this has some active expansion and substitution slots.

Often an introductory section of [Stop! Don't touch me there! This is my no-no-square [alternately 'private square']] is included, followed by [R-A-P-E] + many options for the final piece, some of which are fairly explicit. Variations reported online include: ["R-A-P-E, get your penis out of me!"], ["R-A-P-E, get this creep away from me!"] and ["R-A-P-E, that is a felony!"] I personally remember learning a different chant that borrowed the same introductory segment and mixed it in somewhere — something like, ["Stop! Don't touch me there! This is my no-no square."] This combination was also recalled by several informants. These seemed to be more commonly shared among girls to other girls, rather than among boys to boys, girls to boys or vice versa, and associated with cheerleading activities and scouting in particular. When asked where they heard it, girls identified the chant as a common schoolyard one that just happened to be brought into the sphere of Girl Scouts and camping.

Often these types of chants would come with dances, or corresponding movements. The more suggestive the movements were, usually the more social responses were gained. It had a competitive spirit: one informant said girls who drew their 'no-no squares' very small or were bold in their movements won some social status and often took initiative leading the games or conversations, especially Truth or Dare games including things like eating toilet paper/notebook paper or licking the floor. (It's similar to the frog-gut-eating or "rug burn" ordeal mentioned by the Boy Scouts, only instead of competing masculinity, this seems to be competing for a more mature sort of femininity.) The informant who mentioned the "R-A-P-E" rhyme in person said "we really didn't have much of a clue what we were talking about."

While inappropriate rhymes were recalled by former Girl Scouts, other forms of verbal transgression were largely kept to the boys. One of the informants involved with Boy Scouts mentioned that barely veiled rape jokes were tossed at opposing sides during camp games like capture-the-flag. He heard the boys saying the losing team would be "graped," didn't comprehend its meaning and parroted it, only to be shunned by the older scouts as a result. Interestingly, he juxtaposed this with an answer to one of my questions asking each group to predict gender differences about the other: he didn't think that kind of joke would happen in Girl Scouts. Verbal transgression among the boys tended to be veiling insults or threats, rather than altering songs they were given.

In Boy Scouts especially, the youth membership seemed to close ranks and self-police fairly severely when it came to protecting their own brand of transgressive behaviors. One former Boy Scout shared a story about a time the adult leaders intentionally broke the rules and depended on everyone involved to keep it confidential. According to his report, the troop was hiking on a trail fairly high up a mountain in Philmont and the bearline they were using to keep their food safe got tangled, leaving it dangling high off the ground. The boys threw a rope over the line and a team of four of them tied the rope around the one thought to weigh the least, who was then rappelled up about twenty feet in order to retrieve the supplies. Apparently the kid was both skinny and fairly unpopular. The adults turned a blind eye and the boy who had volunteered for the dangerous job measurably increased his social standing by accepting the task and keeping quiet about the risk; everyone got along with him better when he stuck his neck out and earned some mutual respect. The line they used was clearly unstable and there was a high level of risk involved, meaning everyone involved had to keep it under wraps. Even years later, the interviewee said he would not have shared the story if I hadn't told him it would be anonymous. Another former Boy Scout shared a story in which a smaller group of the boys at camp found a dirty magazine and passed it among themselves until it got to the point where the majority decided such a magazine was immoral, at which point they circled up and burned it.

The Boy Scout who shared the bear line tale said that participation in unofficial or rule-breaking activities, paired with the ability to keep them secret, was hugely important for camaraderie. He estimated that boys who didn't participate in these activities didn't usually last more than two years. These bonding activities included bizarre and gross one-off competitive events, anything from playing Capture the Flag with a sock full of somebody's shit, to a group of boys eating a mix of boiled plants, mud, and frog guts, just to prove that they could take it. Other informants reported similarly competitive behaviors that seemed aimed at "proving their masculinity," including giving each other rug burns and trading insults or threats (such as "grape.") Some of these seem idiosyncratic, but they all follow a similar form and function. The form is a competitive game, something gross, wild, or unusual, and the function is to create a barrier or testing bar for full membership in the group. While some girls reported some similar competitive behaviors, they tended to be more mild and less intrinsic, while Boy Scouts seemed more likely to have experienced some form of hazing. Pranking as a transgressive behavior was mentioned by at least seven informants, all of them male. These passing-the-bar moments track interestingly with the hypothesis that Boy Scouts originated partially as a defense of traditional, militaristic, competitive masculinity. (Arneil 55).

The importance of these group rule-breaking behaviors and transgressive bonding behaviors in the social sphere was reinforced by an informant with a negative experience of Boy Scouts. In one of the camps he attended, a strictly held rule was a complete prohibition of phones and iPods on the premises. As soon as he got there, his older brother pulled him and some of the other younger boys aside and showed them he had snuck in his phone, saying that all the older kids regularly smuggled in their electronics. After receiving this information, the interviewee blew the whistle on the tradition and 'ratted them out' to the Scoutmasters. He reported he 'earned a shunning' and a few punches to the arm. Following this, he faced social ostracism and stopped attending scouts at the rank of Tenderfoot, reporting that he was bullied and excluded— and not just by the boys. When he didn't follow through or participate fully in traditions, even the squeaky-clean ones, he was policed more heavily than his peers, faced social shaming, and was relegated to more undesirable chores. In this case, it's difficult to tell how much of the information was idiosyncratic or biased in some way, but the inclusion of the story provides an interesting confirmation of the first informant's hypothesis that failing to participate in both official and unofficial activities would lead to exclusion from the group. The boundaries of commitment to the organization seem to be strictly guarded and watched, usually by the boys themselves.

Boy Scouts interviewed emphasized that their system of conflict resolution was almost entirely self-contained by the boys and their peer leaders (including adults only when drastically necessary), while Girl Scouts seemed to remember that conflict resolution (what little of it there was) was handled solely by adult leaders or parents. I'd theorize that without so many long camping trips away from parents, forcing them to spend time together, the girls had less time to form their own independent groups and systems away from their parents. They tended to regard Girl Scouts as a smaller part of their identity in comparison to the Boy Scouts. Even the boys with less pleasant memories of their time in scouting seemed to be affected by an overarching sense of either belonging or not, while Girl Scouts' internal social divides and niches were more stark, splitting the group noticeably. While the barriers constituting this divide allowed for some variation, one former Girl Scout said that her troop from 4th-6th grade was divided neatly into two groups: the "popular" and the "unpopular." The difference? Three separate sources, from different areas of Missouri and different Girl Scout troops, agreed on the existence of this division and reported the "popular" girls wore athletic wear and the "unpopular" ones didn't. They consistently signaled belonging to a specific group of people and prioritized that group over the Girl Scouts, announcing membership to each of these with their attire. One informant stated they 'were a different group than me.' When pushed, the differences this group displayed in order to set them apart were difficult for her to describe— "you just got this feeling that you were like the mud on their shoe." However, it was universally unspoken from one group to another, and never got to a point of outright conflict. At least four of the girls described this internal division. This was best illustrated by a quote from one of the girls I interviewed in person:

> I remember there was my group of four girls, and there were other groups of four or five girls. And we stuck to those groups when we went camping and everything. It was like, 'we're the girls who like to read!' 'We're the girls who play sports!'

And then it was like, 'we're the girls who aren't *white!*' It was definitely.... There was that kinda stuff going on. (Collected 2019).

Another omnipresent gender discrepancy was bitterness regarding the differences between Girl Scouts and Boy Scouts, localized entirely among Girl Scouts. Overwhelmingly they felt that their activities were gendered unfairly. Their camps were 'cushy' and felt less adventurous, compared to stories heard of the Boy Scouts' camping adventures. While the boys were learning whittling, emergency first aid and survival skills, the girls felt relegated to friendship bracelets, picture frames, and cookie sales. One girl derisively referred to the activities as 'wifey skills' and said she would have wanted to learn how to whittle instead of learning how to sew, but felt she wasn't given the opportunity. Camping was experienced with varying levels of frequency (some Girl Scouts only went once a year, some didn't go at all and went to yearly indoor 'lock-ins' instead) but more structured. Tents were used less than cabins 'near the pool.' One girl said her troop participated in their local parade every year and were consistently told they couldn't throw candy or beads because it was 'against the rules,' while the Boy Scouts were allowed to do this annually. She stated the entire troop found it frustrating and unfair, but the 'rules' around it never budged, in spite of their best efforts to induce change.

This ties closely to the conflicted origins of the organization as a whole; it's both based in women's independence from and adherence to traditional femininity. Girl Scout's push towards left-leaning ideals around the 70's resulted in a shift towards more individualist attitudes, through which they all but abolished visual uniformity and encouraged parents to be around to enforce their own family codes and levels of comfort. Most girls interviewed reported 'helicopter parenting' as an issue that kept them from forming their own self-policing systems within the organization. In contrast, among the Boy Scouts self-policing was a huge part of the deal. Another BS informant reported that once the younger boys at a campout spit in a bucket of water that he and another leader had brought from the well; they reported the incident to the adult leaders, after which they were told to go and mess up the younger boys' campsite. They made a mess with toilet paper and according to the guideline of 'leave no trace,' made the younger boys clean it up as well as fetch their own water from the well. So even the incidents reported to adults were largely handled among the boys themselves, at the behest of those adults. Girl Scouts reported little to no conflict that would result in this sort of situation, and the conflict that was reported was immediately dealt with by an adult with final authority.

In addition, Girl Scouts felt their accomplishments were less respected.

There was less significance attached to coming-of-age rituals such as moving up the ranks or attaining badges. Girl Scouts felt that achieving the Gold Award earned them less respect than boys who earned the rank of Eagle Scout, since the rank of Eagle is acknowledged and commonly known even outside of the scouting world. Between this and the feeling of relegation to "wifey skills," girls overwhelmingly felt that they lacked a sense of unity, pride, and identity from the organization. The ideals that the Girl Scouts set forward created something strongly ironic: as a result of efforts in favor of female empowerment, the girls are more protected, parentally sheltered, largely kept to indoor tasks and baked goods, and encouraged to dress individualistically, which created a fissured feminine social environment based on physical appearance. It's something of a paradox.

I'd argue that this paradox stems from the conflicted origin story Girl Scouts carries with it; while its motto currently is new-age female empowerment, the actuality of its programs (at least around 2008-2012), seems to disappoint this standard. The organization both upholds and belittles cultural expectations of femininity over time, in ways that don't keep company well. Despite the forward social mobility the organization attempts to embrace, its roots are tangled. According to *The Girl Scout History Project*, "Homemaker" was a program focus introduced in 1953. (See photo of the Homemaker badge below.) This coexisted with badges for "good grooming," "housekeeper," "interior decorating," and "dressmaker" ("Girl Scout Badges 1938-1962").

1953 Homemaker (*Vintage Girl Scout Online Museum*)

While the program has now shed these outdated norms, its idea of "girl power" has a strongly gendered correlation to mental accomplishment, rather than physical accomplishment—it's prepared for a world which fights against women being speakers, politicians, or leaders in business. One interviewee said she guessed that the Girl Scout highest award, the Gold Award, is culturally valued less than the rank of Eagle Scout because the work involved with Girl Scouts tends to be more cerebral or theoretical. Physically raising a flag pole or fixing a trail gives the Eagle rank an edge of immediacy and grit that calls attention to it; for some reason, this kind of physical exercise isn't viewed as something girls should have to utilize (if I had time to explore it, I'd like to dive into the idea of this girl power paradox and exactly how that's played out in the Girl Scout community).

The starkest differences between Girl Scouts and Boy Scouts fell into two different categories, which I would argue fall along the ideological divides that created the two organizations in the first place. The first divergence lies in the type and function of transgressive behavior. For Girl Scouts, transgression was largely not allowed among the youth; they had parents hovering at all times, which resulted in a different form of it, mostly in rhymes and rudies such as the Barnie song and "R-A-P-E." The function of these rhymes was to express something that they were actively being sheltered from, mostly violence- whether physical or sexual. It was a small way of asserting independence in a highly structured environment. Among Boy Scouts, there were many more forms of bonding activities, many of them technically against the rules. The Boy Scout troops were much more self-regulated societies, and their border patrolling behaviors were stricter than those of the Girl Scouts; they participated in one-upping each other in dangerous or bizarre activities. The function of this was to exercise this new independence, defend or practice their idea of masculinity, and set the bar for inclusion high in order to protect it.

The second type of divergence lies in gendered imbalance and visual signaling. The Boy Scouts present a united front visually—it's difficult to tell one from the next. Even at campouts where uniforms are not required, many of them dressed in similar ways, signaling they were alike in more ways than they were not. Overwhelmingly, Girl Scouts reported that there were multiple groups coexisting under the umbrella of their Girl Scout troop, and that these groups were signaled by the clothing they wore. This clothing corresponded to interests, socioeconomic status, and after-school activities. The girls were fissured along the same lines they would be at school, trying to navigate an environment in which they are judged and policed by their peers in regards to what they do and how they present themselves. With this in mind, each of these groups represents a complex idea of gender. Boy Scouts was founded on principles of "true masculinity"— boys can get dirty, boys can fight, boys can learn to fend for themselves. Girl Scouts shouldered the enormous challenge of attempting to both embrace and challenge the idea of traditional femininity, resulting in a conflicting set of ideals: girls are told they can do anything, but are simultaneously sheltered and policed to a much greater extent than their male peers. One informant reported that she felt both inspired and restricted by the gendered dichotomy between the two. On the one hand, it was inspiring to be surrounded by women leaders and freeing to be outside of any sort of patriarchal system; and on the other hand, the rules were obviously gendered in a biased way, whether internally or externally. At least between 2008-2013, the system seemed to defeat itself.

Below, I've included some visual references to illustrate my points about each group.

Picture 1: My own Girl Scout Troop, circa 2011, at a bridging ceremony. There's a noticeable distance between each member, hands are folded in front signaling some awkwardness or discomfort. Beginning around this time in troops and schools, makeup, hairstyles, shoes, and clothing began to be identity signals, aimed largely towards other girls. I'm the short one in purple with my hands held in front. Looking back, the visual separation resulting from my age is painfully clear and did create a divide. While the group was small, it was divided in ways I still remember— of the six girls in the picture, three attended the same school & were on the same athletic teams, while the other three attended three different schools and had more difficulty forming strong connections with each other solely in the context of the troop.

(Troop 1316, 2011)

Picture 2: Some members of my brother's Boy Scout troop, posing together after an Eagle Scout ceremony. It's clear they feel much more comfortable with each other, and it doesn't seem like they were asked to pose this way. Visually, they're clearly similar—two are wearing jeans, two are wearing dark green cargo pants. The one behind them seems to be wearing the same dark green pants. While it's cut off, I have other pictures from the ceremony that demonstrate little to no difference in footwear. The uniforms tell us they are a part of the same group, and give status signals like their red kerchiefs and number of badges, as well as the pins on their shirts. Everything they are wearing signals something specific to others in the group.

(Troop 495, 2014)

Picture 3: an antique photo of a Girl Scout troop, probably circa early 1900s, collected from a site called *The Girl Scout History Project*. The visual differences used to be nearly unnoticeable. The things they wear all signal something about the troop they are in, and even the shoes are variations on a particular type, either oxfords or some kind of flats. This photo is before the ideological divide between the two, which took place somewhere around the 1970s, and the uniforms include skirts past the knee. The girls clearly styled their hair and the flag-bearers are wearing white gloves.

(The Girl Scout History Project)

The Girl Scout History Project mentions one "Homemaker" handbook I was unable to track down to read further. Still, its existence is evidence of the ideological divide that began to fissure the goals and ideals of femininity that formed the foundation of the Girl Scouts.

Works Cited

Arneil, Barbara. "Gender, Diversity, and Organizational Change: The Boy Scouts vs. Girl Scouts of America." *Perspectives on Politics*, vol. 8, no. 1, 2010, pp. 53–68. JSTOR, www.jstor.org/stable/25698515.

Devinimidori. "APH: R-A-P-E." *Deviant Art*, 31 July 2010. www.deviantart-.com/

"Girl Scout Badges 1938-1962." *Vintage Girl Scout Online Museum.* www-.vintagegirlscout.com/badges38.html

Margolin, Emma. "Boy Scouts' proposal says it's OK to be gay–until you're 18." *MSNBC*, 22 April 2013.www.msnbc.com/thomas-roberts/boy-scouts-proposal-says-its-ok-be-gay

Robertson, Ann. "Uniforms / So That's in Your Bag, Girl Scout." *The Girl Scout History Project.* www.gshistory.com/category/uniforms/

Sikeston and Sundown
Lauren Wessling-Linhares

This 2010 paper, rooted in family lore about Missouri's "sundown towns" took on extra poignancy with the unrest in Florissant – which shared that history – after the killing of Mike Brown by police in 2014. Based on interviews with people who had personally known the town under that de jure racist regime, and who quoted people they had known, as they had personally heard, the text contains some biases and several racial slurs. An editorial decision was made to delete the offending words but to mark the places of deletion. There were four prime informants interviewed, whose identifying information has been altered or deleted.

Introduction

In 1860 Sikeston was founded by John Sikes upon the declaration, "I, John Sikes, am going to start me a town and I am going to call it the Town of Sikeston" (Blackwell). Prior to Sikes' time, the area had just been known as "Big Prairie," and most of southeastern Missouri was covered in swampland and timber, with a ridge coming out of the swamp where the town was founded (Blackwell). Interestingly, a few years after establishing his town, Sikes was almost hanged by Confederate guerillas in front of his store during the civil war, but was then saved when his wife sent a black slave girl to give the guerillas 100 dollars. After narrowly escaping death once, Sikes was killed a few years later while trying to persuade a drunk friend to saddle up and go home. His concern was repaid with a shot in the back; the friend then vanished.

Stories of Sikeston's founder hint at a town full of folklore almost as rich as the farmland that brought it to prominence. The goal of this paper is to explore folk stories told by people in and from Sikeston but, in order to do so, proper background of the small city has to be established.

History

Until 1872 Sikeston was the terminus for the Cairo and Fulton (later the Missouri-Pacific) railroad and the train was the only means of transport across the vast swampland (Capeci). In the early 1900s a series of dams from the Little River Drainage District project, in combination with timber "barons" and loggers, effectively converted the area (also called "Swampeast" or the "Missouri glades") into fertile farmland (Capeci). Being on nearly the northernmost edge of the Mississippi Delta, an area characterized by fertile lowlands as well as dramatic humidity, temperatures and rainfall, Sikeston was considered to be part of the agricultural "final frontier" (Capeci). The town experienced much prosperity as farmers and laborers moved to the area and the railroad supplied the rest of the nation with crops from the rich land (Depot's History). The Sikeston region became so important to early 20th century agriculture that during World War I the Sikeston Depot shipped more corn and flour than any other depot in the United States (Depot's History).

The end of the war and an increase in use of cotton as a crop brought thousands of planters to southeast Missouri from the southern states. Sikeston had no slave history, being a relatively young settlement, and by the late 1920s had a black population that accounted for nearly 13 percent of total (Capeci). Being a new town, Sikeston was a society formed from people from all over the nation. It transitioned from "[…] frontier to civilization [and] merged Yankee and southern prejudice" (Capeci). This eventually led to bloodshed in the region between 1890 and 1930 due to the "[…] interplay of a volatile population, pell-mell economic development, and occasional political party rivalries" that "[…] also drew on racist beliefs and a historical context shaped long before 1890" (Capeci). While there are only a few cases recorded of violence in Sikeston itself, the surrounding area and rest of Missouri's bootheel had at least 16 lynchings of blacks between 1889 and 1942 (Capeci).

Sunset

Against a tumultuous backdrop the city of Sikeston, and the black population specifically, continued to grow. Most of the blacks lived on the western edge of town, separated completely from the rest of Sikeston by two crossing railroad tracks, in what was called the Sunset Addition, or simply Sunset. Described as shacks and small houses, Sunset allowed the city to be segregated but also had everything blacks needed to live independently (Capeci; Blackwell). The relationship between blacks and whites in Sikeston in the early 20th century could be described as "strained," according to Sue Marble, who was born in Sunset in 1928 (Blackwell). Reportedly, "Blacks stayed among themselves and whites did the same. We [blacks] had everything we needed for our livelihood, and we didn't bother with theirs." Furthermore, to most Sunset residents "Sunset was their turf and Sikeston their city....[They] created a community within a city...[and] preserved much of their folk culture and southern heritage" (Capeci). In general, it seems that while racism and violence may have occurred in this era in Sikeston, a mutual segregation was more prevalent than anything else as "[...] townspeople lived, worked, and played along separate racial lines in a southern caste and class system" (Capeci).

The Cleo Wright Incident

This is the scene in which most of the folklore of Sikeston is set.

While the historical background of Sikeston can be found rather easily, the background and details about the lynching of Cleo Wright were mostly found in a book called simply, "The Lynching of Cleo Wright." The author, Dominic Capeci Jr., used personal interviews with many of the people present and personally involved in both the crimes by Wright and crimes done to Wright, to present a detailed account of the situation. The following account is drawn largely from Capeci, with additional notes from Blackwell.

Following the Great Depression and the beginning of World War II, an already strained Sikeston finally boiled over. Almost a year before the bombing of Pearl Harbor, members of Company K, formed as a National Guard unit in Sikeston, were mobilized, leaving many women home alone to deal with children and war-time life on their own. In the middle of the night on January 25, 1942 (shortly after the attack on Pearl Harbor), Cleo Wright, a 26 year old black man and Sunset resident, broke into the home of Grace Sturgeon. Sturgeon lived with her young son and sister-in-law while their husbands were deployed. Breaking in through the bedroom window, Wright attempted to slit Sturgeon's throat and managed to cut open her abdomen with a six inch knife. He then escaped, but was found walking on a nearby street by two police officers, and after Wright resisted arrest, a struggle ensued. One of the police officers was left with a sliced lip and tongue, smashed jaw and teeth after Wright attacked him with a hidden knife.

Wright fared far worse with four point-blank shots fired through his abdomen and several blows to the head by a flashlight and a revolver. While Wright was treated at the hospital and then put in jail, most of Sikeston's residents had already heard about his misdeeds, and by 9:00 AM a crowd had already started to form outside of City Hall. Eventually, Wright admitted to attacking the woman due to some "bad whiskey," and as word spread through the mob of four to five hundred people, it was not long until the angry mob pushed through the line of law enforcement officers that were guarding the building. The mob broke into Wright's holding room and dragged him out of City Hall and down its steps by his feet so that his head hit each step. They then "hooked his legs behind the car bumper" of a waiting maroon sedan before dragging him through the streets of Sikeston on the way to Sunset with the intent to burn him.

Citizens followed in a "parade of cars" as Wright was dragged through several streets in Sunset before the cars stopped near the schoolhouse — within view of two churches and the Missouri-Pacific Railroad tracks (Blackwell). A crowd of three to four hundred white residents circled around Wright as he was doused in gasoline and set aflame. Wright's remains were left in the street until the late afternoon, when a city dump truck hauled them away. People who came to Sunset to view the carnage also witnessed a semi-exodus; about a hundred black people, mostly seasonal and migrant workers, left Sikeston permanently that day. While there were some black residents of Sunset who prepared for further combat with the lynch mob, no further violence occurred after Wright's death.

Sikeston soon became infamous, even internationally, for the events surrounding Wright's death. A local prosecuting attorney who witnessed the actions of the lynch mob while trying to protect Wright before the mob dragged him from City Hall managed to bring the case to a grand jury, but jurors refused to indict anyone for the lynching (Blackwell). The case proceeded to a federal grand jury in Saint Louis and received much media attention as it was the first time the federal government had become involved in a civil rights case (Blackwell). In fact, while no indictments were returned and ultimately no one was punished for Wright's murder, the case being brought before the federal court set a pattern for future civil rights cases (Capeci).

While Wright's crimes, and those of the unnamed lynch-mob members were heinous, and motives have been broken down and every minute detail of Wright's life analyzed, the most important thing to remember is that it did happen. Wright's motives can be presented relatively simply; he seems to have been intent on burglary. The impetus driving the lynch mob most certainly was due to racist traditions. These traditions are harder to dissect.

In order to examine Sikeston folklore, interviews were conducted with four willing participants: three men and one woman; two had lived in Sikeston their entire lives. One was a previous resident, and the last a frequent visitor. More interviews were attempted but most people were unwilling to participate, frequently claiming that the stories they knew were "things you don't need to hear." (This is understandable, considering the subject matter of the stories I did manage to collect, and the fact that I appear to be an innocent young girl to most residents there.)

Interviews were informal, held mostly at an elderly citizen's birthday party, and each participant was asked, "Can you tell me any stories about Sikeston?" Each participant had a story about the lynching as well as lore about Sunset.

Participant One told me that Sikeston is "still fairly deeply segregated" and "thrown back 15 years from everything." They mentioned the lynching of Cleo Wright, but did not know his name or when it occurred other than that it was "pretty recent." According to them, a black man had done something "bad" and was taken into police custody, then beaten (implying that the police did it) and dragged through all the brick paved streets of downtown Sikeston before being set on fire while being hanged downtown. Participant Two knew the story as well, but swore the black man was set on fire while being hanged in Sunset. Participant Three mentioned that the black man had first raped a woman before being taken into custody, beaten, dragged through the streets while on fire, then hanged. The last participant said the black man had broken into a house, was taken into custody, beaten, dragged through all the streets of Sikeston and then lynched, and that this event occurred in 1960.

The four participants' accounts of Cleo Wright's death show stability and variation. **All four** tell of a black man who was arrested, beaten, dragged behind a car through some part of Sikeston and then hanged. Interestingly, the case report on Wright's death mentions nothing about actually being hanged, but refers to his murder as a lynching (which can mean death by hanging, burning, or shooting and usually in front of a mob) – though to most people "lynching" is probably synonymous with being hanged. The stories exhibit variation from what "actually happened" and are embellished with the black man being hanged at the end, but most likely only due to a misunderstanding of the word "lynching." Also, all four versions of the lynching simply refer to Wright as a black man and don't mention an actual name. None of the stories mention that a mob was involved and most seemed to imply that the local law enforcement almost supported the lynching (though mob action might be implicit in "lynching"). Amongst themselves the stories also vary in their account of the order of events: one story claims the man was burned while being dragged around the streets; another claims he was burned in an event by itself and yet another claims he was burned while being hanged.

"Sunset" and "Sundown"

There could be several reasons that people still tell the story of Wright's death, especially as it was always the first story that came to mind when participants were asked about Sikeston lore. While none of the participants mentioned it, the story managed to receive international attention and is an important part of Sikeston's history, and many people probably know that it was an important event and just enjoy telling something local and gruesome.

Interestingly, while Wright's murder is treated as lore in Sikeston it also managed to create lore about Sunset. Besides each interviewee's account of the lynching, they all told stories of how Sunset received its name. There were two different versions. One participant claimed that the day Wright was killed the black residents of Sikeston were told, "Don't let the sun set on your ass, [epithet deleted], or they're gonna lynch you," and that that threat was the reason that blacks moved to their own segregated part of town. Another participant claimed that, "back then blacks weren't supposed to be in town after the sun set," and that's why they moved to the edge of town."

None of the participants mentioned whether white people or black people came up with the name for Sunset first, but historically the area was simply known as Sunset Addition by all parties. Historically, Sunset got its full name long before Wright's murder, and according to Blackwell, "There are [people] today who incorrectly but perhaps understandably believe the Sunset Addition got its name that day." In fact, Sunset's name could be the result of its location: historically and in the present day sprawl of Sikeston, Sunset is the westernmost point of town. Basically, the sun always set over that area, and blacks could have decided to live in a community there on their own, without threats from white folks.

However, it is also possible that at one point in time Sikeston was a "sundown town," or a place where blacks really were told that they weren't allowed within city limits after dark (Loewen). Sundown towns arose all across the nation in this same era (1890-1940), after the Civil War and Reconstruction and as race relations grew worse everywhere. "Official" sundown towns usually had a sign posted at their city limits that said something like, "[Epithet deleted], Don't Let the Sun Go Down On You In ...." Loewen provides a list of historic sundown towns, but it is generally hard to prove whether a town is or was ever officially one. In fact, most of the time local historians leave out any sundown policies the town ever had because they don't want it to reflect poorly on the town, and there are even authors that admit that they knew of sundown policies but didn't want to print them (Loewen). Therefore, it is entirely possible that Sikeston was a sundown town when Sunset was created and that no one knows or will admit that that's how it received its name.

Another version of how Sunset received its name as told by the interview participants is an inversion of the first: all four participants told me that white people do not go through Sunset anymore, especially after the sun goes down. In fact, most participants said, "You know why it's called Sunset don't you?[...] because you should never be there after it gets dark." It seems that while originally it was believed that Sunset was created as a place for blacks to go after they were kicked out of town after dark, in modern day the story is inverted, and now it's a place that whites should not go after dark. In fact it seems the area is almost revered for being poor and dangerous. Sunset was described by one interview participant as "vacant lots, a couple of things you'd actually call a house, and the rest are shacks. The rest are frame and tar paper. The very definition of dirt poor," and on a drive through the area it was strongly stressed that the car windows be closed and all doors locked. White Sikeston residents fear Sunset now, as was especially evident when two participants responded with extreme shock upon finding out I had been through the area. Multiple participants claimed that they'd heard that the Sikeston police and fire departments refuse to drive through Sunset for fear that they will be shot or have things thrown at them. I did not study crime reports for the area, relative to the rest of the town. It's possible that the claim has some foundation in fact, that it represents embellishment, or that it's a localized detail of a standard tale to discourage "trespassing" in an area where one doesn't belong.

The two different versions of how Sunset received its name are a form of naming folklore. The stories serve their function well and seem to logically describe why Sunset is called Sunset. Additionally, the second story (admonishing white not to go to Sunset) also serves as a cautionary tale, reminding people that Sikeston is still basically segregated, even though its reasoning about Sunset's name is untrue. If Sikeston were actually known to be a sundown town, the first version of Sunset's naming lore would probably be true. However, the truth behind the lore is not important, but the fact that the lore is still told is very important. It represents a view that probably still believes that segregation should exist and that wants to recognize and remember a violent past, possibly to reinforce racist ideas.

In summary, the folklore told about Sikeston serves several purposes. Being a small, growing town in a relatively turbulent region during the early 1900s ultimately led to violence and the lynching of a black man. While this event achieved international notoriety, it also spawned stories about the event that exhibit stability and variation both amongst themselves and with regards to the account of what really happened. Stories of the lynching are still told seemingly as cautionary tales, but also managed to create naming lore about Sunset. The two different versions of naming lore logically serve their purposes as well as also seeming cautionary and perhaps necessary for remembering racist beliefs that may or may not still exist.

References

Blackwell, Sam. "Sikeston's History as Rich as its Swamp-turned-farmland." *Southeast Missourian*, 11 November, 2001. Web www.semissourian-.com/story/50133.html.

Capeci, Dominic J. *The Lynching of Cleo Wright.* Lexington: The University Press of Kentucky, 1998.

"Depot's History" Sikeston Depot Museum: Sikeston Cultural Development Corporation. Web. www.sikestondepot.org/history.htm. Last updated 2008.

Loewen, James W. *Sundown Towns: A Hidden Dimension of American Racism.* New York: The New Press, 2005. Loewen maintains a companion website at sundown.tougaloo.edu.

Appendix: Interview Notes for Sikeston Stories

"Well, the only two that come to mind, and granted, you have to understand that this is a fairly deeply segregated town.... The earliest one goes back to the origination of the little community off to the west called Sunset; that's where all the black folks live at primarily.

If you ask somebody how that name was arrived at, they told them that's where they need to be because they'd say, "don't let the sun set on your ass [epithet deleted], they're gonna lynch you"—the message being "don't be in town after sunset." Now the name is thought of more as (for white folks) "Don't be in that part of town after sunset," or else bad things would happen to you. Even the people that live there call it Sunset."

The other story involves Sunset itself and the 1960 election with JFK. And this is in the civil rights movement and all that. And the Democrats were all about the civil rights and whatnot. And Democrats had a pretty good [hold] on the south at that point anyway because of the still anti-republic feelings from the war 90 years previous [Civil War]. The Democrats had such a push to get JFK elected but the area had turned against the Democrats because of their involvement with the civil rights movement. To get all the votes possible.

The rumor was that they'd pay the people living in Sunset 5 dollars and a bottle of wine to come out and vote. Also if they didn't vote they'd "Get the shit beat outta them."

Grandma [identifier deleted] used to pick cotton and she'd drag Jerry (my grandma's brother) down on a cotton sack while she walked down the rows of cotton. She'd have one bag across her chest (cross body bag) to put the cotton in and dragged her son in the other one on the ground because the ground was so smooth from weeding and tractors going through.

To this day Sunset is vacant lots—a couple of things you'd actually call a house and the rest are shacks. The rest are frame and tar paper. The very definition of dirt poor.

Me: so is everyone in Sikeston racist?

D: [sensitive to the subject] Now, you have to understand that people up north will identify everything as racist. Just mentioning skin color will get you accused of racism even when you just call someone a "black guy." "They play that [their race] to get what they want"

Informant A: I think Sikeston is more racist than other towns that I've known.

Informant B: Well, yeah, it's thrown back 15 years from everything. St. Louis is more racist than Memphis.

White flight – white people moving out when black people move in to an area.

The lynching of Cleo Wright – the last lynching in Missouri took place in Sikeston in 1942.

Informant B: There you go. Sunset.

Me: Are there any actual stories of people being hurt in Sunset?

Informant D: Not that I'm aware. I know the policemen and firemen don't like going in there.

From Informant C: Whiskey instead of wine for voting blacks. People (I guess Democrats) would pick up the "farmhands" and drive them to every election center in the area. Would end up being more votes than the population but they didn't regulate that back then. Blacks loved election day because they got to be driven around all day and drink whiskey.

"Dubious past" – 1960 lynched the last person in MO -when dad and I told Informant C we drove through Sunset, even during the daytime, recently, he was extremely surprised we would have done it.

Derrick- A guy got drug around Sikeston (the guy that got hung).

Me: Cleo Wright?

[Identifier deleted] found out that they drug him through the brick streets, beat him, hung him, then burned him.

From Informant C: Arthur Bruce was the police chief in the early 60s and lived on the corner of West St. and North St. and would patrol the street from his house to the police station and kept all Sunset "residents" in Sunset.

Kenney Ellison got shot in Sunset. (His father murdered a girl, then died in jail.) And he [Kenny Ellison] died, but "apparently he had it comin."